SONGS FROM AN EMPTY CAGE

The C. Henry Smith series is edited by J. Denny Weaver. Volumes to date have been released by Cascadia Publishing House (originally Pandora Press U.S., a name some of the earlier series books carry) and frequently copublished by Herald Press in cooperation with Bluffton University as well as the Mennonite Historical Society. Bluffton University, in consultation with the publishers, is primarily responsible for the content of the studies.

1. Anabaptists and Postmodernity
   Edited by Susan Biesecker-Mast and Gerald Biesecker-Mast, 2000

2. Anabaptist Theology in Face of Postmodernity:
   A Proposal for the Third Millennium
   By J. Denny Weaver, 2000

3. Fractured Dance:
   Gadamer and a Mennonite Conflict over Homosexuality
   By Michael A. King, 2001

4. Fixing Tradition: Joseph W. Yoder, Amish American
   By Julia Kasdorf, 2002

5. Walker in the Fog: On Mennonite Writing
   By Jeff Gundy, 2005

6. Separation and the Sword:
   Radical Confessional Rhetoric from Schleitheim to Dordrecht
   By Gerald Biesecker-Mast, 2006

7. Searching for Sacred Ground:
   The Journey of Chief Lawrence Hart, Mennonite
   By Raylene Hinz-Penner, 2007

8. Practicing the Politics of Jesus:
   The Origin and Significance of John Howard Yoder's Social Ethics
   By Earl Zimmerman, 2007

9. Peace to War:
   Shifting Allegiances in the Assemblies of God
   By Paul Alexander, 2009

10. Songs from an Empty Cage:
    Poetry, Mystery, Anabaptism, and Peace
    By Jeff Gundy, 2013

SONGS FROM AN EMPTY CAGE

POETRY, MYSTERY, ANABAPTISM, AND PEACE

Jeff Gundy

Foreword by
Scott Holland

The C. Henry Smith Series
Volume 10

Cascadia
Publishing House
Telford, Pennsylvania

Cascadia Publishing House orders, information, reprint permissions:
contact@CascadiaPublishingHouse.com
1-215-723-9125
126 Klingerman Road, Telford PA 18969
www.CascadiaPublishingHouse.com

Songs from an Empty Cage
Copyright © 2013 by Cascadia Publishing House,
a division of Cascadia Publishing House LLC
Telford, PA 18969
All rights reserved.
Copublished with Herald Press, Scottdale, PA
Library of Congress Catalog Number: 2013008433
ISBN-13: 978-1-931038-97-3; **ISBN 10:** 1-931038-97-X
Book design by Cascadia Publishing House
Cover design and composite image by Merrill R. Miller, with photo by Miles
Beverley/iStockphoto/Thinkstock

The paper used in this publication is recycled and meets the
minimum requirements of American National Standard for Information
Sciences—Permanence of Paper for Printed Library Materials, ANSI Z39.48-1984.

Grateful acknowledgment is made for permission to quote materials listed in
"Credits and Permissions" at back of book.

Library of Congress Cataloguing-in-Publication Data
Gundy, Jeffrey Gene, 1952-
  Songs from an empty cage : poetry, mystery, anabaptism, and peace / Jeff Gundy.
    pages cm. -- (The C. Henry Smith Series ; Volume 10)
  Includes bibliographical references and index.
  Summary: "The author employs a theopoetic approach to engage ultimate questions
while probing the intersections of poetry with Anabaptism, Mennonites, mystery,
and peacemaking"--Provided by publisher.
  ISBN 978-1-931038-97-3 (6 x 9" trade pbk. : alk. paper) -- ISBN 1-931038-97-X
(6 x 9" trade pbk. : alk. paper)
  1. Religion and poetry. 2. Peace in literature. 3. Anabaptists. 4. Mennonites. I.
Title.

PN1077.G78 2013
809.1'9382--dc23

2013008433

20 19 18 17 16 15 14 13   10 9 8 7 6 5 4 3 2

To
Keith Ratzlaff,
Jean Janzen, and
Julia Spicher Kasdorf,
who taught me that Mennonite poetry was possible.

CONTENTS

Foreword: God As World's Poet, by Scott Holland   11
Series Editor's Foreword   13
Acknowledgments   15
Introduction: Poetry, Mystery, Anabaptism, and the World   17

PART ONE: PROLEGOMENA

Chapter One: Notes Toward an Anabaptist Theopoetics • 31

Chapter Two: Declining to Be in Charge • 43

PART TWO: TRANSGRESSIONS AND TRADITIONS

Chapter Three: The Hammer and the Free Spirit • 55

Chapter Four: The Marriage of the *Martyrs Mirror* and the Open Road, or, Why I Love Poetry Despite the Suspicion That It Won't Save Anybody • 74

Chapter Five: "Truth Did Not Come Into the World Naked": Images, Stories, and Intimations • 87

Chapter Six: Notes Toward the Heretical Sublime • 102

PART THREE: POETRY, PEDAGOGY, PEACE

Chapter Seven: Adding Real Beings to the World: Teaching Peace, Writing, and Human Exchange • 127

Chapter Eight: On Jesus and Teaching • 138

Chapter Nine: Toward Post-Peace Poetry: or, What to Do with the Drunken Soldiers? • 143

PART FOUR: MUSIC, METAPHOR, MARTYRS, MYSTERY

Chapter Ten: Sound and the Sixties: Sex, God, Rock and Roll, and Flourishing • 169

Chapter Eleven: The Rule of God and the Ruby: The Theopoet Talks Back • 182

Chapter Twelve: The Farm Boy's Thoughts Turn Toward Beauty • 204

Chapter Thirteen: The Baptism in Dark Water: Apophasis, Mystery, and the God Within • 214

Chapter Fourteen: Looking in the *Mirror* • 230

Chapter Fifteen: Who Knows Who Is Calling? • 244

Chapter Sixteen: Voice and Imagination: Meaning Besides Truth • 257

Bibliography 273
Index 283
Credits and Permissions 291
The Author 293

FOREWORD: GOD AS WORLD'S POET

Although many of us writing in the evolving field of theopoetics do not share Alfred North Whitehead's longing for a grand metaphysics, we do find pleasure in quoting his thoughts on God as the poet of the world, "God's role is not the combat of productive force with productive force, of destructive force with destructive force; it lies in the patient operation of the overpowering rationality of his conceptual harmonization. He does not create the world, he saves it; or more accurately, he is the poet of the world, with tender patience leading it by his vision of truth, beauty and goodness." For those unfamiliar with Whitehead, this overpowering rationality is not to be equated with the cool reason of static truth claims. It is instead a deep relational understanding of the interconnected web of life in which any conception of God cannot be separated from the evolutionary flux and flow of embodied life in the material world.

God may be the poet of the world but the world itself does not speak. We therefore look to poets and preachers, artists and intellectuals, scientists and gardeners, powerful uneducated persons, the young, and mothers of families to help us name ourselves and render God's name in history. Poet Jeff Gundy has now given us his beautiful and brilliant theopoetics and in so doing offers his readers an artful spirituality, a fresh theology and a thoughtful poetics of God, world, self and other.

Although religion has always emerged and evolved within the play, work and sometimes war of the infinite multiplicity of the metaphor, theopoetics became a distinctive model for religious and theological reflection at some very generative conferences at Drew University in the 1960s. The early theopoetic writers were Stanley Hopper, David Miller, and Amos Wilder. David Miller, who grew up in a Church of the Brethren pastor's home and graduated from the denominational seminary, reminds us that theopoetics was a response to "the death of God movement." As such, there was a recognition, following the Brazilian theopoet Rubem Alves, that the birds had flown from their cages and that God-talk must now be uttered out of and before the void.

Gundy has seen the empty cages and understands the difference between the disciplines of theology and poetry and theopoetics. The former seeks to poeticize and underwrite a given theological tradition with great rhetorical flair. Theopoetics, in contrast, contending that religion's nearest analogue is art, practices theology as a *poiesis*: an inventive, intuitive, and imaginative act of composition performed by authors. Since theology is a kind of writing Gundy looks most to theologians who practice theology as imaginative construction, such as Gordon Kaufman and Grace Jantzen, rather than those who earnestly seek to recover the primitive church paradigm for faith and practice, like John Howard Yoder. Gundy knows any ecclesial theology worth living cannot be pried apart from a cosmology of this sensuous living world.

As a practicing preacher, I can confess that Gundy's theopoetics is a welcome word for many exiles from the established church as well for many young seekers of beauty, truth, and goodness. The polygenesis of religion, radical cultural pluralism, and the ecstasy of polydoxy have trumped the old anxieties of orthodoxy for many of us. Reading Gundy's *Songs*, I smiled in delight and satisfaction at a writer whose deep soul is simultaneously Romantic, Anabaptist, and Transcendental.

Songs is a gift to me professionally. I will use it in a Theopoetics class at Bethany Theological Seminary and the Earlham School of Religion. Gundy's work has also been important to me personally. Many years ago as a pastor of both Mennonite and Brethren congregations, this caged bird felt no longer able to sing the old theological songs from the pulpit and began to experiment with a more theopoetic genre. Happily, at that time I became conversation partner with three strong Mennonite poets: Gundy, Julia Kasdorf, and Jean Janzen. Their work, witness, and friendship have made me a more artful theologian and a more poetic preacher. Thus, like Gundy, although my heart often leans to the heretical left, in the great romance of faith I still believe in the Communion of Saints.

—*Scott Holland, Professor of Theology and Culture*
  Bethany Theological Seminary

SERIES EDITOR'S FOREWORD

"God never wrote any theology. All theology was written by people in an effort to say something about God or related matters." The speaker was a well-known womanist theologian that I had invited to address my class. Her comment came in response to my question whether there were any creeds or theological formulas that applied universally in all times and places. I approved her answer. It allows the theologian to find new ways to express theological truth in ever changing contexts. Jeff Gundy most certainly agrees with my guest and the implication of her answer, as would many theologians, at least in the abstract.

But Gundy approaches such an understanding not from the side of theology but from his stance as a poet who has thought deeply about some of the big, deep and perplexing issues of theology. Precisely because of Gundy's approach all theologians, particularly those like myself who strive to write with convincing clarity and logic but whom Gundy suspects of claiming to know too much, should read *Songs From An Empty Cage*. If there are any doubters, this book makes quite clear that all theology is, as Gundy quotes Gordon Kaufman, "human construction."

Meanwhile beyond theologians, poets, and other writers who already know Gundy's work will relish this book—its humor, its rich language, its poetic imagery, its processing of images and ideas, and much more that a non-poet cannot describe adequately. As one of the anonymous reviewers wrote, "My reaction to the manuscript was one of rapt suspense and then eventual rapture."

Gundy has written in the relatively new genre of theopoetics. A non-poet's definition of theopoetics might be that it is a hybrid of poetry and theology. But to call it that misses the mark. It is an entire way of thinking. From the side of poetry, it shows that ideas are more than abstractions. They have form—verbal, visual, sensual—and are thus experienced as least as much as they are thought. What one learns from the theology side of theopoetics has at least as much importance. One observes that theology is more than an abstraction. It is a way of thinking, visualizing, and sensing images of God. And at that juncture, theologians should become aware that traditional theology—which Gundy fears is too often bound to efforts to bring closure to arguments—is a way to think about the divine but is only one of multiple ways to consider God. Thus for theologians, theopoetics will underscore their (sometimes reluctant) admission that theology is one form of truth but ought not be confused with TRUTH itself.

Traditional theologians will certainly be interested in Gundy's theopoetic interaction with John Howard Yoder. The resulting view of Yoder depicted in theopoetics is not quite the Yoder that I see, but then again neither are the other "Yoders" depicted in recent efforts to describe Yoder theologically.

One of the engaging elements of Jeff Gundy's theopoetics is his acceptance and use of the sense of many poets that they need to challenge established orthodoxies, thus his embrace of the category of "heresy," his support of the "transgressions" of poets, and his interest in ancient writings deemed heretical. Gundy is aware, of course, that merely adopting as true the opposite of what is presumed orthodox still allows the dominant view to determine truth in a back-handed way. Thus this book's discussion of what some have deemed "heresy" invites every reader to self-reflection about what he or she does accept as the basis of truth from which one can live. It is an invitation to a reflective life of *living for* rather than a mere reactionary life defined by being against.

I have enjoyed working with Jeff to implement suggestions that came from the anonymous reviewers of the manuscript. It is a pleasure to welcome this volume to the C. Henry Smith Series. I am grateful to Bluffton University for its financial contribution to the publication of this book in the C. Henry Smith Series.

—*J. Denny Weaver*
  C. Henry Smith Series Editor

ACKNOWLEDGMENTS

Many thanks to the editors and organizers of these publications and events, where some of these pieces first appeared, all in somewhat different versions.

Chapter One: Presented in condensed form at "Mennonite/s Writing VI: Solos and Harmonies," Eastern Mennonite University, 27 April 2012. Published in *Conrad Grebel Review* 31.2 (Spring 2013): 130-42

Chapter Three: Published in *Crosscurrents* 55.1 (Spring 2006): 80-97.

Chapter Four: Presented at "Mennonite/s Writing: Beyond Borders," Bluffton University, Oct. 27, 2006. Published in *Conrad Grebel Review* 26.1 (Winter 2008): 59-71.

Chapter Five: Published in *The Work of Jesus Christ in an Anabaptist Perspective: Essays in Honor of J. Denny Weaver.* Ed. Alain Epp Weaver and Gerald J. Mast. Telford, Pa.: Cascadia Publishing House, 2008: 371-85.

Chapter Six: Published in *Crosscurrents* 60.1 (Spring 2010): 24-44.

Chapter Seven: Presented at "Teaching Peace: Nonviolence and the Liberal Arts Curriculum," Bluffton University, May 27, 2004.

Chapter Eight: Presented at the Mennonite University Faculty conference at Bluffton University on August 9, 2006. Published in *Higher Learning and the Wisdom of the Cross: Mennonite University Faculty Conference Presentations.* Goshen, Ind.: Mennonite Education Agency, 2006.

Chapter Nine: Published in *Mennonite Quarterly Review* 86.1 (January 2012): 75-96.

Chapter Ten: Presented in a much different version at "Sound in the Land," Conrad Grebel University College, Waterloo, Ontario, June 6, 2009.

For essential conversation, advice, and criticism as I worked on this project, I owe special gratitude to Scott Holland for his scholarly work and personal guidance on the subject of theopoetics, to Gerald Mast for sharing his intricate and wide-ranging knowledge of Anabaptist thought and correcting some of my many errors, and to Julia Spicher Kasdorf for many years of willingness to take me seriously but not too seriously. For long and loyal poetic friendships and ongoing exchanges, thanks also to Keith Ratzlaff and Jean Janzen.

My thinking on the issues taken up in this book has been greatly enriched over the years by conversations and other exchanges with Kirsten Beachy, Trevor Bechtel, Peter Blum, Perry Bush, Susan Carpenter, Peter Dula, Gordon Kaufman, Lamar Nisly, John Roth, Alex Sider, David Wright, and others I suspect I have neglected to mention.

In his role as editor of the C. Henry Smith series and as a friend, conversation partner, and influence of long standing, J. Denny Weaver has provided crucial advice and feedback, especially on John Howard Yoder, as well as indulging my reluctance to become a full-fledged Yoderian.

Susan Carpenter's generous loan of her family's cabin on Snow Road for a week was crucial to early work on this project, and Sally Weaver Sommer's ongoing support as academic dean at Bluffton University has been crucial as well. I am deeply indebted to the Lehman family for a 2011-12 Lehman Faculty Scholarship at Bluffton University, which provided essential time for revision and reworking of several chapters. Thanks to Kathy Landis of Wilderness Wind for inviting me to take part in two summer writing workshops on the Boundary Waters, where I became even more convicted that God dwells in the material world. Special thanks to Peter Blum for helping me wangle an invitation to serve as visiting writer at Hillsdale College in February 2012, where my thinking about theopoetics was honed by many thoughtful questions and conversations with Pete, John Somerville, and other faculty and students. And thanks much to all the editors and conference organizers who enabled me to try out my developing notions in public.

And, as always, deep thanks to my wife Marlyce, who continues to indulge my distractions and obsessions.

INTRODUCTION: POETRY, MYSTERY, ANABAPTISM, AND THE WORLD

Theology wants to be science, a discourse without interstices . . .
It wants to have its birds in cages . . .
Theopoetics *instead,*
empty cages,
words which are uttered out of and before the void . . .
—Rubem A. Alves[1]

Don't despise words.
Poets, the world is noisy
and mute. Only God talks.
—Antonio Machado[2]

Without Contraries is no progression. Attraction and
Repulsion, reason and Energy, Love and Hate, are
necessary to Human existence.
—William Blake[3]

This book has several origins: my love of poetry and all writing that resists the given for the sake of deeper truths; my fascination (mainly intellectual) with transgression, opposition, and "heresy"; my mingled
gratitude, allegiance, and ambivalence concerning Christian tradition
and my particular birthright—historic Anabaptism and contemporary

17

Mennonite practice. What might it mean to pursue a poet's vocation and attempt to be loyal to such a tradition, itself born in rebellion and renewal? Might poetry, among the arts that Mennonites have often regarded with suspicion, further my Anabaptist goals of making peace, working for justice, and spreading the good news, even bring another renewal to a tradition now threatened with bureaucratic ossification? Might Anabaptist zeal and ethical earnestness enrich and deepen the work of poets tempted to idle their lives away in the playgrounds of mere aestheticism? These tensions, I will claim here, can form the sort of Blakean contraries that lead to real progression, if placed into the sort of close contact that takes competing claims seriously without accepting any at face value.

Much of what I undertake here might be described as *theopoetics*, a relatively new term for an old tradition that favors an intuitive, imagistic approach to ultimate questions over narrowly logical and rational discourse. This book seeks to trace and interweave various threads of this tradition in both poetry and prose, drawing on a wide range of historical and contemporary texts. For years, as a poet and a Mennonite, I have studied and written about and out of both of those traditions. For better or worse, I have refused to give up either, even at the risk of being faithless to both, and increasingly become fascinated by the tensions and the possible conjunctions between them.

My passions and obsessions have led to this exploration of the knotty intersections of a wide set of competing claims: poetry, religion, and imagination; history, metaphor and narrative; Gnosticism and Anabaptism; present, past, and future; romanticism, individualism, and community; particularity and abstraction. My ambitions are, it seems to me now, humble and grandiose at the same time: grandiose in that I am really only interested in addressing the most essential questions: what is the nature of this universe, of ourselves, of that not-ourselves that we call God, and how then should we live? Humble, in the deep awareness that for all my wrestling with language, that most essential and frustrating of instruments, I have no final answers, no neat formulae that will render the great mysteries in convenient, lucid language.

Still, I can say a few things that I will seek to demonstrate in more detail in what follows:

• Our most cherished traditions—religious, poetic, and other—all have their origins in transgression, opposition to received wisdom, rebellion of one sort or another.

- These rebellions eventually become themselves ensconced and often stultifying traditions, and their defenders argue earnestly that to change them is to betray them, despite their revolutionary origins.
- Sorting out the worthy, life-giving traditions and transgressions— religious, poetic, and other—from the ossified and/or destructive is, therefore, a matter of considerable urgency.
- The glints and gleams of the best are distributed widely and irregularly amongst the vast human enterprise, but often to be found in the particularly charged language-products we call poetry.
- As we search for what will allow the project of life to persist and to thrive, reason and evidence are utterly essential and yet not enough. We cannot pursue truth without beauty.
- The language we have for God, magnificent and meaningful as it often is, still needs constant renewal and supplement. Revelation is both complete and continuing. If not, why are we alive at all?
- Any particular gathering by a single human agent—no matter how magisterial its claims—must be eccentric, subjective, partial. Mine surely reflects the accident of my birth and heritage, the privileges and limits of my education and location in the American Midwest, my decades of teaching and writing, reading and ordinary life.

With this last point, allow me to say a bit more on how this project came to be. Another narrative of its origin would begin with the irreducible sense of *otherness* that has stuck with me through all else, the sense of being a single, separate person who despite many affinities and allegiances does not fit neatly or completely anywhere. In my late fifties, my children grown, my modest career unlikely to take radical new turns, I have been tempted to sail off into the misty realms of contemplation. I have found myself drawn to mystics, to obscure heretical sects and figures, to oddball misfits and rebel poets who stepped away from the world to critique it. Much of the time I can even convince myself that this path is worth walking; the precedents are noble, after all, and the company is good.

Then I think about the state of the world (fill in your own list of crises and desperate needs here). The violence and disasters, mostly, happen far away from my quiet Midwestern town, my comfortable daily life, but when I speak with someone just escaped from one of the crisis zones, or imagine my children trapped in one of those nightmare scenarios of the near future, sinking into states of mystical oblivion seems idle and frivolous. I ought to be working to change the world, I think, every minute of every day.

But that mood doesn't last either. In the next moment, I find myself caught up completely in the technical problems of putting fresh blacktop sealer on the driveway, stopping up one more leak under the kitchen sink, or patching the cracks in the upstairs bedroom so my wife can repaint it.

And then I read some discussion of what Mennonites and Anabaptists believe, or used to believe, or what they ought or ought not be doing, and all at once I'm taking sides in a 500-year-old argument about how to be faithful followers of Jesus in a world filled with abominations, half-convinced that I must throw off my modern conveniences and compromises and return to the plain ways of my Amish ancestors.

In the next mood, the whole idea of dismissing the rest of the world as an abomination seems to me scandalously arrogant and terminally dumb, and I want only to put on some old Leonard Cohen and watch the hummingbirds zoom around the feeder.

And so on.

None of this is very interesting to me nor (I suspect) to you as an account of my personal tribulations, which are minor and unoriginal. But it has led me to this project. I have tried to avoid merely assembling another string of convenient, reductive dualisms, instead aiming at an exploration of contraries and complexities that might help to trace a path forward, if only the most tenuous trace. Despite my ambitions, I have no grand new answers to the question "How then shall we live?" Those who seek one here may be disappointed at my failure to construct clever, alliterative lists. I can only plead, as A. J. Liebling once did, that "the only way to make clear pea soup is to leave out the peas." I hope that my answers to the questions "How shall we write?" and "How shall we teach?" while still not entirely transparent, may be more useful.

William Blake, in a visionary text from the beginning of the nineteenth century, proposed a marriage of Heaven and Hell. We must note that in marriage neither partner loses his/her identity, but we must also note that Blake was mainly interested in rehabilitating our view of hell and demystifying our view of heaven. Is it possible to somehow find a unifying synthesis, a kind of marriage, of the contraries listed above, even in the space of the page, and how might such a marriage work?

Such a project must at the least be heterodox; for a long time this project was both driven and slowed by my half-guilty, half-defiant sense that it must be heretical, for like Blake I find it difficult to give full allegiance to any one set of beliefs, to take any one human construction of the way the world is as complete or final. Since infancy, I have been hearing competing narratives, often grand and resonant: most crucially, the triumphalist, exceptionalist American story and the Anabaptist version of the Christian story, at least as exceptionalist in its own way, and triumphalist too, if on very different terms.

My daily life is little troubled by these master narratives, and on an intellectual level I find J. Denny Weaver's advice quite persuasive: to quit worrying about them altogether, that is, to avoid granting orthodoxy the power implied by its assumed right to label other views "heresy."[4] Certainly for a long time I have not been unduly anxious about finding my ideas out of synch with the dominant ideologies, religious and otherwise, of our time. Yet I was reminded even in writing this manuscript that authority structures can loom as sudden obstacles even in the lives of comfortably tenured professors like me. When I first submitted an early version, the outside reader spent most of his letter of response complaining that I had failed to appreciate the authority of Orthodox Tradition (capitalizing both terms), and insisting that it was "patently silly and juvenile" for anyone, especially me, to fail to accept that authority. Needless to say, I found myself free to seek another publisher.

And so I plead guilty to such charges. I have been enormously nourished and nurtured by the great narratives of Christendom and Anabaptism, but am no longer able to accept the claim that they settle everything, or that one particular strand is right and all the others wrong. Sooner or later we must make our leaps and claim our allegiances—utter relativism is a master narrative of its own, and a peculiarly debilitating one—but many conversations, and much great literature, art, and music, convince me that we must continue inventing the path forward as we walk it, as we construct history and theology, as we imagine our way toward the attributes and names of God.

My small contribution to this ongoing project owes much to others: among poets, William Blake, Walt Whitman, and Emily Dickinson, those marvelous eccentrics, and too many more to list here, though many will be discussed in these pages. Among critics and theologians, I am especially indebted to Rubem Alves, John Howard Yoder, Grace

Jantzen, Gordon Kaufman, and John D. Caputo, each of them a brilliant eccentric as well, each of them committed to a radical rethinking of what it means to talk about God and about how human beings should seek to do God's will. Scott Holland, Brethren theologian and preacher, has been an especially important guide and inspiration in my own explorations of the territory where poetry and theology overlap and intersect. In very different ways, each works from a sense that as rich and deep as our literary and religious traditions may be, they have left us in crisis on multiple levels—from the ecological to the spiritual—and that this crisis cannot be addressed by simply reasserting old formulas or packaging old wine in new skins.

This sense of both crisis and incompletion has driven my work as a poet; poetry above all comes out of the sense that what we have thus far is not final, that more beautiful things made of words are still necessary. As human beings we seem born to desires that can never be fully satisfied. The ground note of human experience, Simone Weil suggests, is a hunger of the soul that can easily be misunderstood or dealt with in ways that destroy its significance:

> The soul knows for certain only that it is hungry. The important thing is that it announces its hunger by crying. A child does not stop crying if we suggest to it that perhaps there is no bread. . . . The danger is not lest the soul should doubt whether there is any bread, but lest, by a lie, it should persuade itself that it is not hungry.[5]

My first, most frightening negation, then, lies in trespassing what I learned as a child must suffice. The beloved community is vital and blessed, yet not entirely enough. The "Work and Hope" urged in the *Martyrs Mirror* are essential to a meaningful life, yet mere labor is surely not enough, and the hope offered by the spectacle of the martyrs is considerably problematic, as I will explore further. Even trusting Jesus— that beautiful imperative—does not suffice when one's sense of "Jesus" has become a maddening palimpsest of social, cultural, and personal inscriptions. It is vital, then, to allow the soul to admit its hunger, and to go in search of the bread for which it hungers, or (as one song puts it) the water from a deeper well.

This gap, for me, is grounded less in doing than in being. Amid dailyness—and my daily life is as rich, challenging, secure, and pleasant as I have any right to expect—the gap persists. Dare I illustrate with a more or less direct transcription of some idle, erratic notes scrawled during a faculty meeting?

> The tyranny of the urgent has taken over. I regret that I'm not more of what I could be, but at least I'm not you. Or dead. Or adrift among the islets of Langerhans. And while a cell phone warbles and the screen comes down and Gregg fills his cup at the monster coffee urn, I'm internally free, or close, or at least so absorbed in scribbling that I miss saying "Aye" when it's time to say "Aye." Still I am not subject to intrusive advising. Still I have not been either suspended or dismissed. I have not connected any two dots. I have said nothing aloud about the collapse of my inner defenses. I will pick up a report from the stack.

Negation, evasion, extravagance: they're all here, along with their usual accomplices, guilt and defiance. And the sense of being "one of the lingering bad ones," as Emily Dickinson put it, as Walt Whitman's celebration of himself is clearly poised against his awareness of his many transgressions.

In two lengthy recent articles in *American Poetry Review*, critic Steven Antinoff explores something like this problem, which he terms "spiritual atheism," and defines as the spiritual hunger that persists when people find it impossible to believe in God.[6] His discussion is compelling, but atheism is not the problem I address here. My own journey has left me still some kind of a believer, though exactly what kind is a long discussion. Poetry has been, for me, inseparable from the quest for belief and spiritual insight; reading poems and attempting to write my own has been for me a combination of instruction, meditation, and perhaps even prayer that has sustained, nourished, and complicated my life in ways beyond full reckoning.

Why poetry? It is, the current wisdom has it, not for most people, but the province of eccentric professors, alienated hipsters, and assorted other oddballs. Perhaps this is so; I am personally resigned to the perplexed, awkward pause that comes when I am introduced as "our poet." But poetry will not let me go, no matter how few of my neighbors care about it, and (like Mennonites) the band of poets is thinly scattered but fiercely persistent. In a Gnostic, cryptic moment, Harold Bloom suggests that there is much more to poetry than idle word-play or prettiness:

I have come to the conviction that the love of poetry is another variant of the love of power. . . . We read to usurp, just as the poet writes to usurp. Usurp what? A place, a stance, a fullness, an illusion of identification or possession; something we can call our own or even ourselves.[7]

I must admit that poetry plays such a role in my own yearnings. I want to speak and be heard among the cacophonous voices of this world. I want to speak as an American, a Mennonite, a Midwesterner, yet to resist and critique all of these identities as partial and problematic. Nor do I take this as any mark of superiority or uniqueness. I suspect those of us who have awakened to our situations are all this way, incompletely defined by any set of words, any tradition, inhabitants of a world where we both do and do not belong, born into an excess and a deficit that we can never quite name, trail what clouds of glory we may.

At the same time, I will make the case here for a particular, nonviolent sort of power, the power of voice rather than of coercion or violence. For my Anabaptist people, strategies for resisting the powers of the world without taking up the sword have a complicated history. Put very broadly, they evolved from the defiant "bloody theatre" of the Radical Reformation into something much less dramatic, defined for long periods mainly by slogans like "the quiet in the land." While the original Anabaptists were far from quiet—many found themselves martyred or persecuted, and proclaimed and argued earnestly with the authorities—as time went on, most found the bloody pyre unappealing except as an inspiring image of the iconic ancestors. I do not say this in judgment. But they worked and hoped, mainly, that they would be let alone to keep the faith until they were received with rejoicing at the Pearly Gates.

That stance has continued to develop; nonresistance evolved during the last century, for many Mennonites, into more active forms of nonviolent action and witness. The most influential Mennonite theologian and ethicist of our time, John Howard Yoder, insisted that working not just to maintain communal purity but to aid the poor and to promote justice and peace was simply to follow the example and teaching of Jesus, and that all serious Christians surely ought to be pacifist.

In the next generation of Mennonite theologians, my former colleague J. Denny Weaver has developed an Anabaptist theology of nonviolence with clear affinities to Yoder's, and Chapter Five of this volume was written in response to his work. At the same time, many Mennonites, and many more Christians, have been learning from conservative American evangelicalism that good Christians could and should enthusiastically take up their country's weapons, and even issue their own calls to arms. "God is Pro-War," Jerry Falwell famously declaimed in the run-up to the Iraq war, as though he had received a personal email.

All this is both confusing and, many times, depressing. Even the current mainstream version of official Anabaptism, which earnestly incorporates peace work into its bulging portfolio of Work That Must Be Done, often seems wearisome to me in its earnestness, its self-righteousness, its sloganeering and political compromises. I love it, but dutifully, the way one loves a parent who is not aging especially gracefully or a colleague who persists in explaining at length what everybody already knows, and gets it subtly wrong in the process.

So I have imagined what follows in the spirit of *The Marriage of Heaven and Hell* and as the product of a poor and belated ephebe, to use Bloom's term for the one who follows in the footsteps of a strong poet. I see few signs in myself of either William Blake's madness or his genius. Yet I have been granted certain rather astonishing privileges, most notably the gifts of time and learning. I have been able to sit with my books, to leaf through them on days when the only interruptions were of my own devising, to record my own thoughts and preserve them. This is a great luxury, I know, and one I hope not to have wasted.

This book continues with two prefatory chapters.

Chapter One, "Notes Toward an Anabaptist Theopoetics," offers not a systematic history and definition of theopoetics from an Anabaptist perspective, but an exposition of main themes and ideas that also suggests the contours and most important threads of this book.

Chapter Two, "Declining to Be in Charge," responds to recent concerns about "boundaries" within Mennonite writing circles, and argues for esthetic and ideological pluralism.

The next section contains four chapters, each originally written for another occasion but extensively reworked for this book. These chapters mingle historical, literary, and theological investigations into a wide range of sources and events, and explore issues of heresy, rebellion, and forms of writing that aspire to revise the fundamental ways we think about the world.

Chapter Three, "The Hammer and the Free Spirit," explores "heresy" as a sometimes necessary, if perilous, human action, and the "free spirit" thread in history. Is it possible to break free of social constraints without slipping into violence and disaster? Perhaps . . . if nonviolence and community are part of one's heresy.

Chapter Four, "The Marriage of the Martyrs Mirror and the Open Road, or, Why I Love Poetry Despite the Suspicion That It Won't Save Anybody," makes a case for poetry as unbound to narrative and "common sense," suited to the integration of visionary and practical texts and images, and necessary to contend with the perils of our time and to envision a plausible future.

Chapter Five, "'Truth Did Not Come Into the World Naked': Some Images, Some Stories, and an Immodest Proposal," examines the need for metaphor, story, and image as ways of mediating between human beings and what we name as truth. Language must constantly be refreshed, renewed, and re-examined—even terms as familiar as "Christian."

Chapter Six, "Notes Toward the Heretical Sublime," goes deeper into the energy of transgression, opposition and heresy, with special attention to William Blake, John Howard Yoder, and Stanley Hopper. It offers more discussion of "theopoetics" as category and practice, with examples from Mennonite and other poets.

The next cluster deals especially with peacemaking and nonviolence in teaching and writing. Although this entire project rests on my conviction that active nonviolence, while not easily practiced or even defined, is crucial, I have long pondered a knotty set of questions about what it means to pursue peace in classrooms and in the written word, especially in a Mennonite context.

Chapter Seven, "Adding Real Beings to the World: Teaching Peace, Writing, and Human Exchange," considers teaching as a human activity, with reference to Anabaptism and to Surrealism—both radical movements that hoped to change both the lives of individuals and the world at large. If teachers hope to change the world, they must change lives, but lives are changed only through personal encounters.

Chapter Eight, "On Jesus and Teaching," asks a simple question: when we invoke the name of Jesus, just who do we mean? It makes a difference.

Chapter Nine, "Toward Post-Peace Poetry: Or, What to Do with the Drunken Soldier," explores recent claims that Mennonite poets write little peace poetry, and argues that in the current situation "peace poetry" must be understood as much more than poems directly addressing or opposing war. Recent work by a number of Mennonite poets shows their commitments to examining and resisting many types of violence.

The sequence of chapters in the second half of the book especially pursue a deeper understanding of theopoetics.

Chapter Ten, "Sound and the Sixties: Sex, God, Rock and Roll, and Flourishing," examines music by Leonard Cohen and others on the relation between physical and religious desire. With special reference to Anne Carson and Grace Jantzen, it explores the centrality of desire, rightly understood, in building the beloved community.

Chapter Eleven, "The Rule of God and the Ruby: The Theopoet Talks Back," that while John Howard Yoder's contributions to Anabaptist theology and ethics are crucial, his views on language, poetry, and metaphor would benefit from some expansion and supplementation, here provided especially by the Sufi poet Rumi.

Chapter Twelve, "The Farm Boy's Thoughts Turn toward Beauty," considers the long Anabaptist suspicion of beauty as a category, and contends that we neglect it at our peril, both physical and spiritual. Might it be, as Dostoyevsky claimed, that "Beauty will save the world"?

Chapter Thirteen, "The Baptism in Dark Water: Apophasis, Mystery, and the God Within," asks how much *can* we know? As Rubem Alves and Wallace Stevens suggest, resting more willingly in mystery may be the best way to approach God.

Chapter Fourteen, "Looking in the *Mirror*," takes a fresh look at the familiar image and narrative of Dirk Willems from *Martyrs Mirror*, and less familiar stories from that often-invoked but rarely read text, with Rubem Alves' open-ended approach to story in mind. What about those who chose survival rather than martyrdom?

Chapter Fifteen, "Who Knows Who Is Calling?" further examines the idea of an "apophatic theopoetics" and the problem of knowledge claims and particular voices, with special attention to theologian Grace Jantzen, Walt Whitman, and contemporary poet Anne Carson.

Chapter Sixteen, "Voice and Imagination: Meaning besides Truth," offers a culminating exploration of three important contemporary theopoets: William Stafford, Li-Young Lee, and Jack Gilbert.

Notes

1. Rubem Alves, *The Poet, The Warrior, The Prophet: The Edward Cadbury Lectures 1990* (London: SCM Press, 1990), 99.

2. Antonio Machado, *Border of a Dream*, trans. Willis Barnstone (Port Townsend, Wash.: Copper Canyon, 2004), 357.

3. William Blake, *Jerusalem, Selected Poetry and Prose,* ed. Hazard Adams (New York: Holt, Rinehard and Winston, 1970), 124.

4. J. Denny Weaver, email message to the author, 2 February 2012.

5. Simone Weil, *Waiting for God,* trans. Emma Craufurd (New York: Harper-Collins, 1951, 2001), 162.

6. Stephen Antinoff, "Spiritual Atheism: Part One: Reading Kafka for Breakfast, Swallowed Up for Lunch: A Special *APR* Supplement," *American Poetry Review* (May/June 2006): 27-32. "Spiritual Atheism: Part Two: The Quest for Atheistic Salvation," *American Poetry Review* (July/August 2006): 23-35.

7. Harold Bloom, *Agon: Towards a Theory of Revisionism* (New York: Oxford, 1982), 17.

Part One
Prolegomena

CHAPTER ONE

NOTES TOWARD AN ANABAPTIST THEOPOETICS

For years now I have found myself pursuing large questions about God and human beings and the cosmos, in and through poems and essays written from a poet's perspective, and as humbly as my wild ambitions will allow. I have been guided by many fellow travelers and experts in this pursuit, some poets, some theologians, some not readily categorized, and I have followed Scott Holland's lead in particular as I began to use the term "theopoetics" for this endeavor. Like many useful words in the hands of intellectuals, however, theopoetics is subject to much pulling and hauling regarding its precise definition. "A useful working definition of the term would be the study and practice of making God known through text," writes L. B. C. Keefe-Perry, keeper of the website theopoetics.net. "Used as an adjective, a theopoetic text is one that reveals some aspect of the divine."[1]

Immediately both my academic and poetic sides begin to fuss and quibble; this definition seems inordinately inclusive— it has far too much *theo*, and too little *poetry*, for my liking. But as a theopoet, I desire to resist abstract definitions and their tedious, artificial clarity anyway. So I might begin this effort to unpack something of what I mean by "theopoetics" by (partly) disagreeing with Keefe-Perry and postulating, too simply, that theopoetics happens where poetry and theology cross paths, and especially when poetic methods of exploration are brought to theological questions.

Unlike the great theopoets Dante and Milton, and the great Mennonite theonovelist Rudy Wiebe, I am not good at grand narratives, so I will not try to offer one of those here. Like Walt Whitman, I contain multitudes and my contradictions are many. Like William Blake, I am also ready to accept, however uneasily, that without contraries there is no progression—and the conversation on this subject is bound to include many such contraries. We must keep trying to explain, but theopoetics is suspicious of orderly, logical argument, and so I will offer not an argument nor even, as I once envisioned, a manifesto. I do love manifestos, but mistrust them as well; they are generally both too large and too small to contain their own discourse. They creak and crack, and whatever is in them spills off into the sand. Still, if the water lies deep and a leaky bucket is all we have, it is worth dropping it into the well, just to see if we can bring up something.

Here are some notes, then, toward what I might presumptuously call an Anabaptist theopoetics.

1. One origin of theopoetics is in the suspicion that our God-talk is mostly really human talk, that the Great One may not be obsessed with the creation of orderly institutions and systematic belief systems, that revelation is continual and ongoing. Or so I claim, knowing that such generalities must themselves be cast under suspicion the moment they are uttered. "To generalize is to be an Idiot," William Blake beautifully (if paradoxically) said.

2. As theopoet I am skeptical of overarching truth-frames and master narratives, even the narrative of skepticism. Theopoetry kneels at no altar except its own necessity, which is born of intuition and craft, attention and introspection, memory and learning, restlessness and desire.

3. So much religion feels like the will trying desperately to do the work of the imagination. Theopoetics says: enough of duty, enough of obedience to people who presume to speak for God. Enough listening to the licensed and certified. Time to pay attention to the world, and to listen to its many voices. If it doesn't taste good, spit it out. Don't trust anyone who has more answers than questions. Don't trust anyone who tells you to hate.

4. The vast and orderly systems so beloved of the systematizers and rationalizers, their elaborate and sensible explanations of the darkest mysteries, too often seem mere efforts to build little houses and pro-

claim them the world, to paint the ceilings blue and call them the sky, to drink grape juice and call it wine.

5. The difference between such voices and those that speak with the essential wildness of poetry is unmistakable, and not a matter of form. Consider recent demand by certain church fathers that nuns should pay less attention to caring for the poor and the sick, and more to policing the sexual habits of others. Then consider the parables of Jesus. Yes, these are dramatic examples, and there is murkier territory between—but we are moving quickly today.

6. Even community, discipleship, peace, those worthy and essential aims, take on a new aspect under the spell of the theopoetic voice. They do not vanish, but the poem will not be bound to them; it insists on its freedom to say anything, to imagine anything, to question anything, if only for the sake of testing, tasting, discovering.

7. I am happy enough on many days to sit in the balcony if the singing is good, to bring a cheese-laden casserole and stay for the potluck. But just when the rest are settling in to discuss their grandkids and the weather, I feel a great urge to take the wrong coat from the rack and disappear into the winter sunshine.

8. As theopoet I am not missional. I make no claims on those who find all this odd if not ridiculous, those content with their lot, those at ease with the turn of the lectionary and with the comforting buzz of the familiar assurances and admonitions. God bless and keep them. I speak here only for myself and for some others, those whose brows also sometimes furrow even during the sweetest hymns, those who have spoken the creeds and the verses and found their thirst still not entirely quenched.

9. I know—quite possibly all this yearning is merely the result of too much leisure, liberal education, assimilation, and insufficient persecution, of just the sort Thieleman van Braght warned us against in the *Martyrs Mirror.* If I really want to be faithful, I can hear him sternly instructing me, I ought to forget all this frivolity and figure out how to get myself thrown in jail, if not burned at the stake. At the least, I should learn to trust in the Mission of the Church, as it has been explained by those duly trained and certified to do so.

10. But could it be that even the beautiful, true stories we have do not include everything that we might need to know? That new stories, new songs, and new readings of the old are still necessary?

11. Could it be that we should also praise the non-martyrs, the ones who shinnied down their ropes and high-tailed it back to Moravia, the ones who let the authorities baptize their babies but kept sneaking off to the cave anyway? These, after all, are our literal ancestors.[2]

12. Could it be that outside the *Ordnung* there might be other or-ders as true-hearted as our own? Could it be that despite Thieleman van Braght the church is both visible and hidden, that none of us can say what the true path for our neighbor might be, except that we do our best to love each other?

13. Could it even be that the human order, and all our fussy conver-sations about God, are just one minor node of the great and vast cre-ation, one we might profitably regard from a broader perspective? William Stafford heard these words "On a Church Lawn":

> Dandelion cavalry, light little saviors,
> baffle the wind, they ride so light.
> They surround a church and outside the window
> utter their deaf little cry: "If you listen
> well, music won't have to happen."
>
> After service they depart singly
> to mention in the world their dandelion faith:
> "God is not big; He is right."[3]

14. In a more prosaic voice, the ecologist/philosopher David Abram laments our long inattention to the vast realm of life and being outside the human:

> How monotonous our speaking becomes when we speak only to ourselves! And how *insulting* to the other beings—the foraging black bears and twisted old cypresses—that no longer sense us talking to them, but only about them, as though they were not present in our world.[4]

15. The theopoet returns to the old words and finds new secrets hid-den in them, ways of experiencing the earth and the skies and the ten thousand things not as mere matter devoid of "soul," but as creation, whole and entire and scorned, dismissed, or ignored only at our peril. Listen to these words from long ago, enshrined in Proverbs, now dusted and revealed to shine by a fresh translation:

The Secret One through the ecstatic mother founded the earth,
through consciousness he made the skies go around,
by secret knowledge the oceans broke open,
and the clouds let the dew down.
—Proverbs 3: 19-20, trans. Aaron Blon[5]

16. The theopoet attempts, with mixed but occasional success, to
resist dwelling either in the dead past or the unreachable future. "God
himself culminates in the present moment," said Thoreau, burrowing
with his head into the mysteries of things and language, fishing in the
stream of the moment, sounding Walden Pond and keeping careful
records of both the interior and exterior weather.

17. Thoreau's neighbors thought him odd. He *was* odd, as true
poets are; the well-adjusted and compliant satisfy themselves with the
ordinary gruel of community and convention, or (as Thoreau sus-
pected) endure their quiet desperations, perhaps consoled by dreams of
pie in the sky, perhaps not. Kabir said this:

The idea that the soul will rejoin with the ecstatic just because the
    body is rotten—
that is all fantasy.
What is found now is found then.
If you find nothing now, you will simply end up with an apartment
    in the City of Death.
If you make love with the divine now, in the next
life you will have the face of satisfied desire.[6]

18. Often, the theopoet is a lone walker who hears memory and desire shouting and stirring, who hears the whispers and cries of wind and
birds, who dwells in the lovely, rich, perilous welter out of which new
things made of words are born. The Mennonite theopoet Jean Janzen
describes this quest well:

But most intense of all is the longing to know how to live this life,
and to find what is secret and hidden, which pulls us to the deep
and watery places. This is the life of the writer, to continue that
restless inquiry, and to find, if not the secrets, the connections
which make life more whole. [7]

19. Alone, with crowds of the dead and the living babbling and bub-

bling up inside, the theopoets do their part. For the work of the tribe is not only what happens in committee rooms and church kitchens and sanctuaries, not only in letter-writing and demonstrations, visiting the sick and clearing the wreckage after the tornado, necessary and good as all these are. The work of the tribe also happens on the edges, in wandering away, in dreaming, says Rubem Alves, in a passage that uncannily echoes the ur-Mennonite story of Dirk Willems on the thin ice of the pond:

> Truth appears as we stumble, when the frozen surface of the lake cracks and we hear its voice: dreaming . . .
> We are saved by the power of dreaming. Dreaming is the power which resurrects the dead. [. . .]
> So the eucharist: an empty, silent space for our dreaming, before the Absent One—like the dead man of the sea.
> Theology wants to be science, a discourse without interstices
> . . .
> It wants to have its birds in cages . . .
> *Theopoetics* instead,
> empty cages,
> words which are uttered out of and before the void.[8]

20. "There is more day to dawn. The sun is but a morning star," said that old pagan Thoreau. When will we wake up? When will we shake ourselves free of the mud and dust of tradition, leave our noisy overheated rooms, head out to encounter for ourselves the Great One who is both Father and Mother? She has spoken before, though for centuries the words here survived only hidden in a clay jar, and even the name given her ("The Thunder, Perfect Mind") bends and boggles our categories:

> I am the first and the last.
> I am the honored one and the scorned one.
> I am the whore and the holy one.
> I am the wife and the virgin.
> I am <the mother> and the daughter.
> I am the members of my mother.
> I am the barren one
> and many are her sons.
> I am she whose wedding is great,

and I have not taken a husband.
I am the midwife and she who does not bear.
I am the solace of my labor pains.
I am the bride and the bridegroom,
and it is my husband who begot me.[9]

Yes, this voice refuses to be orderly and reasonable. Yes, this voice is mainly but not entirely female. Yes, it seems entirely worthy of our praise.

21. Could it be that God has work for us beside "saving" our souls? Rainer Marie Rilke claimed so, in a poem that feels to me both beautiful and true:

Just as the winged energy of delight
carried you over many chasms early on,
now raise the daringly imagined arch
holding up the astonishing bridges.

The poet's work begins in delight and desire, but to build "the association beyond words" requires more than "being carried along":

Take your well-disciplined strengths
and stretch them between two opposing poles.
Because inside human beings
is where God learns.[10]

22. Could it be, as some have been saying for a very long time, that the One we worship is outside, under every stone, within every tree and brook? "How do you know but ev'ry bird that cuts the aery way, is an immense world of delight, clos'd by your senses five?" So asked the mad and holy Blake. More calmly, just as extravagantly, here speaks David Abram:

The ineffable and sacred One toward which all monotheisms direct themselves . . . is still whispering even now, beckoning to us from beyond the monotonous hum and buzz of our worded thoughts, inviting us to free our senses from the verbal husk into which we've retreated. . . .

An eternity we thought was elsewhere now calls out to us from every cleft in every stone, from every cloud and clump of dirt. To lend our ears to the dripping glaciers—to come awake to the voices of silence—is to be turned inside out, discovering to our astonishment that the wholeness and holiness we'd been dreaming our way toward has been holding us all along; that the secret and sacred One that moves behind all the many traditions is none other than this animate immensity that enfolds us, this spherical eternity, glimpsed at last in its unfathomable wholeness and complexity, in its sensitivity and its sentience.[11]

23. Yes, this is not precisely what I was taught before the ritual of baptism, nor you, I suspect. Is it what I "believe"? How can I answer that? I can only say that discovering others working to revise and rethink our views of fundamental questions—including the nature and place of "belief" in our lives—has been liberating and transforming for me. One of the most provocative of such thinkers is Grace Jantzen, who undertook a marvelously ambitious and nuanced project in theology and religious history (unfortunately cut short by her early death). Jantzen advocates a "deliberate feminist effort to restructure the religious symbolic," based not on "the justification of beliefs which separate the 'true' from the 'false'" but on "an imaginative longing for the divine in a reduplication of desire not content with the old gods," seeking a new future in which all living beings might flourish.[12] The question is not what we believe, Jantzen insists, but what we desire for ourselves and others, and how we act in the world.

24. Where might such beautiful, unorthodox images and ideas lead us? Keats claimed that what the imagination seizes as beauty must be truth. He did not mean that lightly. If the world, and God, are bigger and wilder and stranger than we can imagine, what makes us think that we can bind it with propositions and belief-systems? Gérard de Nerval:

> Do you think you are the only thinker
> on this earth in which life blazes inside all things?
> Your liberty does what it wishes with the powers it controls,
> but when you gather to plan, the universe is not there.[13]

25. This theopoet loves and embraces some theologians: besides Grace Jantzen and John D. Caputo (to be taken up soon), I recently, belatedly discovered the rebel priest Matthew Fox. He mistrusts St. Augustine, asceticism, and the doctrine of original sin, and praises the bounti-

ful universe which is, in fact, our home, despite the efforts of reductionists and tyrants to deny that we are part of something bigger, stronger,
and stranger than any human structure. Fox argues that scientism and
authoritarian patriarchy have cost us dearly:

> The cosmos has been lost in the West, and especially in religion
> and its rituals. . . . One reason has been the Newtonian parts
> mentality of the scientific era . . . which does not allow one to feel
> the mystery and the interconnectedness of microcosm and
> macrocosm. Another reason is patriarchal politics: . . . a threat-
> ened ecclesial establishment trying to control those who suggest
> that life is bigger than controls, that life is cosmic for everyone.[14]

26. Even the Mennonite quasi-patriarch John Howard Yoder, of
course, sings the praises of not being in charge, listening with patience,
and following the grain of the universe. The Yoderian Jesus is a nonviolent revolutionary as well as Savior, the Yoderian community one of
nonviolent witness and communal service, the Yoderian world one in
which through faith we see that "The rebellious but already (in principle) defeated cosmos is being brought to its knees by the Lamb."[15]
When Yoder begins to explain how the fellowship should be regulated, I
do my best to listen and sit still. But the bald cypress outside the window
is waving in the wind, the muddy water of the creek is hurrying off to the
north, and the buzzards are back from the south. None of them seem re-
motely interested in wrestling with the Lamb.

27. There are many varieties of humility, of yieldedness, of pride.
This theopoet is convinced that the "humility" that despises the self and
the body, and the "humility" that demands that others submit to the
group in all things, are as far outside the perfection of Christ as the
sword. With Matthew Fox, I believe that true humility is close to the
earth, does not regard the body as an enemy, and is ready always to praise
the Great Being within and around all things. I will readily confess that
I know this Being through the many things and creatures of the cosmos
and through the words and images that God's creatures offer up as part
and parcel of this creation, and that I continue to love the world though
I lament the many ways that its glory is pierced and wounded.

28. What is it that makes me unwilling to yield myself up fully to
anything less than everything, unable to surrender to Community or
Discipleship or Nonresistance or even to the Messiah who is, so often,

described and defined by others as though their version of him is as precise and authoritative as a stop sign or the Ohio Revised Code? What is it that makes me yearn always for the mysterious, elusive Jesus, the one described in the Gospel of Thomas, itself hidden away in the desert for more than a millennium? In its noncanonical but beautifully eloquent verses we read of a Jesus who said, "It is I who am the light which is above them all. It is I who am the all. From me did the all come forth, and unto me did the all extend. Split a piece of wood, and I am there. Lift up the stone, and you will find me there"[16]

29. Walt Whitman lived while the scrolls of Nag Hammadi slept in their red clay jar. He never read the words of Jesus about turning the stone and breaking the branch . But his "Song of Myself" and other poems are central texts for this theopoet, at least, and much of what I have written here is in homage to him. The grand "I" of "Song of Myself," Whitman insisted, was not merely himself but the voice of all people, all times, all places, "For every atom belonging to me as good belongs to you." In the poem's visionary final stanzas he also imagines a marvelous reunion:

> I depart as air, I shake my white locks at the runaway sun,
> I effuse my flesh in eddies, and drift it in lacy jags.
>
> I bequeath myself to the dirt to grow from the grass I love,
> If you want me again look for me under your boot-soles.
>
> You will hardly know who I am or what I mean,
> But I shall be good health to you nevertheless,
> And filter and fibre your blood.
>
> Failing to fetch me at first keep encouraged,
> Missing me one place search another,
> I stop somewhere waiting for you.[17]

30. The name of God is a call, not a presence, says John D. Caputo, and what we seek is not physical reunion but a uniting of desire and deed in "making truth come true":

> The world quivers quietly under the weak force of an event, made
> restless by the silent promptings of God's divinely subversive call.
> But is it really God who calls? Who knows who is calling? . . .

No matter. We have been delivered from the search for the name of God by the event. . . . The truth of the event releases us from the order of names and transports us to another level, where truth does not mean learning a name but making truth come true, making it happen.[18]

31. We know so little. The world is so large, and the spaces within as well, and this world is but a grain of sand on the edge of one small sea. The infinities within and around us may be terrifying, but they are exhilarating to contemplate and to explore, as best we can. Let us take to the open road, to the wide and unbound world. Let us listen for the call, and turn the stone.

32. Poetry, my friend Dean Young insists, is about the making of birds, not bird cages.[19] I suspect I will never make a real bird—but the gifts of voice and attention and imagination have been given to me, and to all of us, and why would God give such gifts if not to be used, if not for the making of songs and stories that have not yet been heard? Cages are useful, perhaps needful at times, but so are windows, doors, and wings.

33. Not so far away, as God measures distance, planets spin under strange suns, and perhaps creatures who look nothing like us—or a great deal like us—tell stories of One who came among them, bearing wisdom and offering a difficult, joyful new life. With voices unlike any we have known, perhaps, they sing and praise, so sweetly that the fabric of the cosmos shivers and wavers. And if we pause in our daily busyness and bluster, if we still ourselves deeply enough to listen, we might catch an echo of their song.

Notes

1. L. B. C. Keefe-Perry, "Theopoetics: Process and Perspective," *Christianity and Literature* 58.4 (Summer 2009): 579. This essay, available online, offers a concise overview and history of theopoetics, mostly from the theological side, perhaps especially useful to those who may find my approach abrupt and contentious.

2. See Chapter 14 for more on this point.

3. William Stafford, *The Way It Is: New and Selected Poems* (St. Paul, Minn.: Graywolf, 1988), 55.

4. David Abram, *Becoming Animal: An Earthly Cosmology* (New York: Pantheon, 2012), 175.

5. Robert Bly, *The Soul Is Here for Its Own Joy: Sacred Poems from Many Cultures*

(New York: Ecco, 1999), 128.

6. Robert Bly, *The Kabir Book: Forty-Four of the Ecstatic Poems of Kabir* (Boston: Beacon, 1977), 24.

7. Jean Janzen, *Elements of Faithful Writing* (North Newton, Kan.: Bethel College, 2004), 3.

8. Rubem Alves, *The Poet, The Warrior, The Prophet: The Edward Cadbury Lectures 1990* (London: SCM Press, 1990), 99.

9. James R. Robinson, "The Thunder, Perfect Mind," *The Nag Hammadi Library,* revised edition (HarperCollins, San Francisco, 1990), n.p. http://www.gnosis.org/naghamm/nhl.html. 4 April 2012.

10. Rainer Marie Rilke, *Selected Poems*, trans. Robert Bly (New York: Harper & Row, 1981), 175.

11. Abram, *Becoming Animal,* 178-81.

12. Grace Jantzen, *Becoming Divine: Toward a Feminist Philosophy of Religion* (Bloomington, Ind.: Indiana University Press, 1997), 99.

13. Robert Bly, *News of the Universe: Poems of Twofold Consciousness* (San Francisco: Sierra Club: 1980, 1995), 38.

14. Matthew Fox, *Original Blessing* (New York: Tarcher/Putnam, 1983, 2000), 75.

15. John Howard Yoder, *The Priestly Kingdom: Social Ethics as Gospel* (Notre Dame: University of Notre Dame Press, 1984), 53-4.

16. Robinson, "The Gospel of Thomas," *The Nag Hammadi Library*, verse 77.

17. Walt Whitman, *Leaves of Grass and Selected Prose,* ed. John A. Kouwenhoven (New York: Modern Library, 1950), 23, 75.

18. Caputo, *The Weakness of God: A Theology of the Event.* (Bloomington: Indiana University Press, 2006), 199.

19. Dean Young, *The Art of Recklessness: Poetry as Assertive Force and Contradiction* (St. Paul: Graywolf, 2010), 88.

TWO

DECLINING TO BE IN CHARGE

John Roth's introduction to the special issue of material from the 2006 "Mennonite/s Writing: Beyond Borders" conference begins on a triumphalist note: "During the past fifty years, Mennonites in North America have participated in a literary renaissance unparalleled since the Dutch Golden Age in the seventeenth century." Immediately, though, the tone turns subtly cautionary:

> Today, as then, the flourishing of Mennonite literature has emerged against the backdrop of remarkable economic affluence and steady cultural assimilation. And today, as in the past, the ascendancy of Mennonite literature is both a reflection of unsettling transformations and a sign, potentially at least, of a new movement of the Spirit within this 500-year-old tradition.[1]

The earlier time, of course, was when Thieleman Van Braght produced the *Martyrs Mirror,* itself an act of resistance to worldliness and assimilation, though made possible by the material resources provided by that worldliness and the education and wealth it provided. Roth's comments seem more worried than celebratory, however. Could it be because the new Mennonite writing (at least the literary productions; we should remember, certainly, that formulaic Amish romance novels and cookbooks are still the best sellers) tends to be progressive rather than conservative, because it is often skeptical and ironic, because it is insufficiently earnest and pious? Are current Mennonite writers like those Golden Age Dutch that Van Braght sought to admonish? Will their souls be lost to Mammon and The World, and will their dangerous texts drag unwitting readers along with them?[2]

A useful discussion of recent conferences and conversations follows, in which Roth takes his cues from Hildi Froese Tiessen's important "Beyond the Binary" essay from the 1997 Goshen conference and the "Beyond Borders" theme of the most recent gathering. Roth is clearly nervous about the idea of dismantling borders, noting uneasily that the literary folks don't seem to *argue* with each other, or with what he takes as a rather monolithic "academic culture," the way the historians and theologians do:

> In contrast to the long and vigorous debate among Mennonite historians about what it means to do "scholarship for the church," or the sharp critique John H. Yoder and Stanley Hauerwas have leveled against the disciplinary assumptions in theology and ethics, Mennonite literary theorists seem surprisingly uncritical about the academic disciplines that inform their work. Moreover, despite a growing sophistication in the technical tools of critical analysis, the general tone of the essays, like the "Mennonite/s Writing" conferences themselves, tends to be highly positive, perhaps even self-congratulatory, in regards to contemporary Mennonite writing. . . . If there are no borders, one might ask, do any criteria remain for distinguishing between good and bad literature?"[3]

Roth then (somewhat confusingly) cites my venerable, satiric poem "How to Write the New Mennonite Poem" (he leaves the word *New* out of the title) as, in his view, having established something like a permanent rule: "no self-respecting poet will refer any longer to traditional Mennonite ethnic markers in a manner that might be construed as uncritical or nostalgic." Given that this maxim is itself a sort of "border," Roth suggests, the poem is "evidence in itself that a principled rejection of borders—or even the goal of moving 'beyond borders'—cannot ultimately sustain a literary renaissance."[4]

I never dreamed that I had such power. But if John Roth, august historian and church leader, esteemed editor of *MQR*, beloved teacher, longtime colleague, friend and sometime conversation partner of mine, and semi-official arbiter of things Mennonite, has granted it to me . . . I am afraid I must still decline, though with all due gratitude.

Let me explain. Every serious writer knows the inescapable set of tensions between freedom and constraint, individualism and community, exploration and separation. As Robert Frost famously put it— while notably refusing to come down clearly on either side of the argument—"something there is that doesn't love a wall," but "good fences make good neighbors." Different writers take up wildly different positions on this problem, but in this imperfect world nobody with any sense proposes abolishing all borders. Most would agree, however, that it is sometimes essential to *cross* boundaries, to inquire into the different varieties of borders that exist (national, cultural, theological, aesthetic, pragmatic, etc.), and to ask whether all are equally necessary and equally useful. John Roth himself has been one of the most active proponents of international Anabaptism and of listening carefully to voices outside the North American Mennonite enclaves of Lancaster, Elkhart, Newton, and Harrisonburg. I appreciate his efforts to draw together Anabaptists of all stripes and especially to connect to plain groups, despite their resistance to higher education and to many sorts of creative work.

To question the sentimental use of Mennonite markers in a poem, though, is nothing like making permanent rules for one's peers and successors. I can say confidently that in writing my poem I had no desire to forever rule out, or in, any particular aesthetic strategies for the writing of poems—as if any self-respecting poet would pay attention to such a rule anyway, except possibly to take it as a challenge, and attempt to flout it as colorfully and brilliantly as possible. And because I am a poet, not a bishop, if and when such a thing should happen I will be happy and grateful that my poem played some part in enabling the next poem. If I think the poems are bad, I may say so, but only on grounds of taste and aesthetics. There is no Ordnung for poets, at least none that I recognize, and certainly not one that I have any desire to create or enforce.

At the same time, the nature of language and of art mean that there are always limits, many of them unspoken, on what poets and artists can do successfully as art. If I throw a shovelful of dirt and sticks in a bag and claim it's a poem I might be going "beyond borders," but it's hard (though not impossible) to imagine this being taken seriously as a poem. On the other hand, literary history shows that even those forms and modes we now consider time-honored, if not worn-out, from the sonnet to the novel, were once received skeptically as radical innovations. To attempt to legislate limits, or to proclaim some forms or subjects as simply not allowed, is the province of bishops and critics, not poets.

A conference slogan, though public, is hardly the place for fine-grained analysis and argument about which borders require transgressing and which not. Still, Roth's little piece—and I would not put too much weight on what he himself calls its "cursory observations"—got me thinking about other matters related to the Mennonite literary scene. I have myself been more cautious than Roth about using language like "literary renaissance," partly because of my awareness of the continuing difficulty that writers face in getting their work into print, and of the continuing indifference of large numbers of Mennonites to new creative work. Yet Roth is surely right that striking numbers of Mennonite writers in the U.S. and Canada have indeed become established, respected, and even famous. When I began trying to write in the 1970s there were scarcely any Mennonite writers in the United States who were publishing outside of the church press; now there are too many to name, and more emerging all the time.

Some further reflections from someone who has been, I suppose, an insider at least in the American growth of Mennonite writing seem warranted. First, I resist accepting Roth's "steady cultural assimilation" as a full or accurate narrative. My parents and three of four grandparents were birthright Mennonites who lived most of their lives in central Illinois, and were not so deeply affected by the plain-dress movement of the early twentieth century as those in the East; although my mother wore a covering to church until our church agreed to make them optional in the 1960s, she then put it away for good and has never shown any sign of regret. The Mennonites I grew up among saw themselves as set apart by their Mennonite identity, mainly took the church's peace teachings seriously, and went only reluctantly and skeptically into the great cities nearby. Yet in other ways they were quite influenced by powerful forces of mainstream American culture: they loved, played, and followed organized sports; listened to the radio and eventually to television; and took on the temperance and revivalism of evangelical Christianity as their own.

I was born in 1952, and during my youth the great migration away from the farm was in full swing. Following other ambitious young men and women from my area to Goshen College led to my experiencing a very different set of influences, including both the counter-cultural movements of the 1960s and a deeper immersion in Mennonite history and theology. I turned away from both abolitionism and revivalism, along with agrarian separatism, and found myself swimming the turbulent seas of poetry, literature, history, and philosophy.

The differences between me and earlier generations of my family, then, surely have much more to do with levels and types of education (and perhaps ambition) than with a simple or linear process of moving into mass culture. My *resistance* to some aspects of American mainstream culture (especially those associated with right-wing evangelicalism) is surely greater than theirs, though my involvement with other aspects, including literature, other aspects of intellectual culture, and some strands of music, is greater as well. At the same time, thanks to the time and research skills that my education and position have provided, I have been able to study Mennonite history and theology in considerably more depth than they did. I have also learned theoretical perspectives and approaches that make it impossible for me to view the Anabaptist heritage in any sort of simple, un-problematized way. What does "assimilation" mean, then, for us?

The same would not be true of all Mennonite writers, of course. Some have left the church entirely and bitterly. Some worship with other denominations but remain closely attached to and engaged with Mennonite communities and issues. Some still fervently identify as Mennonites (though as I have written elsewhere, what that *means* to Mennonite writers is so varied that it's problematic to use the same term for all of its manifestations).

On another level, there is hardly one monolithic American culture to be assimilated into. The literary culture (itself subdivided into many camps, groups, and cults) is quite distinct in its values, folkways, and patterns of behavior from corporate culture, for example, and both are distinct from the dwindling farm culture that was the majority Mennonite experience not long ago. And no one who pays any attention can avoid noticing the dramatic gap between political parties and sensibilities, which threatens to make civil discourse between their adherents impossible.

As for my poem, it was hardly written from a position of authority, though it certainly does express suspicion about a sort of Mennonite writing that trades on easy nostalgia and sentimental regard for traditional ways. It may have served a sort of minor cautionary function for young Mennonite poets who stumble across it, but I have yet to hear from anyone who felt his or her yearning to write about buggies, quilts, or Dirk Willems—nostalgically or otherwise—stifled by its stern edict. At the 2006 conference in Bluffton, newer poets and writers such as Esther Stenson, Jessica Smucker, Nathan Bartel, Jennifer Conrad, Melanie Cameron, G. C. Waldrep, and many others read work that engaged Mennonite markers and issues in all sorts of ways, and in a wide range of poetic modes and styles, from the reverently plain to the wildly experimental.

Roth is right, indeed, that the Bluffton conference was more celebratory than critical—as was the one held at Eastern Mennonite in spring 2012, and the smaller gathering in Winnipeg in 2009. One might mark this down to the rampant individualism of writers, or to the relative youth of this movement. It may also reflect that the goals of creative writing differ from those of writing history or theology: given the necessarily personal and idiosyncratic nature of creative work, there is much less pressure to be "right," or to quibble in public over fine distinctions. Poets and fiction writers, in my experience, can much more readily and at less cost than intellectuals in some other fields admit to having each a distinct version of the world. Having observed and sometimes been drawn into heated public debates among theologians and historians, I am not sure that this is a bad thing. The agonistic, adversarial approach that treats intellectual exchange and discourse as a ritualized form of combat is itself, it seems to me, one of the worst assimilations that some Mennonite intellectuals have suffered. Even some of those who claim an absolute commitment to nonviolence seem to find the arena of the academic conference or the scholarly monograph a place where attack and defense are appropriate metaphors.

Grace Jantzen suggests that this adversarial method of argument is at least as old as Zeno. Following John Robinson, she notes that "Seeing argument and the pursuit of truth as a battle in which positions are set up, attacked, defended, held or demolished became standard methodology in philosophical writing."[5] She also suggests (as I discuss elsewhere in this book) that this view of argument is part and parcel of a larger, male-dominated symbolic that is obsessively preoccupied with violence and death.[6]

It seems a very good thing, then, that the Mennonite writing scene should be more cooperative and less gladiatorial. Yet there certainly have been conflicts and tensions, especially around those books that have achieved wide readership. Miriam Toews' widely praised, controversial 2004 novel *A Complicated Kindness* led to a lively colloquium published online in *Mennonite Life,* and Rhoda Janzen's best-selling memoir *Mennonite in a Little Black Dress* has led to much spirited conversation. Still, it is worth noting that exchanges of this sort among Mennonites today could take place without anyone proposing that Toews or Janzen be thrown out of the church entirely—quite unlike the controversy over Rudy Wiebe's *Peace Shall Destroy Many* (1962), which led to his leaving his position as editor of the *Mennonite Brethren Herald.* One reason, of course, is that neither Toews nor Janzen are currently active members of Mennonite churches anyway.

At the 2006 Bluffton conference, John Ruth and Rudy Wiebe engaged in a memorable and somewhat contentious conversation (published in revised form in *Conrad Grebel Review*), but even that exchange seemed like the occasionally testy but mostly playful and respectful maneuvering of two venerable patriarchs from different tribes and with vastly different histories and sensibilities, rather than an all-out struggle for dominance.[7]

There are, I think, multiple reasons that writers have not contended among themselves in the agonistic way that historians and theologians struggle over Bender's Anabaptist Vision, polygenesis, atonement theory, and any number of other issues. What I suspect may be among the most important I must offer as an undefended speculation, since I have neither the time nor the resources for a full sociological analysis: Many of the most prominent Mennonite writers are women, and in their interactions with other writers they have been more interested in finding allies and friends than in competing for supremacy. While Ruth and Wiebe engaged in the memorable dialogue described above, it must be noted, poet Jean Janzen (the third member of the panel) offered a number of fascinating insights and anecdotes whenever she could find a gap in the discourse.

Another is surely that this generation of Mennonite literary figures and critics, by and large, identifies less closely with institutional Mennonite power structures than did the historians and theologians who dominated the last half-century of Mennonite intellectual life, and they thus have less invested in any particular orthodoxy or set of Anabaptist doctrines. Is it accidental that none of the most widely known Mennonite creative writers teaches either at Goshen College or Eastern Mennon-ite University—the schools where links between denominational and intellectual activity have been the strongest, and pressure to conform to orthodox expectations the highest?

In fact, many of the best-known Mennonite writers have devoted considerable energy to critiquing aspects of Mennonite and Anabaptist culture and practice. Consider Rudy Wiebe's *Peace Shall Destroy Many*, Di Brandt's *questions I asked my mother*, Patrick Friesen's *The Shunning*, Julia Spicher Kasdorf's *Sleeping Preacher*, Miriam Toews's *A Complicated Kindness*, and Rhoda Janzen's *Mennonite in a Little Black Dress*. Each of these texts portrays a Mennonite community that is life-sustaining and faithful in some ways but deeply flawed in others; their critiques are cast in narrative and lyrical terms, and they are very different, yet each em-phasizes the human costs of adherence to strict, sometimes repressive doctrines and practices. These writers—and many others—are all en-gaged in serious wrestling with their religious, personal, and literary tra-ditions. They have often chosen to follow their own paths as creative writers rather than enter into academic debates about which path is the best one, or attempt to define some definitive writerly Truth against all the other truths. But this seems to me a sign of vitality rather than weak-ness.

In my own work as critic and as local organizer for the 2006 confer-ence, I have worked at remaining open to many different sorts of good work. Of course I have my own sense of literary merits, but in dealing with Mennonite writers and texts I have tried to encourage what seems to me the best work and simply pay less attention to what seems less ex-cellent. (My taste is both fallible and fungible, and I learn over and over that some texts take a while to teach me their virtues.) Surely there does need to be conversation and argument about good and bad—or, per-haps, bad, good, better, and best, or more or less interesting, or "what I like," "dazzling but disturbing," "earnest but not exciting." . . . The cat-egories multiply quickly, once "right" and "wrong" are not the most im-portant terms.

The aesthetic and ideological pluralism of Mennonite literature may worry John Roth, but it seems to me its greatest strength. As that writing continues to flower, debate about the merits of particular texts and approaches will surely continue and increase, and I welcome those conversations—the more intense and passionate, the better, as long as

they are accompanied by the recognition that none among us is the final
arbiter or the One in Charge.

Notes

1. John Roth, "In This Issue," *Mennonite Quarterly Review* 82.1 (Winter 2008):
3.

2. During college, an older couple, one of them on the faculty, admonished my
then-girlfriend not to let me "drag you down in the hole that he's in." As I write this
we are nearing our 38th year in that hole; mostly the view has been surprisingly good.

3. Roth, 4.

4. Roth, 4-5.

5. Grace Jantzen, *Foundations of Violence (Death and the Displacement of Beauty)*
(London and New York: Routledge, 2004), 158.

6. See Jantzen, 158 ff.

7. See Julia Spicher Kasdorf, Moderator, "Literature, Place, Language, and Faith:
A Conversation between Jean Janzen, John Ruth, and Rudy Wiebe," *Conrad Grebel
Review* 26.1 (Winter 2008): 72-90, for an edited transcript of this conversation.

Part Two
Transgressions and Traditions

CHAPTER THREE

THE HAMMER AND THE FREE SPIRIT: TOWARD A PRACTICAL HERESY

"There is a crack in every thing God has made."
—Ralph Waldo Emerson[1]

I was scraping white paint from the business end of my hammer when it hit me—not the hammer, but the idea I'd been waiting for all summer. I'd spent the time at my usual odd welter of projects (and some loafing). In May, right after the college year ended, I helped my son tear down the engine of the Volvo we got cheap because it had serious issues. Then I replaced the small, high windows in our family room with a beautiful (if overpriced) bay window so that we could see the back yard and put up some bird feeders. In July I worked on my sister's utility room with my dad and brother, rebuilding a closet and laying a new tile floor, and then put down new floors in our upstairs bathroom and our kitchen. Now I needed the hammer to drive stakes to frame the little patch of concrete I was hoping to pour in the neck where our driveway widens and we always end up driving off the edge into what's supposed to be grass but is usually mud.

In between all these tangible projects, I was reading arcane texts about remote times and places, especially about various heresies and heretics. I found stories of people whose beliefs were often extreme, sometimes touching, sometimes ludicrous, sometimes frightening, and whose ends were often sad, violent, or both: the gnostics, the Cathars, the Free Spirit heretics, the Anabaptists who included many of my own ancestors, many others. My search led me into all sorts of other scattered texts and authors: Heraclitus, Lao Tzu, the poet Antonio Machado, and social critics like Raoul Vaneigem and Greil Marcus. In between, I spent a week in the woods at a nature writing workshop and took a trip with my wife to Quebec, including a pilgrimage to the Lady of the Harbor in Montreal, immortalized in Leonard Cohen's "Suzanne." By the hammer moment I was spinning, mind and body, among all these various interests, intentions, demands, and desires.

I started pondering all this a couple of years ago when a student turned up one day in a black T-shirt that read "Heretic in Good Company." It listed many great and unconventional men and women—Luther, Calvin, Joan of Arc, Meister Eckhart, Margaret Porette, Peter Waldo, Menno Simons, even Jesus himself. The point is one I've been muddling over ever since: Many of the ideas and ideals that human beings now cherish most dearly were first received as the rankest of heresies, their proponents attacked, imprisoned, tortured, even killed. At least one corollary seems equally clear: very likely we are still doing the same thing, deriding as heresy or dismissing as crazy ways of thinking that will prove themselves out over time, and win wide if not universal acceptance.

This is not just some otherworldly, arcane business, although reading the heresy debates of the past can boggle the mind and the spirit. The intensity of the rhetoric, often, seems inversely proportional to the significance of the issue. But while the terms and the sides have changed, the days of religious wars are not over. Even in these post-Christendom times, the ways we organize the human world still often depend on our religious beliefs and assumptions, especially in societies like the United States (and much of the Muslim world) where religion continues to play an enormous, if enormously complicated, role in public life and discourse.

My own Mennonite tradition has been entangled in questions of heresy from its start, nearly five centuries ago, in a set of related groups who came to be known as "Anabaptists" for their practice of baptizing (or re-baptizing) adult believers. These rebels saw themselves as pious believers who only meant to renew the church, but their rivals—not only Catholics but the newly emerging Lutherans and Calvinists and other emerging reformers as well—saw them as threats to both the religious and the social order. Part of the threat was theological; some Anabaptists adapted decidedly unconventional beliefs.[2] While these theological issues generated vast numbers of tracts, pamphlets, and books, however, the true issues had—and have—less to do with abstract theological questions than with their implications.

As Humpty Dumpty said to Alice, the real question is who is to be master. Like Calvin, other authorities of Europe saw in Anabaptism a radical threat to the order of things—for the Anabaptists claimed that their first loyalty was to Christ rather than to the State, and that when the two conflicted there could be only one choice. The Anabaptist refusal to swear oaths, based on Jesus' "Let your yea be yea, and your nay be nay," also threatened social cohesion, particularly the bonds that held peasants in sworn obedience to their masters for labor and as soldiers. The Christian must obey his conscience before all secular authority—the logic was dangerously simple and dangerously lucid, as was the insistence that true Christians must take Jesus' words and example seriously and refuse to take up arms or to kill. If the broad range of citizens came to believe so, who would till the nobles' land and fight their wars?

The loose but fervent movement that led George Blaurock, Felix Manz, Conrad Grebel, and the handful of others to pouring water on each other's heads in an upstairs room in Zurich in 1525, and made the rebel Dutch priest Menno Simons into a fugitive, was vigorously opposed wherever it cropped up. Manz became the first martyr in Zurich when he was drowned in the River Limmat, and thousands more followed. But the spectre that most terrified Europe was not that of these radical but nonviolent reformers. Far more unsettling were the apocalyptic Anabaptists—a minority among a minority—who came to believe that, given the impending millennium, God's chosen could freely use the sword against their enemies. Their most spectacular moment began when a group of radical Anabaptists seized power in the small north German city of Münster in 1534. Political maneuvering soon developed into a full-scale insurrection; the rebels eventually instituted community property, polygamy, and absolute rule, even conducting spot executions in the city's main square.

Drawing zealots to the city from across northern Europe, the Anabaptists held out for more than a year against the besieging armies of Bishop Waldeck. Eventually the city was retaken, hundreds killed, and three ringleaders paraded around Europe in chains for months and then executed; their bodies were hung in cages from a Münster church tower. Much of Europe came to believe that this was the true and appalling face of Anabaptism. As A. G. Dickens remarks,

> In the imaginations of many otherwise gentle and moderate men, Anabaptism seemed . . . a vast international conspiracy to tear down the fragile social structure of Europe. In that setting, some degree of persecution hence became quite inevitable and it was by no means wholly religious in character.[3]

The violence of Münster (and elsewhere) was as great a shock to the developing Anabaptist movement as to its opponents. In response, most became more committed to nonviolence than ever. Menno Simons' belief that nonresistance was essential to true Christians was both clarified and intensified by the violence of these uprisings, which included the death of a Peter Simons who may have been his brother. Still, Dickens is right about the public impression: for centuries the term *Anabaptist* conjured up images of wild-eyed heretics wielding bloody swords rather than the publicity-shy tradesmen and farmers who made up the heart of the movement. Ever since Münster most of the various descendants of Anabaptism have preached and practiced nonviolence—if not with perfect consistency, at least with persistence. But such bad press is hard to fight. How many of us base our views of our enemies on the worst things they have ever done, and our views of ourselves on the best things we hope someday to accomplish?

The particular issues over which the religious combatants of Reformation Europe killed each other seem mostly quaint if not trivial today. But structurally similar conflicts continue to threaten us all. Zealous religious fundamentalists, Islamic and Jewish and Christian, influence world affairs out of all proportion to their numbers. Yeats put it most succinctly, though we are long past the historical moment he wrote of: The worst are still full of passionate intensity.

Liberal tolerance is not extinct—probably in some form it is still the majority view—but the variously intolerant wield a great deal of power and plenty of weapons. Not least among these weapons is the shared conviction, across a wide range of political and religious fundamentalisms, that their own violence is holy and their cause just, while their enemies are heretical, infidels, or under the spell of the Devil, and can and should therefore be assaulted with whatever force is required to destroy them. Shortly after 9-11, a church near me proclaimed on its sign that "Allah is not America's God."

The problem of heresy is also a problem of orthodoxy and of the place of diversity of belief and practice in civil society. While certainly some heresies have been genuine dangers to the social order, many others were repressed mainly because they threatened entrenched power elites, however oppressive. Some of these which managed to persist have brought great gains in human freedom and dignity. Above all, I mean to argue, it is intolerance and the drive for enforced purity that separate dangerous ideologies—*both* orthodox and heretical—from the useful ones. Good heretics may offer pointed critiques, but they do not force their views on others, whether with swords, hijacked airliners, cruise missiles, or Bradley fighting vehicles.

Sarah Lammert, as a Unitarian no friend of rigid dogmas, argues that there are essentially two religious impulses. The first, she says, attempts

> to control the human spirit and force people to behave morally . . . under the guise of a demanding and unforgiving God who re-quires above all that we believe certain things and act certain ways, interpreted by the authority of a hierarchical religious insti-tution.

The alternative impulse, Lammert suggests,

> is to free the human spirit to directly encounter the mystery of being-ness . . . that appears under the guise of a loving God (or Goddess, or Creator Spirit, or Spirit of Life) who requires only that we dedicate our hearts and minds toward spiritual growth.[4]

Anabaptism has not always furthered this second impulse rather than the first. Though it began as a revolt against religious hierarchy, even its nonviolent practitioners have often imposed their own rigid moral structures and strictures; its cherished egalitarianism and empha-sis on community have often become in practice the rule of the few over the many. But the revised and possibly heretical practice I have in mind would be much indebted both to Anabaptism and to something very much like the second impulse Lammert describes, whatever the cost to order and conformity.

The refusal of worldly power and organizational authority is a key feature of the Sermon on the Mount and Jesus' career as radical teacher and unconventional revolutionary. Anabaptists have from the start considered the life and teachings of Jesus the most essential guides for living as true Christians. But parallel teachings can also be found throughout the religions of the world. The *Tao Te Ching* offers one classic exploration of ruling through a humility and resistance to abuse of power that in some ways may be even more radical than the New Testament. Often its imagery is water-related, as in this intriguing passage which suggests that the best way to rule is through humility:

LXVI

The reason why the River and the Sea are able to be king of the hundred valleys is that they excel in taking the lower position. . . .
Therefore, desiring to rule over the people,
One must in one's words humble oneself before them;
And, desiring to lead the people,
One must, in one's person, follow behind them.[5]

Such paradoxes are typically dismissed as amusing but useless by those who claim to be "realistic." When the going gets tough, we learn early, only sissies are squeamish, while true heroes unleash all the violence they can muster against the evil-doers, then return to their grateful women and children and a world made right once again. The myth of redemptive and controllable violence is deeply ingrained in American culture: just a short time until we eradicate our enemies, and then all will be peaceful. One more just and necessary war, and then all will be well. You know the arguments.

But I am convinced that the most dangerous people on the planet, whatever their nation or creed, are those who not only dream of making things perfect but have plans to enforce their version of perfection on everybody else. The dream of *eliminating* evil and ushering in a realm of eternal peace and justice is seductive, but it has never been, and I think will never be, successfully uncoupled from violence. We would be better off if George W. Bush (and many others in high places) had pondered more deeply the great cautionary tale on this theme—Melville's *Moby-Dick*—before vowing to carry on unremitting warfare until the evil they found personified in those they named enemies was destroyed.

I was working on the concrete because the old job—hastily poured at least twenty years ago, before we bought the house—had cracked into five or six pieces. To make things worse, the biggest piece had somehow gotten itself undermined on the outside, so that with the right pressure it became a sort of small teeter-totter. Just before we left on vacation, my wife drove over the outside edge, the piece tipped up, and the inside edge caught the tie rod under the car. It made a big clunk, poked a hole in the rubber bellows around the tie rod, and must have also stressed the seal on the steering rack—because when they called me out to check, sticky red power steering fluid was puddling on the driveway. With much wailing and gnashing of teeth we examined the damage, and pondered what to do—would our beloved but temperamental Volvo make the 2000 miles we planned to drive, or would it need a new steering rack in some isolated corner of Quebec?

I took the car to our local mechanic, who was leaving for the weekend in a couple of hours and wanted nothing to do with my panicky entreaties. Finally, after a sweaty hour under the car trying to figure out just how bad it was, I poured in a bottle of power steering fluid advertised to have mysterious leak-sealing powers, duct-taped the bellows, and put a spare can of fluid in the trunk. We drove off for Quebec, had a grand time, and the level never dropped a millimeter, though the engine oil kept dripping from the other leak I haven't been able to find—oh, never mind. When we got back, I knew it was time to deal with the driveway.

In his classic *The Pursuit of the Millenium*, a history of heretical movements of medieval Europe, Norman Cohn devotes a long section to the "Heresy of the Free Spirit"—the adherents of which tended to claim that the secret knowledge of Christ would enable them to "become God," to dispense with labor and other obligations and free themselves from moral codes, especially those governing sex. This "Elite of Amoral Supermen," as Cohn terms them, also (often) claimed to be free to lie, steal, and murder, at least according to the accounts of their more orthodox opponents.

Cohn then turns his attention to the Anabaptist movement, duly noting its generally communitarian and egalitarian origins. In his lengthy discussion of the Anabaptists of Münster, though, Cohn suggests that the two heresies intersected disastrously in the Münsterite leader Jan van Leyden (also known as Jan Bockelson) as what began as a communitarian ethos was overtaken by a pathology that combined elitism, violence, and absolutism—a disastrous mix held together by a fervor that I only reluctantly call "religious." After proclaiming himself King of the New Jerusalem, Cohn notes,

> In language worthy of any adept of the Free Spirit [Jan van Leyden] explained that pomp and luxury were permissible for him because he was wholly dead to the world and the flesh. At the same time he assured the common people that before long they too would be in the same situation, sitting on silver chairs and eating at silver tables, yet holding such things as cheap as mud and stones.[6]

But must the Free Spirit lead us to the bloody square of Münster? Must all attempts to build a visionary alternative to the status quo be derailed into self-destructive violence and abuse of power? Whatever the difficulties, both external and internal, the impulse to seek relief from the weight of the world and the labors of daily life in some kind of visionary break from the ordinary is very old and not inevitably, or even primarily, religious in origin. Mircea Eliade's classic *The Myth of the Eternal Return* traces the yearning in a great number of early societies for a return to a paradisal world without labor or death. Raoul Vaneigem, the "Situationist" philosopher best known for his involvement in the 1968 student uprisings in Paris, argues that the Free Spirit movement was driven by a version of this yearning, something more sociological than theological:

> The attitude that plunged Christianity into the most complete disarray came from the most ordinary of resolutions, and from the most popular and shortest of credos: "Enjoy life and laugh at everything else." In the eyes of the Church there was no more urgent task than to silence anyone who encouraged the idea that such freedom could be pursued without fear or blame, or without any constraint whatever; hence it smothered and destroyed them or clothed them in the tawdry religious garb of heresiarchs.[7]

In his *Lipstick Traces: A Secret History of the Twentieth Century*, Greil Marcus also argues that the Free Spirit movement was one manifestation of an ancient and recurring theme. A rock music critic turned historian, Marcus sees 1970s punk music as another recurrence of an anti-social, absolutist, nihilist impulse which he finds popping up throughout history—in the Ranters of seventeenth-century England as well as in the Dada and surrealist movements. Marcus points to the slight but uncanny coincidence that Johnny Rotten, Sex Pistols lead singer, who proclaimed himself "an antichrist," was given at birth the name John Lydon, nearly identical to Münster leader Jan van Leyden. "So much for one true Christ, for one true antichrist," Marcus writes. "And to root motives in a mere coincidence of names is specious—but serendipity is where you find it. John Lydon was raised a Catholic; when in 1980 two born-again Christian rock critics . . . asked him if he suffered remorse for his blasphemies, Lydon said he did, and disavowed nothing."[8]

Marcus claims that a wavery but unbroken line at least two millennia old connects a startling variety of extravagant religious, literary, and musical expressions:

> Little Richard's glossolalia could be traced back thousands of years to gnostic chants that moved through time till they became the sort of prayers offered by mystics like John of Leyden, after which they found their way into Pentecostal churches, where Little Richard learned the language of "Tutti Frutti."[9]

An underground link between these varieties of enthusiastic expression, oddly, might help to explain why rock music and its various successors have been so bitterly denounced by the self-appointed defenders of orthodoxy: like the fourth-century bishops who attacked the Gnostics, like Calvin and Zwingli attacking the Anabaptists, the self-righteous recognize on some level that the most serious threats to their authority come from the "heretical" variations that claim their home turf. The rock concert and the Pentecostal service have obvious ritual similarities, and both are consciously designed to obliterate ordinary consciousness, to replace it with something else. Even more restrained and liturgical observances, and (near some other extreme) the austere Sunday morning meetings of my plain Mennonite youth, may differ wildly in style but still share more than we think with more exuberant rituals.

Critics like Marcus and Vaneigem (and me) often are to be found walking a fine line, compelled by common sense to keep a certain distance from the obvious excesses and disasters of the Free Spirits, yet entranced by their iconoclastic energy. Vaneigem glimpses within the movement "the most unfathomable parts of life, those parts of living that could not be expressed in either economic or religious terms . . . Its trail is crisscrossed with gleams of light that are inexplicable to historians." Whatever its excesses, he celebrates its desire, expressed through "the emancipation of sexual pleasure and the nourishing of love," to "transcend a life turned against itself, and to annihilate the pitiful pairing of oppressive God and oppressed nature."[10]

I do not know how thorough Vaneigem's acquaintance with Emerson, Thoreau, and Whitman might be, but in singling out for praise the sexual freedom and "no work" elements in Free Spirit thinking—especially the latter—he sounds very much like a Transcendentalist at some moments. Vaneigem concludes *The Movement of the Free Spirit* with a meditation on time: "There is no eternity," he writes, "save that which lies at the heart of the present moment, in the unfettered enjoyment of the self."[11]

A century and a half earlier, that great loafer Whitman had left his newspaper work to contemplate at his leisure a spear of summer grass, the possibilities of unrestricted love and sexuality and the infinitude of the single, separate person. The ambiguously free spirit Thoreau had likewise abandoned his father's pencil factory for the broad margins of life at Walden Pond. Among much else, *Walden* objects to hard, dull labor for the sake of some future good; instead, Thoreau insists that "God himself culminates in the present moment, and will never be more divine in the lapse of all the ages."[12]

Yet of course Thoreau left Walden after two years and spent several more constructing the text that would record, amplify, reshape, and mythicize his experience there. Whitman wrote and rewrote *Leaves of Grass* all the way to his deathbed. Every moment through which we live may indeed be a divine culmination, but still we experience a long succession of them. And the problem of how to sustain freedom of spirit over time—on every level from the practical to the abstract—haunts every manifestation of the movement in one way or another. How to carve out a place to exist, in the face of inevitable hostility, without violence? How to maintain an alternative community without merely reproducing one or another version of oppression?

Vaneigem sees one of the key problems: the full equation of self with God—which apocalyptic Anabaptists as well as the more radical Free Spirit heretics either flirted with or openly proclaimed—leads inexorably to the sort of destructive "freedom" that destroys others and ultimately the self as well. "To proclaim oneself God is fatally to inherit his lie or, if you prefer, his authoritarian truth. To behave as master of things and creatures . . . dismissing all guilty conscience regardless of one's actions, is to pledge allegiance to the artificial processes of denatured nature," he admits. Against this danger, Vaneigem can offer only a murky route toward real "fulfillment of life"—something to do with "an alchemy of individual fulfillment . . . achieved by a gradual relinquishment of the economy's hold over individuals." But he insists that however questionable their actions, "followers of the movement of the Free Spirit identified, with remarkable lucidity, all that is negative: work, constraint, guilt, fear, money and possession, keeping up appearances, exchange and the striving for power."[13]

Finally, the experience of physical love is Vaneigem's great hope for a kind of sensual salvation. Somehow, through "the intensity of attention each individual gives to the refinement of his own pleasures" he claims we may "learn to abolish guilt and discover innocence" and overcome the fragmentation of our mental and physical lives. "There, finally, in outline, is the universe of the gift. It is not the sacrifice implied by the law of the exchange, but love of the self emancipated from individualistic selfishness and its exclusive appropriations; self-love that is enriched by what it offers."[14]

Perhaps lacking such faith in the transformative power of sensuality, I can at least agree with him that "the universe of the gift" and the sort of self-love "emancipated from individualistic selfishness" seem worth pursuing. My own heresy, then, might begin by dispensing with the goal of ushering in a Golden Age—especially by force. But it would include an urgent commitment to many small, incremental moves toward justice and harmony, all based on the principle of the Golden Rule and the recognition that nothing and no one can be abused without cost to the whole. If we cannot eliminate strife, we surely have options about the means we employ in seeking the good and the just. We should look through the available heresies for those that advocate without violence, those that are open rather than closed, those that offer rather than demanding. Most heresies have their martyrs—we should choose those whose martyrs shed only their own blood. Dirk Willems is a better role model than Joan of Arc.

The problem of time remains. The dream of release from the harsh wheel of everyday existence remains forever potent, all the more so because it has proven so difficult. As Marcus finally concludes, this is the rock on which the pure Free Spirit impulse founders: it cannot be sustained, because it has no program beyond a harsh cry of rebellion and refusal of obligation. "This is the secret the Sex Pistols didn't tell, which they only acted out," he notes:

> the moment in which the world seems to change is an absolute, the absolute of passing time, which is made of limits. For those who want everything, there is finally no action, only an endless, finally solipsistic reckoning. . . . There is a hint of transformation here, of resentment, leading—who knows where? There is the certainty of failure: all those who glimpse possibility in a spectral moment become rich, and though they remain so, they are ever after more impoverished. [15]

I know the tug of the ecstatic moment as well. Yet I must finally stand up for muddling through, for giving up the search for an ultimate ecstasy or a perfected society in this world, for the difficult but necessary balancing of high expectations with acceptance of human imperfection. The drive for absolute perfection, of the moment or of the world, will take us nowhere that we want to be.

To find support for such a murky program among the early Anabaptists, I might turn to the most mystical, Hans Denck, who has long been dismissed as too esoteric by scholars intent on defining a pure "Anabaptist Vision" largely oriented around ethics and practice. But Denck has begun to reemerge as a figure with much to teach. In 1526 he compiled a long list of conflicting passages in Scripture, not to destroy the faith by exposing contradictions but in pursuit of a larger if elusive truth:

> Two opposing texts must both be true. But one is locked up within the other as the lesser within the greater, as time within eternity, place within infinity. . . . O, how blessed we would be if, in recognizing how little we have, we would decry our poverty and hunger after the bread of life which is the Christ of God our Father . . . for he is inclined to give only to the hungry.[16]

In an earlier essay entitled "Heresy and the Individual Talent" I constructed a playful but partly serious manifesto for what I called "Anabaptist Surrealism," noting that those two movements, while wildly disparate in many ways, both traced their roots to Zurich in times of great stress and strife, and both shared the impulse to practice—or at least to envision—radical new ways of organizing a human society whose members would not systematically exploit and kill each other. I proposed that the earnest, sometimes dour Anabaptist commitment to plain speech, action, and attention to the specific directives of Jesus would be well leavened by the surrealist love of chance, whim, dream, and humor, and the surrealist recognition that reason and will—even or especially in the service of religious faith—are unreliable as any other masters, the more so the more absolutely they are served. Reciprocally, I think that the Dada/surrealist resistance to war and bourgeois conventionality, often so energetic and so desperately incapable of envisioning practical alternatives, might be well informed by Anabaptist models of community, nonviolence, and service.

Now I find myself trying to envision something that would go well beyond surrealist Anabaptism, something that would hold together these and many other seeming tensions and contradictions—not by main force but by a determination to make the holding together of apparent opposites a main value. Surely the problems of mind and body, spirit and flesh, cannot be solved once for all, and can hardly even be meaningfully addressed within the prison of those mistaken categories. A human consciousness reflecting on nature is only in some Descartian delusion an isolated spark utterly separated from the object of its reflection.

I found unexpected support for these groping thoughts in James Agee's often-praised but under-read classic, *Let Us Now Praise Famous Men*. As he comes to know more and more about the desperately pinched lives of the sharecroppers he and his collaborator Walker Evans lived among, and struggles to find language that might capture something of their realities, Agee notes his desire to escape the usual dualistic expectations in his writing about these people and their lives. "For I must say to you," he writes, "this is not a work of art or of entertainment, nor will I assume the obligations of the artist or entertainer, but is a human effort which must require human co-operation."[17]

Among all the complicated and sometimes partial accomplishments of his text, I would note especially Agee's insistence (shared by Evans) on evoking the *particularity* of their subjects, the individual human beings they lived and talked and ate with, observed and photographed. Agee acknowledges that such particularity is not to be captured in any final way inside the pages of a book, but he insists that at least it be recognized:

All that each person is, and experiences, and shall never experience, in body and in mind, all these things are differing expressions of himself and of one root, and are identical: and not one of

these things nor one of these persons is ever quite to be duplicated, nor replaced, nor has it ever quite had precedent: but each
is a new and incommunicably tender life, wounded in every
breath, and almost as hardly killed as easily wounded: sustaining,
for a while, without defense, the enormous assaults of the universe.[18]

Never "quite to be duplicated . . . each is a new and incommunicably tender life." This is a core insistence of my heresy as well. We are all
one, and none of us is the same as any other, and so any one-size-fits-all
dogma is bound to fail.

Even the welter of revolutionary movements that was early Christianity, as Elaine Pagels has demonstrated most deftly, was soon regulated and made to conform to the bureaucratic need for a set of doctrines
and practices that could be easily promoted and enforced. I learned from
childhood through college that my ancestors wanted to recover the purity of "the early church," but Pagels' *Beyond Belief* demonstrates that
even the earliest church was no single, simple, pure thing, but a complex
mix of all sorts of ideas and impulses, texts and stories.

The Gospel of Thomas, rediscovered in 1945 with a trove of Gnostic
texts near Nag Hammadi in Egypt, contains many familiar sayings of
Jesus, but the context is quite different from the canonical New Testament gospels. The author of *Thomas* makes no effort to tell Jesus' life
story, instead offering a long, only casually organized set of "the secret
sayings which the living Jesus spoke and which Didymos Judas Thomas
wrote down." Many are enigmatic even by biblical standards, pointing
toward a mystical illumination more often associated with Eastern religions: "Jesus said, 'Let him who seeks continue seeking until he finds.
When he finds, he will become troubled. When he becomes troubled,
he will be astonished, and he will rule over the All.'"[19]

While scholars still argue over exactly what sort of gospel it is, most
agree that *Thomas* is at mostly mildly "gnostic" in the sense that word is
used by its enemies. It contains little of the exotic mythologizing and
anti-materialism of more extreme Gnostic texts, instead emphasizing a
spiritual journey toward full knowledge of the divinity within, leading
toward illumination rather than deification. In her earlier book *The Origin of Satan,* Pagels discusses another apocryphal text and its refusal of
the dualism of good and evil and the externalizing of evil. As she points
out, Satan never appears in *The Gospel of Philip.* Instead, the Father and

the Holy Spirit direct events:

> *The Gospel of Philip* offers an original critique of the way all other Christians, orthodox and radical alike, approach morality. . . . both orthodox and radical Christians assume that morality requires *prescribing* one set of acts, and *proscribing* others. But the author of *Philip* wants to throw away all the lists of "good things" and "bad things". . . . For, this author suggests, what we identify as opposites—"light and dark, life and death, good and evil"—are in reality pairs of interdependent terms in which each implies the other.[20]

Is it possible to refuse the harsh dualism of Good and Evil without concluding that all things are permitted to the elite? Can we live free of legalisms without slipping into the heresy of the Free Spirit? Pagels believes that the gnostic texts offer "the transforming power of love" as a crucial stabilizing principle: "For [*Philip*] the question is not whether a certain act is 'good' or 'evil' but how to reconcile the freedom *gnosis* conveys with the Christian's responsibility to love others. . . . The central theme of the gospel *of Philip* is the transforming power of love: that what one becomes depends upon what one loves"[21]

This may seem simple, then: Love, and do what you will.[22] Margaret Porete suggests in her *The Mirror of Simple Souls*—for which she was killed as a heretic in 1310—that the soul transformed by God will be freed from desire: "Ah! Gods, said Divine Love, who reposed in the annihilated soul, what a long road and what a great distance it is from such lost life to free life, to free life which wants nothing to do with lordship! And this wanting nothing sows the divine seed, taken from the divine will. Such a seed can never fail, but few people are able to receive it."[23]

The problem, perhaps, remains one of sorting—not the sheep from the goats, not the "good" from the "bad" in some absolutist sense, but the loving and the lovely from all the rest. Even the soul that "wants nothing" must live in the world, must make choices and judgments. Put differently, the problem may be to operate somehow *without* the kind of easy categories for judgment on which we so easily come to rely. If we refuse to separate the Elect and the Damned, the Saved and the Abomination, the Good, Bad, and Ugly, how do we create the mental sets that we need to operate in the world?

We might consider something like the Halfway Covenant, the long-ago compromise made in the Puritan churches of New England when they faced a crisis. Their theology held that only true believers could be full members of the church, and that only those who had gone through a clear, identifiable conversion experience were truly believers. But as time went on, and more and more adults in the community had not experienced conversion and were only partial members of the church, the problem of what to do with the children of those adults became acute. Could and should such children be baptized? The crisis was political as well as religious, because in Massachusetts colony only full church members could hold public office, and so the group available to rule kept shrinking. Yes, said those who devised the Halfway Covenant, let us draw the circle wider lest it constrict to nothing. No, argued others, including the great preacher Jonathan Edwards, we must draw a firm line between those who belong and those who do not.

This fundamental question is still being contested, *mutatis mutandis,* in many different contexts. By now you know where I stand: by my lights, surely Edwards was wrong and his more open-minded opponents right (though my Anabaptist joker cannot resist noting that the whole problem becomes moot if we simply abandon the dubious practice of infant baptism). But if we are to baptize some while they still gaze at the world with the wide clean eyes of babes, why not admit them all? As the man said, God will sort them out.

Poorly organized, outnumbered, and divided amongst themselves, the Gnostic groups withered along with many other early sects, especially after Constantine made Christianity the official religion of the Roman Empire early in the fourth century. As the church became The Church, many and various dissenters were labeled heretics and bitterly, sometimes violently opposed. Their texts were excluded from the canon, forbidden, destroyed; for centuries they were known almost only through the reports of their enemies. Still, there were always a few who resisted the categories of orthodox belief and practice, and refused to recant their most dangerous intuitions.

John Calvin's arch-enemy was Michael Servetus, who wrote a widely read book questioning the doctrine of the Trinity (and, almost incidentally, accurately describing the circulation of the blood seventy-five years before Harvey published his similar account). During Servetus' trial for heresy, which was to end in his being burned at the stake, Calvin asked this question: "What, poor man, if one stamped his foot on this floor and said he trod on God, would you not be horrified in having subjected the majesty of God to such unworthy usage?" Servetus replied: "I have not a doubt but that this bench, this table, and all you can point to around us is the substance of God."[24]

What if, indeed, all is of the substance of God? Not only you and I, but all the Republicans and Democrats, punks and preachers and executives, terrorists and soldiers and the mothers and fathers and children of soldiers and terrorists, Muslims and Christians and Jains and Hindus and atheists and agnostics, all the fishes and birds, the wheat and the corn and the weeds and the tall pines and the very soil from which they grow? If this is so, if we come to believe that this is so, then we might well choose to plant our feet with care, to treat the world and all its things with care. Such a heresy I believe we might be able to use to live, and to live well.

For a long time I have treasured Leonard Cohen's song "Anthem" especially for its chorus: "There's a crack, a crack in everything—that's how the light gets in." Not until recently did I learn that long before, in his essay "Compensation," that old dreamer Emerson wrote something similar: "There is a crack in every thing God has made."

The essay is a meditation on this world and the next, written in resistance to the idea that the good may suffer here but will be rewarded in heaven. To the contrary, Emerson claims, we need not make "the immense concession that the bad are successful; that justice is not done now." "Every act rewards itself," he insists; "the world will be whole" no matter how partly and selfishly we seek to act: "You cannot do wrong without suffering wrong. . . . The exclusionist in religion does not see that he shuts the door of heaven on himself, in striving to shut out others. Treat men as pawns and ninepins and you shall suffer as well as they. If you leave out their heart, you shall lose your own."[25] The essay ends with a complaint about our resistance to change and growth:

> We cannot part with our friends. We cannot let our angels go. We do not see that they only go out that archangels may come in. We are idolaters of the old. We do not believe in the riches of the soul, in its proper eternity and omnipresence. . . . We linger in the ruins of the old tent where once we had bread and shelter and organs, nor believe that the spirit can feed, cover, and nerve us again. We cannot again find aught so dear, so sweet, so graceful. But we sit and weep in vain. The voice of the Almighty saith, "Up and onward for evermore!" We cannot stay amid the ruins. Neither will

we rely on the new; and so we walk ever with reverted eyes, like those monsters who look backwards.[26]

What might it mean, to move out from the ruins, to find our way forward and discover the riches of the soul? To say with Servetus that all things are "of the substance" of God is not to say that we, or the benches and buffets of the world, "are" God; certainly it is not to say that we can all claim vast cosmic powers. Perhaps it merely but crucially means that our work is to cherish all the things of God as best we can.

I spent as much time chipping paint off the hammer head as I did driving the stakes to hold the frame for the concrete. I had to go to a wedding that afternoon so I was in a hurry, but I mixed up five bags of ready-mix one at a time in the rusty bed of the old wheelbarrow I'd borrowed from my friend Gregg. I shoveled the sloppy mix into the hole and smoothed it down, first with a scrap two by four and then with a trowel I'd bought a year before to apply linoleum cement but never used. I made a fairly neat job of it, and even used an old tool I found hanging in the garage to scribe an expansion joint across it at what I guessed was the right spot. Before I went inside to change I covered the spot with plastic to keep out the rain, and put some rocks and a bucket around the edge to hold down the plastic and discourage the family from driving over it too soon. When it had dried it didn't look bad at all, certainly better than before, though I realized too late that water tended to puddle along one side. Within two weeks there was a crack across one corner.

Notes

1. Ralph Waldo Emerson, "Compensation," *Selected Writings of Emerson*, ed. Brooks Atkinson (New York: Modern Library, 1940), 170.

2. One especially controversial Anabaptist idea was *psychopannychia* or "soul sleep"—the idea that after death the soul would sleep until the body was resurrected at the Last Judgment. "These babblers have so actively exerted themselves," John Calvin complained, "that they have already drawn thousands into their insanity."

3. A. G. Dickens, *Reformation and Society In Sixteenth-Century Europe* (New York: Harcourt, 1966), 137.

4. The Rev. Sarah Lammert, "Unitarianism and the Radical Reformation," *The Unitarian Society of Ridgewood*, 12 January 2003. Web 12 August 2004.

5. Lao Tzu, *Tao Te Ching*, trans. D. C. Lau (New York: Penguin, 1963), 128.

6. Norman Cohn, *The Pursuit of the Millennium: Revolutionary Millenarians and Mystical Anarchists of the Middle Ages* (Oxford: Oxford University Press, rev. ed. 1970), 273-4.

7. Raoul Vaneigem, *The Movement of the Free Spirit: General Considerations and Firsthand Testimony Concerning Some Brief Flowerings of Life in the Middle Ages, the Renaissance and, Incidentally, Our Own Time,* trans. Randall Cherry and Ian Patterson (New York: Zone Books, 1998), 103.

8. Greil Marcus, *Lipstick Traces: A Secret History of the 20th Century* (Cambridge: Harvard University Press, 1989), 93.

9. Marcus, 93.

10. Vaneigem, 93.

11. Vaneigem, 233.

12. Henry David Thoreau, *The Illustrated Walden,* ed. J. Lynton Shanley (Princeton: Princeton UP, 1973), 93.

13. Vaneigem, 246; 249; 250.

14. Vaneigem, 256.

15. Marcus, 447. "La Belle Dame Sans Merci," by John Keats, and William Butler Yeats' "The Song of Wandering Aengus" both tell the tales of men who have moments of bliss with beautiful, otherworldly women, then pine away the rest of their lives in vain efforts to recapture that moment (and the woman).

16. Denck, *Selected Writing of Hans Denck,* ed. and trans. Edward J. Furcha and Ford Lewis Battles (Pittsburgh: Pickwick, 1975), 135.

17. James Agee and Walker Evans, *Let Us Now Praise Famous Men: Three Tenant Families* (New York: Ballantine, 1939, reprint ed. 1966), 102.

18. Agee and Evans, 53-4.

19. James R. Robinson, ed., "The Gospel of Thomas," *The Nag Hammadi Library,* rev. ed. (HarperCollins, San Francisco, 1990). http://www.gnosis.org/naghamm/nhl.html.4 April 2012.

20. Elaine Pagels, *The Origins of Satan* (New York: Vintage, 1996), 171.

21. Pagels, *Origins,* 172.

22. If I draw mainly on Christian texts and heresies, it is because these are the traditions I know best, not because I claim any exclusive truth to be found in them. In fact, if I would claim anything, it would be that there is as much to learn from the errors and excesses of my tradition as from its insights and triumphs. I would say the same of all the other traditions.

23. Qtd. in Vaneigem, 141.

24. Lawrence Goldstone and Nancy Goldstone, *Out of the Flames: The Remarkable Story of a Fearless Scholar, a Fatal Heresy, and One of the Rarest Books in the World* (New York: Broadway Books, 2002), 183.

25. Emerson, *Selected Writings,* 171; 180.

26. Emerson, 188.

FOUR

THE MARRIAGE OF THE *MARTYRS MIRROR* AND THE OPEN ROAD, OR, WHY I LOVE POETRY DESPITE THE SUSPICION THAT IT WON'T SAVE ANYBODY

What is the grass? [. . .]
How could I answer the child? I do not know what it is, any more than he.
I guess it must be the flag of my disposition, out of hopeful green stuff woven.
Or I guess it is the handkerchief of the Lord [. . .]
—Walt Whitman, "Song of Myself"[1]

It would be useful, I think, to construct a sober, measured and objective analysis of the condition of Mennonite Literature, and I wish I were capable of that. I have tried repeatedly to think systematically and categorically about Mennonite writers and writing, subjects that have fascinated me for more than twenty years. But the current flowering of all sorts of Mennonite-related writing, while certainly a welcome thing, has made neat systematizing all the more difficult. Sooner or later, all my efforts at such a scheme have come to resemble Jorge Luis Borges' imaginary Chinese encyclopedia, which classifies animals into these remarkable categories:

1. those that belong to the Emperor, 2. embalmed ones, 3. those that are trained, 4. suckling pigs, 5. mermaids, 6. fabulous ones, 7. stray dogs, 8. those included in the present classification, 9.

those that tremble as if they were mad, 10. innumerable ones, 11. those drawn with a very fine camelhair brush, 12. others, 13. those that have just broken a flower vase, 14. those that from a long way off look like flies.[2]

Instead of a clear and plausible scheme, then, I can only offer some presumptuous, idiosyncratic generalizations and contentious opinions and speculations about narrative, poetry, writing, souls, and such matters, drawing freely on the work of some of my illustrious forebears and fellow travelers both within and without the various Anabaptist enclaves and entourages.

1. I love poetry because it does not have to be narrative. The longer I live, the more often I feel weary of stories, all of them: not only the old master narratives but the new and allegedly hip and humble substitutes too, including my own. All right, I have a secret fondness for my own, but I don't trust them. Donald Barthelme once proclaimed "Fragments are the only forms I trust."[3] Many days I think he was onto something.

As Scott Holland points out, narratives and narrative theology can be instruments of oppression as well as liberation.[4] Hitler told a clear story, and so do many groups whose narratives deserve to be read only with a great deal of skepticism. They are all false stories, or so it seems to me, but the attraction of clear, simple, and false versions of the world seems to be more or less eternal. W. H. Auden said of the tyrant whose epitaph he wrote, "The poetry he invented was easy to understand."[5] He did not mean this as a compliment.

Immediately I must hedge. Yes, this is too strong. How could we live without story? As Barry Lopez has pointed out, storytelling is crucial to resistance, and resistance is crucial to us all.[6] I believe him. It's *bad* stories, wrong-headed stories, alluringly simple stories, especially those that insinuate that violence of various sorts is a sometimes unpleasant but efficient and reliable way of solving human difficulties, that must be resisted. But indulge me a little.

One key difference I wish to propose between two kinds of story—the kind of narratives that trouble me, and what I will provisionally call "poetic" approaches to the great questions—is that poetry resists spurious clarity. "The poem must resist the intelligence almost successfully," wrote Wallace Stevens, one of the most exacting, if perplexing, religious poets of the last century. Stevens claimed that once it became impossible (as it did for him) to believe in the old ways, we would need to *make up* something we could believe in, even though we knew we had made it up. His "Notes Toward a Supreme Fiction," as the title suggests, talks around this subject for twenty-eight pages without anything resembling a clear definition, though there are many statements like "Perhaps / the truth depends on a walk around a lake . . ." and "The poem goes from the poet's gibberish to / The gibberish of the vulgate and back again."[7] Frustrating, yes; yet such circumlocutions and obscurities have an appeal to me that the clear and relentless alternatives just do not match.

Anabaptists of a certain bent, or twist, might notice some affinities between Stevens' exploration of the "supreme fiction" and Gordon Kaufman's claim that theology is a "constructive activity of the imagination,"[8] not a deductive process of sorting around through canonical texts and ideas in search of the perfect synthesis of what has already been said and done. But more on this in a moment.

2. Even when they're telling stories left and right, poets often can't keep them straight, either internally or externally. As frustrating as this slop, mess, and contradiction may be to those who yearn for order and reason, it reminds us just how much our lives elude our desire to make them into satisfactory narratives. Here I would modestly propose that the idea that one coherent, all-encompassing story subsumes the entire universe *and* is simple enough for human beings to wrap our petty little minds around is—at least slightly and more likely insanely—presumptuous anyway. Find a dark spot some night, if you can, and contemplate the stars. Think about their distances, and how far and long all that brilliant light must travel to reach us so dimly, and how it scatters in all directions. Try to imagine everything that's going out there, and what sort of narrative you might offer that would do it justice from here.[9]

I had a memorable conversation once with an aspiring evangelical science fiction writer, who told me that he had figured out that there was no need to imagine any other Truth than the singular narrative of the New Testament: "Earth," he proclaimed, "is the Jerusalem of the universe!" He seemed quite pleased with this notion; I found myself wanting to say, "Don't you think God might make alternate arrangements for beings billions of light years away?" I didn't then, though I am now. We all have the right and the need to carry our own stories, and to offer them to others. But come on.

3. Here are some stories:

A. My great-grandfather George, a gentle and brave Mennonite pastor, preached earnestly in favor of abstinence.

B. One stalwart of his congregation would rise after such sermons and declaim, "A little wine never hurt anybody!"

C. As we all know, Jesus' first miracle was to change water into wine, almost certainly so people could drink it. It seems hard to evade the idea that he was drinking himself.

D. George had a habit of going down to the tavern on Sunday afternoons to visit with the men, and sometimes he'd convince one to go home to his wife instead of drinking up all his wages.

These *all* seem like good stories, don't they? But how do they fit together? What do we *do* with them?

4. Compare the Gnostic Gospel of Thomas to the canonical gospels. It disregards Jesus' life almost entirely, consists entirely of sayings and the fragmentary parabolic stories Jesus tells. If Thomas were the only gospel we had, we would be impoverished, but as a supplement to the others, its compendium of enigmatic proclamations and cryptic narratives complicates and enriches our lives. There is something liberating in the nearly arbitrary, seemingly disorganized catalog Thomas offers, as if its author had been an anachronistic imitator of Walt Whitman. Can you read number 77 without thinking that it has the whiff of the authentic?

> Jesus said, "I am the light that is over all things. I am all: from me all came forth, and to me all attained.
> Split a piece of wood; I am there.
> Lift up the stone, and you will find me there."[10]

5. Consider the book of poems as text: most authors struggle and strive to assemble many short poems into a coherent order, but most readers will not read all the way through, front to back, no matter what. They will browse, skip around, start in the middle or at the end, and it might even be *better* that way, despite the author having labored mightily to make it some sort of linear whole. You can read one or two poems, put the book down and ponder them for a while.

6. Although I do like fragments, my purpose here is not to make more of them than they will bear. Nor am I expressing more than personal skepticism about the impulses to grand, epic constructions that have yielded so much wonderful writing. I am speaking, personally and

eccentrically, in praise of small (and large) wholes that may or may not tell stories directly or indirectly, modest (or grand) artifacts whose apparent borders open onto large landscapes or contain impossibly many rooms, like Dr. Who's phone booth. I'm speaking in favor of many such pieces, in many voices, one after another, as diverse and polyphonic as possible, holding in abeyance our urge to rectify, unify, organize, rationalize. If I have a vision for Mennonite/s writing, and for writing in general, that's it. If we must have epics, let them be like *Leaves of Grass*, filled with bold claims and their contraries, accepting their own contradictions as part of the essential multiplicity of this life.

7. Among the fundamental tools of even the largest narrative are omission and excision: whatever fits into the story matters, all the rest must be placed outside. If you think about it carefully, the percentage of exclusion even the most generous narrative requires is astonishing. It's a rough business. And narratives that claim universality, as all the good ones do ("Yes, this is our story, but it's your story too, even if you were born in the Lesser Magellenic Cloud, photosynthesize instead of eating, and will change genders twice before you find the two others you will need to reproduce") are the kindest and the cruelest of all in the way that they seek to bend all realities and identities to our own definitions. We can try to convince a good outside midfielder that baseball is the *real* game and she's really meant to be a second baseman: it might even work, until she has to turn the double play.

8. But as this rather strained athletic analogy may or may not suggest, I really mean less to critique narrative than to speak for metaphor, for both reckless adventures into it and for more careful attention to it. To start at the top, surely *all* of our talk about God is metaphorical, almost by definition. Yet we often behave as though it's ordinary, instrumental language, as though we have the sort of reliable information about God that we do about how much rain we got yesterday or whether the mail has arrived. Or we slide into various embarrassing, even painful metaphors. While writing this very paragraph, I heard this in a song: "Jesus built a bridge to Heaven, with three nails and two cross ties." Try to picture *that*.

Gordon Kaufman writes of the risks of reification, of

> taking the content of a symbol . . . to be a proper description or
> exact representation of a particular reality or being; in Kant's apt
> phrase, it is "treating our thoughts as things." We reify the sym-

bols "creator" and "lord" and "father" when we take them to mean that God *really is* a creator/lord/father. . . . This religious symbolism has had repressive and oppressive power . . . not so much because of its particular content as because that content was reified: God was taken to be *in actual fact* a kind of creator/lord/father "out there" who really established—consciously willed and deliberately created—the patterns of order governing life here on earth.[11]

Whether or not we accept the rest of Kaufman's argument that God is more accurately described as the "spontaneous creativity" at play in the universe than as creator/lord/father—a long discussion, I know—surely he is right about reification and its repressive and oppressive force. But we can hardly do without metaphor either.

9. Poetry is of use, then, as a way of thinking and working in metaphor with some rigor, and of letting the imagination do the work it was, apparently, made to do. Metaphor and metaphorical thinking are ✳ absolutely essential to human life, especially spiritual life. Poetry—art, really—defamiliarizes metaphors that have gone dull and stale and brings new metaphors into being. Robert Frost claimed that unless we become "at home in the metaphor," we are not safe anywhere: "Because you are not at ease with figurative values: you don't know the metaphor in its strength and its weakness. You don't know how far you may expect to ride it and when it may break down with you. You are not safe with science; you are not safe in history."[12]

I believe, with some others, that metaphorical language used in this way is essential. Far from being the opponent of religion, metaphor may even be, as Marion Woodman puts it, "the literal language of the soul."[13] Canadian Mennonite poet Patrick Friesen puts it a little differently: "Poetry as the childish immediacy in apprehending earth and self. Poetry as a genuinely spiritual activity, probably opposite to institutional religion."[14] Walt Whitman's great innovation, the first great flowering of poetry in America, lay in his trust of the imagination as the necessary servant of the soul rather than the enemy of faithfulness. And it was in the encounter with the physical world, he thought, that the soul grew: "Wisdom is of the soul," he writes, "is not susceptible of proof, is its own proof . . . / Is the certainty of the reality and immortality of things, and the excellence of things; / Something there is in the float of the sight of things that provokes it out of the soul."[15]

In an even more famous but endlessly suggestive passage, Whitman improvises answers for the child who asks him "What is the grass?"

> How could I answer the child? I do not know what it is, any more
>   than he.
> I guess it must be the flag of my disposition, out of hopeful green
>   stuff woven.
> Or I guess it is the handkerchief of the Lord,
> A scented gift and remembrancer, designedly dropt.
> Bearing the owner's name someway in the corners, that we may see
>   and remark, and say, *Whose?*
> Or I guess the grass is itself a child, the produced babe of the vegeta-
>   tion.
> Or I guess it is a uniform hieroglyphic. . . .
> And now it seems to me the beautiful uncut hair of graves. . . .
> I wish I could translate the hints about the dead young men and
>   women,
> And the hints about old men and mothers, and the offspring taken
>   soon out of their laps. . . .[16]

Whitman is famous, especially among his skeptics, for his "imperial ego" and his naïve optimism. But notice how provisional and impro-visatory his answers are here, though they gradually become more confi-dent. "I wish I could translate the hints," he writes, and then proceeds to do just that—but only a victim of the Fallacy of reification could mistake these images for a creed or a dogma.

He does puzzle. Like most Americans of his day, Whitman was steeped in Christian ideas of the afterlife, so what can he mean when he says that to die is *luckier* that any one supposed? What could be luckier than eternity in Heaven? Can it be "luckier" to slide into the earth and be translated by worms and lesser creatures into some other form of life, to become a spear of summer grass, the uncut hair of a grave? Perhaps even more beautiful, and equally strange, is the passage in which he describes an uncanny physical encounter with his soul:

> I believe in you my soul, the other I am must not abase itself to you,
> And you must not be abased to the other.
> Loafe with me on the grass, loose the stop from your throat,
> Not words, not music or rhyme I want, not custom or lecture, not

even the best,
Only the lull I like, the hum of your valved voice.
I mind how once we lay such a transparent summer morning,
How you settled your head athwart my hips and gently turn'd over
  upon me,
And parted the shirt from my bosom-bone, and plunged your
  tongue to my bare-stript heart,
And reach'd till you felt my beard, and reach'd till you held my feet.[17]

Donald Revell remarks on the oddly *absolute* quality of this passage: "The pace is uncontrollable: not a poem, but a world; and not another world, but *this* one. . . . In the embrace of Self and Soul, poetry is present at the creation of the world, an instance that happens never to end."[18] Whitman has in mind nothing less than a revolutionary revision of our notions of physicality and transcendence, the profane and the sacred, and of the very meanings of time and life, as D. H. Lawrence noticed: "His morality was no morality of salvation. His was a morality of the soul living her life, not saving herself. . . . The soul living her life along the incarnate mystery of the open road."[19]

12. Compare another great gay poet, Oscar Wilde. His late *De Profundis*, written after his years spent in prison, is a long meditation on suffering he knows he *deserves* in some sense. The laws against "sodomy" make no sense to him, but he knows he has done wrong: "I became the spendthrift of my own genius . . . Desire, at the end, was a malady, or a madness, or both. I grew careless of the lives of others. . . . I ended in horrible disgrace. There is only one thing for me now, absolute humility."[20]

We might notice, first, how different Wilde's situation is from that Anabaptist suffering which is felt to be undeserved, inflicted from outside by The World upon the pure and faithful. Wilde's humility is driven by his realization that he *has* done wrong, and is far different from the ideological humility that Mennonites have so earnestly demanded of themselves, or mostly, really, of others within the tribe. If you believe that you suffer because you are pure and holy, how can you be truly humble? The far deeper humility his ordeal has forced upon him led Wilde to see empathetic identification with the other as the very essence of Christ:

the very basis of Christ's nature was the same as that of the nature
of the artist—an intense and flamelike imagination. He realized
in the entire sphere of human relations that imaginative sympathy

which in the sphere of art is the sole secret of creation. He understood the leprosy of the leper, the darkness of the blind, the fierce misery of those who live for pleasure, the strange poverty of the rich. . . .

Christ's place indeed is with the poets. His whole conception of Humanity sprang right out of the imagination and can only be realized by it.[21]

13. But wait, you say, the imagination makes narratives, is indispensable to narrative. Even this essay is constructing its own story as it goes, recasting and appropriating others at every step. Granted—and a beautiful thing a good story is, surely. Let me register my own love for the wildest and weirdest of narratives—what could be wilder and stranger, for starters, than the biblical narrative, with its huge cast of heroes, sinners, misfits, kings, and rebels, culminating in the greatest teacher, preacher, and counter-cultural rebel of them all?

For a Mennonite example, I might offer Keith Miller's *The Book of Flying*, a beautifully written and conceived "fantasy" novel.[22] It is about a young man who goes on a journey and eventually gets wings and learns to fly, but that is like saying *Moby-Dick* is about a whale hunt. What I love in *The Book of Flying* is what I love, really, about literature: that its textures of language and turns of plot and the characters it creates, fallible and lovable and frightening as they are, feed my soul. I come away from it convinced that hidden but necessary parts of my being have been nourished and have grown. This is the place, I think, where poetry and religion meet: in the care and feeding of souls.

So, in the tradition of both Walt Whitman and Keith Miller, let me say a few more reckless things about souls. In the classic Mennonite human/psychological economy (and I think this is the prevailing Christian one as well), the standard metaphor for the soul is as a precious, delicate, and helpless thing whose main function is to be saved, the way peaches exist only to be canned, never eaten fresh, in the well-managed Midwestern kitchens of Jean Janzen's wonderfully metaphorical "Peaches in Minnesota."[23] In this scheme the ego is a sort of Christian soldier who must be clothed in the armor of God to resist the blows of the world and the snares of the flesh, though it must also submit to the community ("gelassenheit") and do its work without question.

14. But this is deeply unhealthy. Bottled up or canned, deprived of challenge and exercise, the soul withers and sickens, even becomes in-

sane, like the captive narrator of Charlotte Perkins Gilman's great story "The Yellow Wall-Paper." Notice that she is confined to an upstairs room, where she rattles around like a marble in a gourd, or a soul in a body. Pressed to control everything within and without and to submit at the same time, the ego grows muscle bound, anxious, and weary, prone to injury and ill-equipped to deal with the inevitable reverses of life.[24] Thwarted and denied, the body seeks paths around the blockages, as water tests every possible way through or under or around a levee.

15. When the old song said "Feed your heads" it was onto something. The soul is meant to be fed, to grow, to sustain the ego, to stretch and explore, to learn and to teach. And this is why poetry and art are not frivolities but essentials. Art, at least real art, contends with the great mysteries without retreating nervously into formulas and postures. Poems, at least real poems, do not pretend to know more than human beings can truly know, but explore and investigate everything in their tentative, necessary ways. And the food they offer grows in this vast and frightening realm that begins where our desire to know surpasses our knowledge. "The purpose of art," wrote James Baldwin, "is to lay bare the questions which have been hidden by the answers."[25]

16. One of the great guides to this arena of interior and exterior exploration was William Blake. I am still trying to unpack his visionary *The Marriage of Heaven and Hell*, thirty years after Nick Lindsay introduced me to it. Blake wrote in opposition to the windy, sentimental mysticism of Emmanuel Swedenborg, who (Blake thought) was far too enamored of angels and of legalism. Energy, Blake insisted, was not evil, but "eternal delight." "Those who restrain desire do so because theirs is weak enough to be restrained," he claimed, "and the restrainer or reason usurps its place and governs the unwilling. And being restrained, it by degrees becomes passive till it is only the shadow of desire."[26]

I cannot give Blake the attention he deserves here.[27] But I think now that we need a new marriage, not of heaven and hell, but of a whole series of necessary contraries. We are already making our way, surely, and this is good. Writers bring things into being by imagining them, in mysterious but palpable ways. I know, myself, not only of "imaginary gardens with real toads in them,"[28] but of imaginary villages with real Mennonites in them, beings of weight and depth who breathe and speak, argue and make love, transgress and repent, witness and worship and bear their kind. Saying does not just make it so, but it is a start.

So let us imagine—deeply and calmly and wildly—the marriage of Anabaptism and surrealism. The marriages of truth and desire, of the blessed community and the lonely wanderer, of Demut and Hochmut, Gelassenheit and Pride, the Will and the Imagination. Let us wed the Farmer and the Cheerleader, the Bishop and the Movie Star, the Sublime and the Funky. Let us wed the stories of simple, faithful people and of obnoxious rebels, and of obnoxious simpletons and faithful rebels.

In a good marriage, both partners become more themselves, not less, so we will want no simple dualistic fusion. Living under the sign and specter of postmodernism, we need not and cannot think that whatever oppositions we may construct are either simple or essential. So let us have marriages more transgressively multiplex than we can yet imagine: the marriage of gay and straight and transgendered, of smart, educated, crafty, ignorant, and just plain dumb. Let us have the marriage of all the beasts Borges cataloged so erratically in his imaginary encyclopedia, the marriage of Borges himself and his various imaginary beloveds, and his famous double "Borges," and the double's double, who has no name in this world. Let us have the marriage, or at least the happy mingling, of all the illogical and un-nameable and astonishing beings of this universe that God has so improbably imagined into existence.

Let us imagine and proclaim the marriage of the *Martyrs Mirror* and the Open Road and the Anabaptist Vision and the Supreme Fiction. Of the Hidden Church and the Mansion of Many Apartments and the Cave of the Anabaptists and the Room of One's Own. Of the Gospel of John and the Gospel of Thomas and the Gospels of John Howard Yoder and Gordon Kaufman. Of the precious and precarious visions of Julia Spicher Kasdorf and Di Brandt and Miriam Toews and Jean Janzen with those of Rudy Wiebe and Scott Holland and Patrick Friesen and Gerald J. Mast, and all the other names I know but do not have space to add, and all the names I do not know. And may they all live long and prosper or blaze out gloriously, and be priests and servants of each other and of the whole sad and beautiful world, and contend together about the good and the right and the true and the holy.

For there is much that has been hidden, and it is our work as poets and writers to dig it up. Much has been lost, and our work is recovery. Much has not yet been imagined, and our work is discovery. Much has been misunderstood, abandoned, or ignored, and our work is to grasp and polish and return all that to the world, in its truth and depth and weight, its misery and joy, its beauty and trouble. This is the work that is play, that is profane, that is holy, that is fallen and recovered, captive and free. I do not know much about God, but I believe that this is the work that God would have us do.

Notes

1. Walt Whitman, *Leaves of Grass and Selected Prose,* ed. John A. Kouwenhoven (New York: Modern Library, 1950), 27.

2. Jorge Luis Borges, "John Wilkins' Analytical Language," *Jorge Luis Borges: Selected Non-Fictions,* trans. Eliot Weinberger, Esther Allen, Suzanne Jill Levine (New York: Penguin, 2000), 231.

3. Donald Barthelme, "See the Moon," *Sixty Stories* (New York: Dutton, 1982), 98.

4. "Some expressions of narrative theology can be quite conservative, colonizing, and chauvinistic," Holland writes. "The variety of narrative theology practiced by Karl Barth, Hans Frei, George Lindbeck, Stanley Hauerwas, and some enthusiastic Mennonite disciples unapologetically asserts that the church's story must swallow up the world's story and that the disciple's narrative must eclipse the human narrative." Scott Holland, "Response to Gordon Kaufman," *Conrad Grebel Review* 14.1 (Winter 1996): 51.

5. W. H. Auden, *Selected Poetry of W. H. Auden* (New York: Random House, 1970), 51.

6. Barry Lopez and Christian Martin, "On Resistance: An Interview with Barry Lopez," *Georgia Review* 60.1 (Spring 2006), 15: "The theme of resistance, of course, is very old in the arts, perhaps clichéd, but many people still believe the most important thing for an artist is to resist. If a certain order is in place, and you never question that order, then there's very little for your imagination to do. If your imagination is not alive, part of your interior atrophies. You wake up later in your life and remain angry for years, because you didn't act."

7. Wallace Stevens, *The Palm at the End of the Mind Selected Poems and a Play,* ed. Holly Stevens (New York: Vintage, 1972), 212, 222.

8. Gordon Kaufman, *In the Beginning . . . Creativity* (Minneapolis: Fortress, 2004), 120.

9. Cf. John D. Caputo, *The Weakness of God: A Theology of the Event* (Bloomington: Indiana University Press, 2006), 118: "The idea of one true religion or religious discourse or body of religious narratives makes no more sense than the idea of one true poem or one true language or one true culture."

10. James R. Robinson, ed., "The Gospel of Thomas," *The Nag Hammadi Library,* rev. ed. (HarperCollins, San Francisco, 1990). http://www.gnosis.org/naghamm/nhl.html. 4 April 2012.

11. Gordon Kaufman, *In Face of Mystery A Constructive Theology* (Cambridge: Harvard University Press, 2006), 330; 334.

12. Robert Frost, "Education by Poetry," *The American Literature Archive.* ed.

Brian A. Bremen, http://www.en.utexas.edu/amlit/amlitprivate/scans/edbypo. html. October 16, 2006.

13. Marion Woodman, "Men Are from Earth, and So Are Women: Marion Woodman on the Inner Marriage of the True Masculine and the True Feminine." Interview by James Kullander. *The Sun* 368 (August 2006), 13.

14. Pat Friesen, *Interim: Essays & Meditations,* (Regina: Hagios Press, 2006), 96.

15. Whitman, *Leaves of Grass,* 121.

16. Whitman, 27-28.

17. Whitman, 27.

18. Donald Revell, *Invisible Green Selected Prose of Donald Revell* (Richmond, Calif.: Omnidawn, 2005), 99.

19. D. H. Lawrence, "Whitman," *Studies in Classic American Literature,* Thomas Seltzer, 1923. *American Studies at the University of Virginia.* http://xroads. virginia.edu/~hyper/LAWRENCE/lawrence.html. October 16, 2006.

20. Oscar Wilde, *Collected Works of Oscar Wilde,* (Ware, Hertfordshire: Wordsworth Editions, 1997), 927.

21. Wilde, 937.

22. Keith Miller, *The Book of Flying* (New York: Penguin, 2004). His *The Book on Fire* (Stafford, UK: Immanion Books, 2009) is equally fascinating.

23. Jean Janzen, *The Upside-Down Tree* (Winnipeg: Henderson Books, 1992), 21.

24. Cf. Friedrich Hölderlin, *Hyperion and Selected Poems*, ed. Eric L. Santner (New York: Continuum, 1990), 68: "Reason without beauty of spirit and heart is like an overseer whom the master of the house has set over the servants; he knows as little as they do what will come of all their endless toil, he only shouts: 'Get busy,' and is almost sorry to find the work being accomplished, for in the end he would have nothing more to oversee, and his part would be played."

25. James Baldwin, *Creative Process* (New York: Ridge Press, 1972), 17.

26. William Blake, *Jerusalem, Selected Poems and Prose,* ed. Hazard Adams (New York: Holt, Rinehart, and Winston, 1970), 125.

27. See Chapter 6 for a more extended discussion of Blake and *The Marriage of Heaven and Hell.*

28. Marianne Moore, "Poetry." *The Norton Anthology of Modern Poetry,* 3rd. ed., Vol. 1, ed. Jahan Ramazani, Richard Ellman, ad Robert O'Clair (New York: Norton, 2003), 439.

FIVE
CHAPTER

"TRUTH DID NOT COME INTO THE WORLD NAKED": IMAGES, STORIES, AND INTIMATIONS

"Don't expect faith to clear things up for you. It is trust, not certainty."
—Flannery O'Connor

1

A few years ago I received an invitation to reflect on J. Denny Weaver's contributions to Anabaptist theology and life. I was doing fine until I encountered the more specific request to "situate your own viewpoint on Christology in relationship to Denny's work." The first word I wrote down was "Yikes."

Let me explain. I have followed J. Denny Weaver's work ever since I became his colleague at Bluffton twenty years ago, and learned a great deal from him. We have had conversations (and occasional arguments), alone and with others, on too many subjects to list. Denny's ongoing theological enterprises, and his many other interests, have influenced and energized my own work in many direct and indirect ways. His determination to construct a thoroughly Anabaptist theology with nonviolence at its center, and his trademark energy and conviction, have been an inspiration.[1]

While I owe Denny a great deal, however, I have long been uneasily aware that my own internal processes are less focused and coherent than his. I have labored to produce more or less academic prose, including a good deal of writing on Mennonite literature and even some which flirts with the boundaries of theology, but these efforts have not led toward a consistent, coherent edifice of thought; instead I have found myself constructing ramshackle improvisations and inquiries, most of which resist clear theses and point-by-point expositions. (I say this as confession, not boast.) For all the attractions of abstraction, I find myself drawn even more strongly toward more concrete language, toward imagery and metaphor. In the gaps between story and meaning, image and interpretation, exploring what resists being truly or fully known, where poetry aspires toward something like theology—that is where I feel at home.

When asked to "situate" my "viewpoint on Christology," then, what first came to mind was my little poem "How the Boy Jesus Resisted Taking Out the Trash":

> O there's not enough to bother with.
> O in a couple thousand years the landfills will be groaning.
> O we're too poor there isn't any trash.
> O what about Naomi what does she do around here.
> O if ever you suspected what's to come you'd put me in the best chair, you'd kill the last goat for supper and feed me the heart and the liver.
> O not now.
> O remember my father's business and all that. Priests and Levites are going to love me, some. Locusts will sing and sizzle. Precious stones will roll toward me like mice. Everybody's pretty daughters will cry because I don't like them that way.
> O I'll change it into figs and honey later, all right?
> O all right.[2]

Now this is not a serious effort to envision the actual life of the boy Jesus; it has more to do with memories of my own sons, smart and obstreperous as they were as children, and my guess that even Jesus might have had his moments of resistance to his parents' instructions. The poem suggests that such resistance might be either funny or annoying, depending on your position in relation to it. In the end, though, my boy Jesus says "Oh, all right," recognizing that the familial power structure does have some just claims upon his time and energies. The poem has a kind of implied narrative but does not even tell a completely clear story, let alone state a thesis and support it. I spend a lot of my time training students to do those things in writing, which may partly explain why I treasure the freedom from such requirements that poems offer.

While few of the preserved sayings of Jesus are very accurately described as poems, it is no secret that his rhetorical style is often indirect and elusive. At times he even seems to suggest this is deliberate; in Mark 4:11-12 he says to the disciples, "To you has been given the secret of the kingdom of God, but for those outside everything is in parables; so that they may indeed see but not perceive, and may indeed hear but not understand; lest they should turn again, and be forgiven." Biblical scholars tend to be uneasy with what seems the plain sense of this passage—that there are some people Jesus does not *want* to understand his message—and some suggest it must be an apocryphal addition. Without delving further into this controversy, let me just observe that any quick turn through the Gospels—or a quick contemplation of the last two millennia of Christian history—will confirm that Jesus did not leave an utterly transparent set of teachings behind.

We might also consider these words from the apocryphal "Gospel of Philip":

> Jesus took them all by stealth, for he did not reveal himself in the manner in which he was, but it was in the manner in which they would be able to see him that he revealed himself. . . . He revealed himself to the great as great. He revealed himself to the small as small. He revealed himself to the angels as an angel, and to men as a man. Because of this his word hid itself from everyone.[3]

We treasure and trust this indirection of Jesus, however frustrating it sometimes is, because we trust his goals and motives—and, perhaps, because we have little choice but to work with what we have. Still, a long if slender thread in our tradition cautions against the wrong sort of God-talk. St. Francis famously said "Preach the gospel at all times and when necessary use words." Thomas Merton expanded on the idea: "[A] saint is capable of talking about the world without any explicit reference to God," he wrote, "in such a way that his statement gives greater glory to God and arouses a greater love of God than . . . hackneyed analogies and metaphors that are so feeble that they make you think there is something the matter with religion."[4]

When I find myself drifting into the fogs of abstraction, I try to re-locate myself in the particular place I inhabit with my physical body. I wrote some of these words in a rented minivan somewhere in Illinois, headed west to my son's college graduation. As we passed through a small town I saw piles of dirt and gravel in a parking lot where a new building was going up. I saw a woman in a yellow vest standing in the middle of an intersection holding a surveyor's stick, yelling numbers to a companion, ignoring the traffic swirling by her on all sides. Soon we were out of town, though, amid ditch grass bushy from the spring rains, not yet laid low by the mowers, and the tender yellowish new corn, two inches out of black earth. Next to me my wife was driving, glancing over to see what I was doing. She didn't ask what I was writing, and I didn't volunteer. Sometimes it's necessary to keep things quiet until their time.

2

More and more I find myself wanting to leave behind all the human contentions that seem, however crucial, so frustrating and irresolvable, and instead head off to split the wood and lift up the stone, to speak of the world as if it was indeed the habitation of the divine. It would not be so bad, surely, to devote one's time to praise of the earth and our companions living, lost, and to come, and all those beings visible and invisible that lead us toward justice, mercy and love. Whitman had such business in mind when he offered this wonderful list of what we should do:

> Love the earth and sun and the animals, despise riches, give alms to every one that asks, stand up for the stupid and crazy, devote your income and labor to others, hate tyrants, argue not concerning God, have patience and indulgence toward the people, take off your hat to nothing known or unknown or to any man or number of men, go freely with powerful uneducated persons and with the young and with the mothers of families, re-examine all you have been told at school or church or in any book, dismiss whatever insults your own soul . . . and your very flesh shall be a great poem and have the richest fluency not only in its words but in the silent lines of its lips and face and between the lashes of your eyes and in every motion and joint of your body.[5]

Whitman also wrote beautifully of the patience and calm of animals—though on that subject I must quibble with him. My neighbor has been keeping his daughter's dog, an exotic, energetic animal whose convictions are simple and absolute. Every time I pass by—which I do three or four times a day—Clarence erupts into a utter fury of barking and leaping, dashing along the fence, turning in tight little circles; he doesn't stop until I'm nearly out of his sight, and no matter how many times I pass by his intensity never diminishes. He is quite convinced that I am a deadly threat with whom no compromise is possible, and that only the noisiest and most muscular public hostility will fend me off. My purposes are utterly irrelevant and unthreatening to his, but he's too busy making desperate threats to learn anything about that.

3

Truth did not come into the world naked, but it came in types and images. One will not receive truth in any other way. There is a rebirth and an image of rebirth. It is certainly necessary that they should be born again through the image. What is the resurrection? The image must rise again through the image.[6]

Late one fall I visited the Oregon Extension—an intensive study program in the mountains of southern Oregon. We stayed at a sprawling dude ranch nearby, which our hosts said was run by a fervently evangelical family; among its features not visible from the house where we stayed were three gigantic crosses atop a small hill. One chilly but sunny afternoon I went for a long walk around the ranch, with Mount Shasta looming out beyond the closer ranges. This poem, "Contemplation at the Bar R Ranch," was the result.

Both the owner and his daughter said we'd have to see the crosses
so of course I tried to avoid them. But wandering aimlessly

after sublimity as I do on free afternoons I followed a sign
that said "Baptismal" down a narrow way

and stepped carefully on rocks across the icy creek.
When I looked up there they were, enormous,

big enough to crucify a pteranodon or a giraffe.
As I climbed the muddy path some part of me said

I have to safeguard my doubts and another remembered
how the old picker said to Goodman *I find*

the prettiest woman in the room and play every song for her.
Too edgy to eat, Salinger's Franny tried to pray

the Jesus prayer all the way through homecoming.
With the sun low behind the crosses I could barely look.

Thin grass, lichens, rocks and gravel lay low all around
stunned by some brutal devotion not their own.

Three weeks to solstice. Faint thin birdsong.
So many trees, so many rocks, so many women

whose lives and bodies I will never touch.
The creek rippled on, Shasta glowed in the chilly haze,

a strand of spider silk glinted in and out of sight.
Breathe in: *This is paradise.* Breathe out: *I must go.*[7]

Theology aims to be clear, precise, exact, and straightforward about its propositions, to bring reason to bear on mystery. Is the impulse to theologize somehow related to the impulse to erect larger-than-life-size crosses in a mountain meadow? The impulse to mistrust large public gestures of piety while seeking to register one's own spiritual intimations and quandaries in the language of poetry? I do not mean these as rhetorical questions. As my poem suggests in its own way, the crosses seemed utterly displaced to me there, a kind of poetry doomed by the clumsiness and crudity of its ambitions. True poetry, I believe, seeks to dwell less obtrusively and more lightly within the mysteries of existence. But why should my views of such matters be trusted?

Poetry dwells among the mystery of language, and what happens to our terms, both abstract and concrete, as we seek to arrange and control them, to use them to speak of phenomena that are not fully contained by any language. Consider what Thomas Merton has to say about one key religious term: "It is a pity that the beautiful Christian metaphor 'salvation' has come to be so hackneyed and therefore so despised. It has been turned into a vapid synonym for 'piety'—not even a truly ethical concept."[8]

This far Merton might seem to be on the same path that Denny Weaver took when he argued that Anabaptists have historically insisted on "keeping salvation ethical" and connected to action in the world, resisting the view that it represents a merely personal exchange between the individual and God. But Merton has a somewhat different dualism in mind. Rather than devaluing the subjective in favor of the ethical, he means to rehabilitate and expand our notions of subjectivity: "'Salvation' is something far beyond ethical propriety. The word connotes a deep respect for the fundamental metaphysical reality of man. . . . It is not only human nature that is 'saved' by the divine mercy, but above all the human *person*. The object of salvation is that which is unique, irreplaceable, incommunicable—that which is myself alone."[9]

When I recently taught a "spiritual memoir" class, it quickly became clear that I had a diverse group. Some were earnest and devout Mennonites, Catholics, and others; some had little religious background; some came in with traumatic experiences that made them deeply suspicious of "spiritual writing." In the first several weeks we explored what that term might mean—especially, I tried to say that we would be best off not to worry about whether we were being orthodox or not. Rather than concentrating on who was saved and who wasn't, I suggested that we try to write with all the clarity, depth, and openness we could manage about our actual lives, feelings, experiences, thoughts, and convictions.

Once people realized that I meant this, the class took off. People found the nerve to talk and write with sometimes astonishing directness and insight about the particular conditions of their lives and their souls, or at least to treat those elements of their lives with more precision, openness, and detail than we were accustomed to. We discovered help in this endeavor in writers like Merton, and others such as Anne Lamott, Annie Dillard, Kathleen Norris, and Cynthia Yoder, very different writers who were all quite open about their own doubts and qualms as well as their faith.

All of these writers seem (I realize in retrospect) to share Merton's interest in what he calls "the human *person*"—a totality encompassing more than the body, the self, or the soul." Like Merton, they all had a large and generous sense of the "unique, irreplaceable, incommunicable" nature of the human person, and all write as though it is both natural and right that followers of Jesus should cultivate our persons rather than stifling or denying large sections of them.

Not until the class was over did I discover a letter from the poet James Wright that touches on similar issues. Wright reflects on the links between his poems and the language of his home town in southern Ohio, which he says has been "ringing somewhere in my head all my life":

> I suppose what I'm saying is that a person—like your young poets—should not be afraid to pour into his poetry all the phrases and sayings and rhythms that in truth mean the most to him, the sounds that he can hear outside of himself—because, if he listens, he'll hear them inside of himself, too. Everybody surely hears some kind of song inside of himself. How amazing if he could only be brave enough to sing it out loud. If he does, often he gets back from other people something like an echo—an echo changed and transfigured by the secret songs of the very people who have heard him sing in the first place.[10]

What poems do, perhaps better than any other mode of expression, is delineate those complicated interior and exterior negotiations that make up our lives and our desires in their fullest sense. At a conference once I was asked, somewhat suspiciously, whether poems represent "subjective" truth—the clear subtext being that this sort of thing, while perhaps interesting, is inferior to the "objective" truth to be found elsewhere. I don't remember exactly what I said, except that I resisted the whole notion that truth could be split into such categories and tried to suggest that truth was much bigger than our language for it. "On the 12:50 Out of Fairfield" by Julia Levine, which dances beautifully among several planes of being and language, helps me think about the subjective and the objective.

Go ahead.
Say you are not moved by the soul

that looks out of every window,
seven cranes lifted like a train of hours

floating into loss, dusk already sifting down
the splintered rafters of your heart.

Say you don't need Heaven, the fictive afterlife
poured with cirrus blue and saints,

to get you through a rape, two deaths,
every lover that left you all alone.

Or say there is not one God,
but a countless shatter of the sacred,

like rain inside a week of rain,
and all the pearly fragments pour down

like desire, too large and brimming
to be held inside one life,

lust like a holy rush of sea
slapping up against the threatened levies

of your flesh, the conductor
singing out the names where longing dwells,

and all the strangers you will never touch
stepping down to stations

swarmed with light.
So, go ahead. Say you are just fine.

Say this is enough, right here, right now.
That you will learn to want

only what you have.
Go ahead. Try.[11]

The fascination and complication of this poem is mostly in its series
of imperatives, addressed to a "you" who seems to be the poet, but is not
limited to her. Say this, say that . . . say that the things and people of the
world do not move you, say that there is no "single God," say that you do

not yearn for more clarity, more certainty, more ease within this lovely world and all the pain and desire its creatures bear. Crucially, all this "saying" happens not in some realm of abstract ideas, but in a very specific place, on a train with rainy fields and cranes outside and other passengers bearing their own secret lives about with them.

The poem asks radical, fundamental questions. How can the moment—which is always all we have, in one sense—ever be enough? How can we ever find anything more? How do all of our categories and theologies and imperatives and taboos, all our language and rules for engaging this world, intersect with the moment as it passes and keeps passing? All of these things are connected, the poem suggests, but not easily or simply; they cohabit each moment inside of our heads, where the world as we each know it happens.

As the ending reminds us, all the imperatives of the poem are verbal utterances, speech acts not meant to be "true" propositionally but to represent the immediate progression of the speaker's thoughts and feelings. All those imperative "Says," however, do surely add up to an effort to bring something into being by speaking it—perhaps a fuller acceptance of things as they are, an end to or at least a softening of yearning and desire and lust. At the same time, the poem evokes and recognizes the power of those elemental human realities, and how intertwined they are. It is no accident that the poem moves so quickly from God to the "holy rush of sea" to the mysterious bodies of strangers. And equally crucial to the poem is its vulnerability, the poet's recognition of her own ambivalence and uncertainty, her own doubts and lusts. Writing is mysterious this way, because it requires both mastery and relinquishing, great knowledge and greater awareness of one's limits.

4

"An ass which turns a millstone did a hundred miles walking. When it was loosed, it found that it was still at the same place. There are men who make many journeys, but make no progress toward a destination."[12]

I walked home for lunch, as I've done a hundred times before—down the back stairs from my third-floor office, through the sculpture garden, past Shoker Science Center and Marbeck Center, across Riley

Creek (still flowing but low; it's been a dry spring), up the hill past the art building. None of this is new to me, and not for the first time I felt that I've spent my life walking in a pointless circle, moving between my comfortable office and my comfortable home, wearing the keys on my keyboard shiny, while the bombs explode in Iraq and politicians posture and desperate people suffocate in shipping containers. How to sum up this world, anyway?

Clarence is on the other side of town now, probably still barking at squirrels and any other living thing larger than a sparrow who passes by. The planet groans as the giant bonfire that passes for civilization blazes on. My green beans and snow peas are struggling out of the ground, despite the dearth of rain. Our aging minivan has a whine in the right rear that starts at thirty-two miles an hour and disappears at thirty-six. One part of my mind wants to take the tire off and check out the bearing, another to settle on the recliner and read Jacob Boehme on the Unity of the All.

Within a few miles of me, I know, some of God's children are hungry, terrified, strung out, utterly broke, crushed by depression. None of them are visible from here. The sun shines softly. The administration led by the most powerful Christian on earth has plans to develop bunker-busting nuclear weapons, lest any place on earth be outside the reach of American power. I try to find something new and inspiring to read, but everything strikes me as either ponderous beyond bearing ("Those in the fourth have forms like human forms and feet like human feet, and wear helmets on their heads, and marble tunics"),[13] or beautiful insights mingled with absurd optimism:

> All movement is a sign of
> Thirst.
>
> Most speaking really says,
> "I am hungry to know you."
>
> Every desire of your body is holy;
>
> Every desire of your body is
> Holy.[14]

Still, the new lilac bush seems to be rooting in, and so do the sunflowers I transplanted from my friend's place in the country. The sun warms the top of my head and all the half-formed desires, fears, and dreams swirling inside, as though all the whole breathing world should answer to that small, dark, teeming space.

5

"When we get our spiritual house in order, we'll be dead. This goes on. You arrive at enough certainty to be able to make your way, but it is making it in darkness. Don't expect faith to clear things up for you. It is trust, not certainty."[15]

I first went on a "poetry night hike" a few years ago, led by my friend Terry Hermsen. I was suspicious about the idea of walking out with a group of people to write poems, but I have now done half a dozen of these hikes, and every one so far has been remarkable in its own way.

Last summer I found myself in charge. I spent days figuring every detail, but miscalculated how long the light would last under the trees and got the group—ten of us or so—started much too late. I had planned a fifteen-minute walk past one waterfall and to another, to read a few poems when we got there and then set people loose to write as the dark came on. But as we walked to the upper waterfall, the light already dimming under the trees, I realized that if we pressed on we would be walking back along the rough, root-laced path in more or less total darkness.

It grieved my heart to stop partway and turn around, but everybody seemed relieved when I suggested it. When we got to the lower falls, which are pretty enough in their own right, I read a couple of poems and we watched the light fade. I stumbled to a sittable rock and got out my little book along with the others.

There's something about writing in a place with trees and rocks and water as the light dwindles. The page gets vaguer and vaguer until you have to rely on muscle memory to avoid writing over your own words and ending up with an illegible scramble. But I always find that as my eyes become less useful, other parts of my being become more alert and more talkative. Still agitated by having messed up, I tried to settle into that twilight state in which all kinds of utterance seem to be possible, the way the sun's absence reveals the stars. As the water murmured along its way I wrote like mad for fifteen minutes or so, paying very little attention to what the others were doing. When I was done, I realized that many of the others were still at it, and even after everyone had put their pens away we lingered for a while longer, soaking in the sensations of the night.

The way back was quiet, and still I wasn't sure how it had gone. I apologized to everybody, several times, and they were gracious, although my naturalist partner Mike suggested that if I had just listened to him things would have gone better. (He had brought along a fancy little LED headlamp and wandered around sure-footedly as the rest of us stumbled on the rocks and roots.)

On the last night we had an open reading, and I read my night hike poem, which has a lot to do with giving up the hope of being too fully in control of anything:

Where Water Finds an Edge
—Blue Hen Falls, June 2004

Nothing like a careful, thorough plan with one large error.
Inside a dog it's too dark to read—here, almost.
Rocks piled around like bad excuses, like my father's brow

as he tries to say gently just how deep and wide my screw-up is.
I stumble for a place to sit and a thin sheet of shale
cracks, breaks—even the skin of the earth can't be trusted.

Every splash is a syllable, not one is a word. But who knows
what Suzanne will show us if we drink her tea,
spend the night and manage not to jump her bones.

Every stone is a section of the mind of God,
every leaning tree and breathing creature.
We need the dark because it makes us clumsy,

because it makes us forget the banks we are rushing between,
muttering about hymns and women while the Falls
open before us. We will not need to be ready

to tumble down. We will shine and shout
and all the damage will be forgotten soon.
The water is not wounded by its breathless journey,

it bears its troubles lightly, it winks to the sun,
it does not falter as the full night arrives.
And the hard ledges glow, long after all else is lost.[16]

The next morning I found myself sitting next to a shy woman I
hadn't gotten to know well, although the night before she had put on a
marvelous performance of a story she'd written. She said to me "Thank
you for your error," so quietly that I asked her to repeat what she'd said.
I still didn't hear her clearly, but it seemed rude to ask again, so I let it
pass. Only later did I realize just what she had said, and what a gift she
had given.

Notes

1. The series of books and articles through which Weaver has worked out this
project, especially the three important recent books *Keeping Salvation Ethical*
(1997), *Anabaptist Theology in Face of Postmodernity* (2000), and *The Nonviolent
Atonement,* 2nd. ed., greatly revised and expanded (2011), provide a model of focused intellectual activity—at once wide-ranging and coherent—that I regard with
little short of awe. Denny's response to my own work, especially his help in shaping
my book *Walker in the Fog: On Mennonite Writing* for the C. Henry Smith Series
which he edits, has also been generous, rigorous, and constructive.

2. Jeff Gundy, *Rhapsody with Dark Matter,* (Huron, Ohio: Bottom Dog, 2000),
54.

3. Willis Barnstone, *The Other Bible,* (New York: HarperCollins, 1984), 90.

4. Thomas Merton, *New Seeds of Contemplation,* (New York: New Directions,
1961), 24.

5. Walt Whitman, *Leaves of Grass and Selected Prose,* ed. John A. Kouwenhoven
(New York: Modern Library, 1950), 446.

6. "The Gospel of Philip," Barnstone, *The Other Bible*, 93.

7. Jeff Gundy, *Spoken among the Trees,* (Akron: University of Akron Press, 2007),
102-3.

8. Merton, *New Seeds,* 37.

9. Merton, 37-8.

10. James Wright, "Ten Letters," ed. Jonathan Blunk, *The Georgia Review* 59, 1
(2005), 37.

11. Julia Levine, *Ask* (Tampa: University of Tampa Press, 2003), 33-4.

12. "The Gospel of Philip," Barnstone, *The Other Bible,* 92.

13. Hildegarde of Bingen, *Scivias,* trans. Mother Columba Hart and Jane Bishop (New York: Paulist, 1990), 141.

14. Hafiz, *The Subject Tonight Is Love: 60 Wild and Sweet Poems of Hafiz,* versions by Daniel Ladinsky (North Myrtle Beach, S.C.: Pumpkin House, 1996), 9.

15. Flannery O'Connor, *The Habit of Being: Letters of Flannery O'Connor,* ed. Sally Fitzgerald (New York: Vintage, 1979), 354.

16. Gundy, *Spoken among the Trees,* 25.

SIX

NOTES TOWARD THE HERETICAL SUBLIME

"If I paint the glass blue," says Alan Watts, "I cannot see the sky."" And this would be true even though I call the glass the "sky.""[1]

1

A tremendous energy comes from the sense of transgression, especially when coupled with the ethical sense that one's transgressions, though "heresies" to the established order, are faithful to a higher power. Whether the sense of transgression or faithfulness is the more powerful driver—a question whose answer seems less than clear to me—it *is* clear that such energy has fueled movements and martyrs throughout history. Some of these transgressors take on the status of heroes, others remain condemned to villain status . . . all depending on the outcomes. They include the original followers of Jesus and rebels and reformers all through the church history, as well as poets of all sorts, especially romantics like Blake, Keats, Whitman, and Dickinson, and neo-romantics like Wallace Stevens. Different as these poet and movements are, all are conscious of their transgressions against orthodoxy, and all are convinced they are being true to some more authentic spirit, reality, and/or experience.

Anabaptism, though its paradigms are obviously, even radically anti-Romantic, contains its own heretical imperative in its call to a utopian purity that requires constant renewal and resistance to "the world." The first Anabaptist rebels, with their manifestos, their baptizing of adults, their refusal of oaths, their breaking of images, their rejection of state churches whether Catholic or reformed, were similarly driven by the conviction that most people had gone terribly astray and drastic changes were needed to set things right. Of course they were heretics according to the established order, and it took them generations to secure their own tiny establishments in the crevices and ravines of that order, to solidify their refusals, negations, and drastic gestures into a new order of their own.

But as the revolutionary moment gives way to the daily, then monthly and yearly rigors of community survival, the revolutionary order must evolve into order of another sort—and eventually come to seem a new oppression to a new generation of rebels. As has been documented and dramatized by many artists and writers, Anabaptism has been no less prone than any other sect become establishment to its own institutional hierarchies and oppressions. Along with participation in the general suppression of women and minorities, Mennonite communities have often been particularly suspicious about artistic expressions not confined to a narrow range of pious and/or utilitarian forms.[2]

Especially for the Swiss Brethren Anabaptists and their American descendants, this shift might be seen, very broadly, as a move toward a "heretical pastoral"—a perhaps brash renaming of the "quiet in the land" syndrome, in which Mennonites and Amish sought to preserve difference and purity through withdrawal, and to establish rural communities where their radical ideas might be lived out with minimal interference. An important variant, which often ran alongside the withdrawal motif, was the eventual negotiation of toleration and varying degrees of cooperation and mutual exchange between Anabaptists and their neighbors. Especially in the Low Countries, in Poland and Prussia, some developed extensive involvements in their wider communities, often trading a measure of assimilation for greater security and prosperity.[3]

My main interest here, however, is not with church history, but with that edge where religious and poetic energies intersect in the drive to imagine and bring into being another world through the language of poetry. In this sphere, poetry and theology become close companions—some would say competitors—and the relatively new field of "theopoetics" offers useful means of exploring some of the varieties of what I will call the heretical sublime.

The founder of theopoetics, Stanley Hopper, argues that while there is a natural tension between poetry and theology when both claim the right to insights into the ultimate nature of things, it makes little sense to resolve this tension in favor of theology. Instead Hopper insists that poetry is the primary discipline, because it is open to psychological and existential depths and mysteries, while standard theology is fixated on logic and reason:

> [W]hen we name the conditions of reality by way of the analytical reason, the soul in its movements returns tautologically upon the circle of definitions it sets out with; likewise our symbolic representations may close us in upon the arc of return implicit in their initial figurations. "If I paint the glass blue," says Alan Watts, "I cannot see the sky." And this would be true even though I call the glass the "sky." When I become aware that it is a glass, I must then shatter the glass as a barrier, in order that I may be open to the sky.[4]

Hopper quotes approvingly Kafka's aphorism about the need to accomplish the *negative*, claiming that when we confront all that we do not and cannot know about God, we must also acknowledge how inadequate reason and evidence are to the ultimate questions posed by life. We must recognize, Hopper thinks (following many postmodern theorists) that all knowledge is constructed out of language but that language itself is built up out of nothing, out of difference and metaphor, and that all of our discourse about ultimate questions is itself metaphorical.[5] Once we do so, he claims, we will naturally turn to the form of discourse most at home in metaphor—poetry—to explore the questions that theology has traditionally claimed as its domain.

This argument has some connections to Mennonite theologian Gordon Kaufman's claim that theology is always a "constructive" human activity and must be recognized as such, though the details of Kaufman's project are quite different than Hopper's. Kaufman dismisses most of traditional theology as the product of the over-reification of metaphors like "lord," "father," and "creator"; God, he insists, is far beyond any such human constructions. The most accurate, best metaphor for God, he argues, is "serendipitous creativity," not lord or father or creator:

> What could we possibly be imagining when we attempt to think of God as an all-powerful personal reality existing somehow be-

fore and independent of what we today call "the universe"? As far as we know, personal agential beings did not exist, and could not have existed, before billions of years of cosmic evolution of a very specific sort, and then further billions of years of biological evolution also of a very specific sort, had transpired. How then can we today think of a person-like creator-God as existing before and apart from any such evolutionary developments?[6]

Despite the apparent congruence of this argument with Hopper's claims for poetry, Kaufman's affinities to Hopper and theopoetics go only so far. Kauffman understands "creativity," in particular, as a much broader category encompassing all sorts of material and intellectual activity, from the development of planets and life to the writing of theology and of sonnets. Generally, he is still committed to rationalism—he remains a theologian, however innovative and iconoclastic—and suspicious of the intuitive processes of poetry. If God is indeed serendipitous creativity, however, it would seem to follow that in creativity we all take part in the work of God. This divinity is within us, though we do not have easy access to it, any more than we can reach within and squeeze a few extra drops of bile from our livers when it might be convenient.

Stanley Hopper, in contrast, turns precisely to poetry in hopes of the large-scale transformation he sees as necessary. "When language fails to function at the metaphorical or symbolic levels," he writes, "the imagination goes deeper, soliciting the carrying power of archetype, translating the archetype from the spent symbolic system into fresh embodiments."[7]

The aim of poetry, then, is not to render or describe or narrate—but to discover a language adequate to being, to bring into this world things made of words that draw us toward the full consciousness of which we can yet only dream. This purpose, Hopper argues, is before and independent of any other function that a poem might have (though a poem may have many other functions as well). And this purpose is also not subject to limits imposed by other realms of human endeavor. In and of itself, then, Hopper claims poetry of the sort he favors is a holy activity, and not to be circumscribed or contested, although of course the success of its execution remains open to discussion and judgment.

Like Kaufman (and an increasing number of contemporary theologians), Hopper believes that the largest errors of conservative religion are over-reification and trust in unexamined metaphor. To claim that the language of the past is sufficient to carry God's project into the future, and that God can be contained in human language in ways sufficient to answer all the important human questions, including who is worthy of salvation and who is not, no longer will suffice. New language, new images, new metaphors are constantly required. The quest is not for an absolute naming or a set of propositions that will make of the Divine a comprehensible system—any such project, Hopper believes, is mistaken in its quest for a certitude that is existentially unavailable to us.

What, then? Hopper turns to the work of Martin Heidegger, who himself looks to the poet Rainer Maria Rilke for a way of addressing ultimate questions. In a letter of Aug. 11, 1924, Rilke writes:

> To me it seems more and more as though our customary consciousness lives on the tip of a pyramid whose base within us (and in a certain way beneath us) widens out so fully that the farther we find ourselves able to descend into it, the more generally we appear to be merged into those things that, independent of time and space, are given in our earthly, in the widest sense worldly, existence.[8]

How much *can* we know, and how clearly can it be expressed? If knowledge were a simple thing, surely there would be less discourse and more clarity. A main principle of theopoetics is that the mysteries of existence—and what we call God is surely the greatest of these mysteries—can be approached only with proper respect for their nature *as* mysteries. Heidegger speaks of the need to address mystery without reductionism: "But we never get to know a mystery by unveiling or analyzing it; we only get to know it by carefully guarding the mystery *as* mystery. But how can it be carefully guarded—this mystery of proximity—without even being known?"[9]

Theology seeks closure and clarity; poetry resists them, resting more readily in uncertainty and incompleteness. Keats's oft-cited idea of "Negative Capability" is relevant: "that is, when a man is capable of being in uncertainties, mysteries, doubts, without any irritable reaching after fact and reason." [10] Also relevant is this section of Robert Bly's "Six Winter Privacy Poems," "Listening to Bach":

> Inside this music there is someone
> Who is not well described by the names

Of Jesus, or Jehovah, or the Lord of Hosts![11]

The idea that God is unknowable in essential ways is a comfort to many poets, a bitter spur and fundamental challenge to (some) theologians. Theology, at least in its traditional senses, must operate as if a great many things about God can be articulated in human language, or give up its entire enterprise; poets (I might claim) are often able to rest more easily and alertly within the mystery, and receive and offer different sorts of information as a result.

Intriguingly, Hopper mistrusts the modernist poetry of both T. S. Eliot—too orthodox—and William Carlos Williams—too secular. Instead, he is a surprising advocate of their contemporary Wallace Stevens. Though Stevens is famous for his abandonment of conventional Christian faith, Hopper finds in his "sense of the dropping away of the entire symbolic world of Christendom" a radical, refreshing opening toward something else: "divinity must be within the world as given," Hopper says, "not superimposed from above or deferred to something remote and static"; "The universe that Stevens cannot find a center in is itself that box of the guitar whose emptiness becomes a Presence when we play things as they are."[12]

Can it be that embodiment and mystery, presence and materiality, are before other orders of knowing? Mennonite theologian John Howard Yoder often challenges orthodox assertions himself, and acknowledged repeatedly that in a relativistic world there is no airtight way to establish truth-claims. Even so, he argues that for confessing believers, "The church precedes the world epistemologically. We know more fully from Jesus Christ and in the context of the confessed faith than we know in other ways . . . the meaning and validity and limits of concepts like 'nature' and 'science' are best seen not when looked at alone but in the light of the confession of the lordship of Christ."[13]

Christians must, surely, privilege the "knowing" associated with "Jesus Christ and the context of the confessed faith" above other sorts of knowing. Still, as I will explore in more detail later, assigning epistemological priority to the church seems to me fraught with peril. Yoder often presents himself as a pragmatic sort, dismissive of mystery and mystification; he insists on viewing practices such as baptism and communion not as "sacraments" whose true significance is in some hidden, miraculous transformation, but as what he calls "ordinary human behavior."

They are, he insists, "not mysterious. No esoteric insight is needed for them to make sense. A social scientist could watch them happening."[14] Similarly, Yoder makes at least one dismissive reference to "mere poetry," in the important essay "Armaments and Eschatology": "To sing 'The Lamb is Worthy to Receive Power,' as did the early communities whose hymnody is reflected in the first vision of John, is *not mere poetry.* It is performative proclamation. It redefines the cosmos in a way prerequisite to the moral independence which it takes to speak truth to power. . . ."[15]

Yoder's language here, and the casual way he tosses aside "mere poetry," suggests why poets often find the rhetoric of theologians frustratingly condescending. Even if Yoder did not "really mean" that all poetry is mere fancy language (as his defenders have tried to convince me), the clear, plain sense of the sentence is that poetry is not important or useful. Yet the claim that follows—that the communal performance of the song is transformative—reflects precisely the power of poetry and other figurative language, in the context of community, to "redefine the cosmos." Such language lays claims whose value as propositional truth finally matters less than their outcomes: it allows, even creates, "the moral independence which it takes to speak truth to power." On this we agree— but why, then, could Yoder not allow that speech of this vital, bodily sort is "indeed poetry" rather than "not mere poetry"? At the least, surely one is not "religious" and the other something else.

Just how primary, then, are intellectual belief-constructions like "the confessed faith"? Does the abstract language of belief precede or hold sway over other forms of language, other mediations between experience and meaning? As Yoder suggests almost despite himself, the performative language of hymns and poems, in which theological assertions are embedded in metaphor and music, often has a force that "mere theology" lacks.[16] Language and cosmos, many believe, are intricately related. Again, Heidegger:

> Only where there is language is there world, i.e. the perpetually altering circuit of decision and production, of action and responsibility, but also of commotion and arbitrariness, of decay and confusion. . . . Language is not a tool at his disposal, rather it is that event which disposes of the supreme possibility of human existence. . . . The being of man is founded in language. But this only becomes actual in *conversation.*[17]

How *does* language function to structure and shape our perceptions and understandings? Heidegger (and much postmodern thinking after him) assigns language a primary role in consciousness. The poet and critic Anne Carson further notes that in this role, language is deeply interwoven with human intention and desire: "It is nothing new to say that all utterance is erotic in some sense, that all language shows the structure of desire at some level."[18] Any linguistic exchange, she suggests, involves a "symbolic intercourse": "writer and reader bring together two halves of one meaning, so lover and beloved are matched together like two sides of one knucklebone." Not only is desire inseparable from language, but so is imagination: "Imagination is the core of desire. It acts at the core of metaphor. It is essential to the activity of reading and writing."[19]

Theologians and church authorities—especially since the Reformation—have often sought to keep imagination and desire out of the church because their church is built on Reason and authority, neither of which can survive imagination and desire. This suspicion goes all the way back to Plato, who banned the poets from his Republic because he knew that those informed by imagination would not yield willingly to the rule of reason and authority. Yet as Grace Jantzen points out, theology is impossible without the *desire* to do theology, if we think about it at all carefully:

> Desire is both the indispensable substratum of rationality and its danger: it is the other of rationality. . . . unless the God of classical theism were desired by contemporary philosophers of religion, unless they wanted this God and no other, they would hardly spend their energy seeking out arguments and evidence justifying their beliefs about "him"—again, this God, and no other.[20]

If there is no language *without* desire, without imagination, then seeking to ignore or evade these categories can only lead to disaster. Anabaptism, perhaps even more than other strains of Christianity, relies on reasoning closely from biblical texts, especially those offering the life and teaching of Jesus, to particular behaviors and practices; in this it is very much an Enlightenment project. One can celebrate its main projects—especially the drive to make Jesus' nonviolence a norm, not to be rationalized away when it seems necessary to kill somebody or other—while sensing a certain lack of imaginative spaciousness within it.

If the positive heresy of Anabaptism in the context of Christendom is that following Jesus is more important than doing the business of the state and the "world," its most problematic aspect, at least for artists, may be its iconoclasm, its mistrust of beauty and the arts and the imagination. Let us turn now to look more closely at the transgressive energy of some particular expressions of the heretical sublime.

2

At the end of my sophomore year in college I took a summer course called "Tradition and the Individual Talent." The title came straight from the famous essay by T. S. Eliot, who despite the radical innovations of his poetry was hardly a revolutionary in other spheres; he famously described himself in the preface to *For Lancelot Andrewes* as "classicist in literature, royalist in politics, and anglo-catholic in religion." But the course had been hijacked by the rebel poet-teacher Nicholas Lindsay; while we read Eliot, we spent more time with others such as William Blake (to whom Eliot condescended mercilessly, as I will discuss below), William Butler Yeats, and Theodore Roethke, all of them far more open than Eliot to unconventional approaches to mystery.

What was Blake's project? His ambitions were immodest, to say the least, though the invocation to his prophetic book *Jerusalem* is a blend of the traditional and the unorthodox:

I rest not from my great task!
To open the Eternal Worlds, to open the immortal Eyes
Of Man inwards into the Worlds of Thought, into Eternity
Ever expanding in the Bosom of God, the Human Imagination.
O Saviour pour upon me thy Spirit of meekness and love!
Annihilate the Selfhood in me: be thou all my life.[21]

Worlds of thought, eternity, the Bosom of God, and the human imagination: all are somehow equivalent, or at least interchangeable, in Blake's rhetoric. A main opposition, as he sees it, involves "Abstract Philosophy warring in enmity against Imagination / (Which is the Divine Body of the Lord Jesus, blessed for ever.)"[22] Blake mistrusted priests and (like a good Anabaptist, though as far as I know he knew nothing about them) saw the collusion of church and state as a betrayal of both. Thus the shocking dystopian vision of "London":

> How the chimney-sweeper's cry
> Every blackening church appalls,
> And the hapless soldier's sigh
> Runs in blood down palace-walls.[23]

In "The Garden of Love," churchly authority is just as shockingly linked to repression and denial; the chapel in this garden has "'Thou shalt not' writ over the door," and instead of flowers there are graves and tombstones, among which "priests in black gowns were walking their rounds, / And binding with briars my joys and desires."[24]

I loved many things in Blake, and was baffled by just as many more. But the single text that struck me most deeply, and which I have returned to many times since, is *The Marriage of Heaven and Hell*. This strange work, a sort of fantastic, composite narrative incorporating long sections of aphorisms and epigrams, is frankly heretical, or at least radically revisionist:

> Without Contraries is no progression. Attraction and Repulsion, Reason and Energy, Love and Hate are necessary to Human existence.
>
> From these contraries spring what the religious call Good & Evil. Good is the passive that obeys Reason. Evil is the active springing from Energy.
>
> Good is Heaven. Evil is Hell.[25]

This is Blake's signature voice, or one of them: brusque, dismissive of "the religious" and "the passive that obeys Reason," bent on a project entirely his own.[26] Rehabilitating what "the religious" dismiss as "evil," Blake offers these further grand generalizations as "THE VOICE OF THE DEVIL":

> All Bibles or sacred codes have been the causes of the following Errors.
> 1. That Man has two real existing principles Viz: a Body & a Soul.
> 2. That Energy, call'd Evil, is alone from the Body, & that Reason, call'd Good, is alone from the Soul.

3. That God will torment Man in Eternity for following his Energies.

But the following Contraries to these are True:

1. Man has no Body distinct from his Soul, for that called Body is a portion of Soul discerned by the five Senses, the chief inlets of Soul in this age

2. Energy is the only life and is from the Body and Reason is the bound or outward circumference of Energy.[27]

Strong stuff, indeed, for a farm boy not yet twenty. It hardly struck me as something I could "believe," yet the sense of authority was undeniable. And somehow it seemed strangely plausible, at least in comparison to all those bland exhortations toward goodness I had dutifully absorbed—which seemed strangely inadequate in their accounts of "evil" to so many of us who grew up in the sixties. Richard Nixon claimed to be fighting evil, Jim Morrison did not, but while both of their voices seemed dangerous, I knew which one seemed also to carry a vital whiff of the imagination.

Blake only gets better: "Those who restrain desire do so because theirs is weak enough to be restrained, and the restrainer or reason usurps its place and governs the unwilling. And being restrained, it by degrees becomes passive till it is only the shadow of desire."[28] Balance between contrary forces is essential, Blake insists—Reason is not bad in itself, but has enthroned itself unjustly and painted Energy as the incarnation of evil . . . in much the way, to add some anachronistic examples, that Captain Ahab did with Moby Dick, and the Bush administration did with any who dared oppose them. As a means of restoring this balance, the Devil gets all the good lines in Blake's version, beginning with this great post- or pre-rational question:

How do you know but ev'ry Bird that cuts the airy way,
Is an immense world of delight, clos'd by your senses five?[29]

A later dialogue between this devil and an angel is even more startling. The devil insists that Jesus himself broke all the commandments:

did he not mock at the Sabbath, and so mock the Sabbaths God?
murder those who were murder'd because of him? turn away the
law from the woman taken in adultery? steal the labor of others to
support him? bear false witness when he omitted making a de-

fence before Pilate? covet when he pray'd for his disciples, and when he bid them shake off the dust of their feet against such as refused to lodge them? I tell you, no virtue can exist without breaking these ten commandments. Jesus was all virtue, and acted from impulse, not from rules.[30]

The text concludes with a prophetic "Song of Liberty," imagining the collapse of the empire of Reason and the restoration of balance, and ending with this lovely coda:

"Let the Priests of the Raven of dawn, no longer in deadly black, with hoarse note curse the sons of joy. Nor his accepted brethren, whom, tyrant, he calls free: lay the bound or build the roof. Nor pale religious lechery call that virginity, that wishes but acts not!
"For every thing that lives is Holy."[31]

In this lyrical outburst Blake presses toward both animism and antinomianism. If every thing is holy, why should some rule over others; why should any obey another? Though Blake was too solitary to be interested in forming a movement, such visionary energy has fueled many rebellions and social experiments. The red-letter cautionary example for Anabaptists has always been what happened at the small north German city of Münster in 1534-5, when a band of apocalyptic Anabaptists took over for over a year and attempted to create a visionary community. Constantly besieged by surrounding armies, with food and able-bodied men in short supply, the leaders eventually resorted to polygamy and public beheadings in the town square in their attempts to hold power. Mennonites have feared such anarchic wildness ever since—and spent centuries trying to deny that such excesses were the natural outcomes of their views.

But might there be a pacifist antinomianism, one in which the only rule is love? The traditionalist answer, unsurprisingly, is "of course not." This perspective is neatly captured by T. S. Eliot's suavely condescending remarks about Blake:

We have the same respect for Blake's philosophy . . . that we have for an ingenious piece of home-made furniture: we admire the man who has put it together out of the odds and ends about the house. . . . Blake was endowed with a capacity for considerable understanding of human nature, with a remarkable and original sense of language and the music of language, and a gift of halluci-

nated vision. Had these been controlled by a respect for impersonal reason, for common sense, for the objectivity of science, it
would have been better for him. What his genius required, and
what it sadly lacked, was a framework of accepted and traditional
ideas which would have prevented him from indulging in a philosophy of his own, and concentrated his attention upon the
problems of the poet.[32]

So says the famous Eliot, whose anxiety at the disruptions of the
twentieth century and desire for the comforts of a received order made
him, eventually, a staunch defender of reason, common sense, and objectivity. Of course, the most cursory reading of *The Waste Land* or "The
Love Song of J. Alfred Prufrock" reveals immediately that the roots of his
own poetry were in none of those things, but in deeply rooted traumas
and wishes that found their way into the startling, unpredictable images
and juxtapositions of these great poems.

Sensing that Eliot was more trustworthy as a poet than as a critic, especially of Blake's work, I was pleased to discover a much less famous but
more sympathetic essay on Blake by the Quaker critic Harold C. Goddard. Rather than holding Blake to the standards of "impersonal reason"
and "common sense"—as if those categories had served the human race,
much less poets, as founts of unimpeachable wisdom—he regards
Blake's lack of respect for "accepted and traditional ideas" as his great
strength, and celebrates his devotion to the imagination as engine of social change:

Imagination can not only cause that-which-was-not, to be; it can
cause that-which-was, not to be. It is this double power to annihilate and create that makes imagination the sole instrument of
genuine and lasting, in contrast with illusory and temporary, social change. . . . For art is the language of the imagination, the
means by which the divine in man communicates with the divine
in man, the coin that enables us to exchange LIFE.[33]

Goddard recognizes, with Hopper, that dismantling of received errors is as necessary as the creation of new insight. Elsewhere he claims
that Blake's scheme, the famous, difficult system he arduously worked
out (so Blake claimed) lest he be "enslaved to another man's," addresses
the key problem that Blake saw in the world, and which is symbolized in
one of the key events of Blake's life: his forceful expulsion of a drunken

soldier from his garden one evening. (Blake was tried on trumped-up charges of sedition following this incident, but found not guilty.) "There is a drunken soldier in the garden of the world at present," Goddard writes powerfully: surely the crucial issue of our day, as of Blake's, is how to contend with those who are both trained to violence and "drunken" enough with the power of violence to think that it actually solves problems.

According to Goddard, Blake's answer to this problem fuses imagination and action, desire and reason, at least within the visionary space of the poem. Blake's "fourfold vision," then, is a climb up a kind of Jacob's Ladder from darkness to vision. Single Vision is standard eyesight. Double Vision is metaphor—cf. the Tyger. The dynamic interplay of images is Threefold Vision, as in dreams. "Whoever has known imaginative love, whoever has created a work of art and felt inspired at the moment he conceived it has an inkling of Blake's state of threefold vision." And Fourfold Vision is "dreaming (or loving, or imagining—they are three forms of the same thing) with such intensity that the dream obliterates daylight as daylight ordinarily obliterates the dream." [34] "If the two worlds remain at odds, if the ship of dreams is wrecked on the rocks of reality, we have at the weakest daydreaming, at the strongest hallucination or insanity. But if the two coalesce, as it were, if the ship sails the seas of reality successfully, we have fourfold vision." [35]

> I give you the end of a golden string,
>   only wind it into a ball,
> It will lead you in at Heaven's gate
>   Built in Jerusalem's wall. [36]

Jerusalem, Goddard argues, "means the City of Perfect Liberty. In other words, it is not just individual, but social ecstasy and vision that Blake seeks. Put more men, more often, into a more elevated state of imagination, and everything else follows." [37]

This *is* a faith, if one of an unaccustomed sort. If Blake offers no action plan for practical political action, his vision is surprisingly pragmatic in its real-world implications, though (as G. K. Chesterton remarked of Christianity) it has mainly proven difficult and been left untried. An antinomianism that would transcend Law through the Imagination, that would bring Jerusalem into being by vision rather than by will? Difficult, surely. Yet this romantic rhetoric of Blake's, Goddard suggests, offers a way out of another problematic dualism: "Our forefathers believed in individual salvation. We believe in social salvation. Either without the other is futile, Blake believes. Indeed 'society' and 'the individual' are simply two more of those abstractions of the Reason that he abhorred. Like Heaven and Hell they must be "married" before there can be creation."[38]

To walk with Blake and to see through his eyes, I might suggest, is to glimpse the "grain of the universe" of which John Howard Yoder speaks—and no less than Yoder, Blake believed and desired that grain to move toward justice and peace. As the image of "fourfold vision" suggests, however, we must not rush too quickly from Book to Ethics, from text to behavior (text written by bodies), without taking sufficient account of the passage through language and imagination without which no text can be written and no effective action can take place.

I had nearly finished this essay when I encountered John D. Caputo's fine essay "On Being Clear About Faith." He argues eloquently and persuasively that while religious language and narratives need not—cannot—be regarded as providers of unmediated Truth, they still have much to offer as they move believers to act on the moral imperatives that they embody:

> What then *are* religious revelations ultimately about? They are centrally made up of important religious narratives that shape the lives of the faithful in that tradition; they are formative not informative. They don't reveal (or "report") secret bits of information to us—like the identity of Deep Throat—about the transactions of angels but they imaginatively embody a form of life. [. . .] Are they true? Yes. But we are thinking about their "truth" in the wrong way if we take them as supplying clear knowledge in a representational theory of truth. Their truth—and this is what I think *vera religio* comes down to—comes in the way of the fruitfulness of the form of life to which they give rise, which they both shape and embody.[39]

Caputo argues, in effect, for a poetic view of religious language, and like Blake, he insists that such a view is more, not less, practical than a rationalist or legalist approach. We need religion because it feeds our souls, and through the feeding of souls we discover that living faith requires much more of us than assent to some set of abstract propositions. We can no more live fruitfully without well-cultivated inner lives than we can drive our cars for a decade without changing the oil or checking the battery. There *are* "ghosts in the house" of our beings, as David Miller argues, and if we fail to converse with them, they are likely to do all sorts of damage. Miller suggests that instead of ignoring, repressing, or seeking to bind these ghosts we ought to "entertain" them, "as a host would entertain a guest."[40] If we to allow the ghosts that inhabit the world, our texts, our selves, to speak openly, he suggests, they may have a great deal to teach us.

3

The turn to theopoetics, if we choose to make it, takes us back to poetry, where communication with spirits of all sorts is ongoing. Mennonite poet Julia Spicher Kasdorf explores this practice memorably in her essay "When the Stranger Is an Angel," which considers both the biblical injunction to offer hospitality to strangers—who may be angels after all—and their potentially transformative power. Speaking of the story of Jacob wresting with the angel and a family story of a visiting hobo, Kasdorf muses startlingly on their implications:

> Perhaps this story—like my father's story—means that we possess a sacred power to make angels out of strangers when we are open to change. This can only happen when we leave the security of the hearth and go out to greet the stranger, when we sit with him and imagine his life, when we are able to question our certainties with him and be taught and changed by the encounter.[41]

Kasdorf's poem "Bat Boy, Break a Leg" returns to this theme, interweaving two encounters with strangers and enacting just this sort of patient openness:

> The student with two studs in his nose
> and a dragon tattoo crawling from his collar,
>   who seems always ready to swoon
>   from bliss or despair, now flits
> At my office door. I will look at his poem
> drawn onto a music score and find nothing
>   to say about chance or HIV.
>   Only later I'll think to tell him

the night before I left home, I slept
sadly in our old house until a wing
    touched my cheek, tenderly as a breeze.
    I woke to black fluttering at my feet,
and a mind fresh from the other side
said *don't turn on the light, don't*
    Wake the man, don't scream or speak.
    Go back to sleep. The next morning
I remembered that people upstate
whack them with tennis rackets, that
    the Chinese character for good luck
    resembles the character for bat—
both so unsettling and erratic—
but it's bad luck to say good luck
    in China, as on stage where they say
    Break a leg, so delicate bats
must be woven into silk brocade
and glazed onto porcelain plates.
    Next morning, I found a big-eared mouse
    with leather folded over his shoulders
hanging from claws stuck in a screen.
All day, my work made me forget, but
    then I'd remember, passing the window
    where he slept, shaded under the eaves.
He was fine. I was fine. Then at dusk,
he was gone, suddenly. Pale boy dressed in black,
    Maybe the best that can be said for any of us is that
    once we were angelic enough to sleep with strangers.
He touched my cheek. I opened the screen.
He flew in his time. We did no harm.[42]

Most notably, this poem not only tests and reaffirms nonviolence, but extends it to animals and other such strangers, without waking "the man" who can be expected to react with an aggressive defense of his home against the intruder. Making peace with bats? Shocking.

Many poems in Jean Janzen's fine new book, *Paper House,* also challenge and even contradict conventional religious thinking, even as they search for signs of holy presence. In the playful "Five Lessons on Piety" a blue jay "screeches his piety, / then steals the bagel from my plate," and

"The old poet strums his guitar and sings / 'O Piety, how close you lie to Heresy.'"[43] The startling "Liminal" investigates the threshold between this world and the next:

> Sometimes it is the scent
> of peach, smooth and sweet
> as a newborn, or the newborn
>
> breathing in soft flutter.
> Or the river, relentless
> and disappearing.
>
> Nothing firm, like granite,
> which bars the entrance, yet
> having been born in fire
>
> could become fire again.
> Then is the doorway everywhere—
> grass, bread, your hand gesturing?
>
> Or language, your voice saying,
> "here it is," a place
> we can almost glimpse.[44]

My own recent poems have also often been investigations of crossings and openings between everyday life and the other realms, interior and exterior, that seem more and more palpable to me. Whatever the reason, I find myself drawn more and more to obscure and ambitious texts and authors, those unwilling to trust that the standard wisdom and common sense exhaust everything that we were meant to know and experience. Like Janzen's "Liminal," although without her admirable economy, "Damselfly" explores thresholds and possible openings into new life:

Damselfly

Beginnings have an irritating but essential fragility, and one that should be taken to heart.
—*Teilhard de Chardin*

Consider that ant swarm on the sidewalk, like spilled brown sugar, and the pale yellow leaves the hackberry casts free in a dry June, pressed to the parking lot.

The gray uneven two-by-fours of the picnic table, no place to set a cup half full or half empty.

A green grain head, waving from the corner the mower can't reach.

Elijah's cloak parting the waters, and Elisha: "Let me inherit a double-share of your spirit." And Elijah: "Your request is a difficult one."

And the bowl with the coiled serpent in its heart. And *This is my body.* And the stones of the creek, surfacing with the drought.

When spoken, the secret is no longer the secret. I am not good at secrets. The God I love speaks only in roars and whispers. The God I love only seems to play favorites.

At nine it is already humid, and the woods are dressed in their seven summer greens. All around me the machines are sorting and sifting, cutting and burning.

I wait a whole minute and a black damselfly crosses the creek and the world begins again and again.

And far away right here in town, the child wakes and rolls and stretches, not yet hungry. Wide-eyed, he waves and coos to bring the day into his blue-tinted room.

And there she is, smiling in the open door.[45]

One spark for my recent thinking has been poet Donald Revell's innovative prose book *Invisible Green.* Discussing poet Ronald Johnson's *Ark,* Revell quotes a passage from Thoreau's journal in which Thoreau drinks at a stream, and imagines that he has drunk more than water: an arrowhead, or some ova, or perhaps seeds of thought. Thoreau muses that those who would drink at "running streams, the living waters" must be ready to "suckle monsters" with unpredictable results. Yet doing so is preferable to drinking from stagnant waters:

> Is there not such a thing as getting rid of the snake which you have swallowed when young, when thoughtless you stooped and drank at stagnant waters, which has worried you in your waking hours and your sleep ever since, and appropriated the life that was yours?[46]

Here the key act is drinking from the fresh stream, rather than from the "stagnant waters" that conceal snakes. Revell offers this reading:

> Thoreau, and with Thoreau, Johnson, here describe practices before Religion, behaviors beyond Law. They were antinomians in the active, innocent sense. (Like Blake before, each propounded the vigor of unoriginal innocence, one whose unharming energies vivify, perhaps even maintain, the originating world-as-found.)[47]

This is the heretical sublime, or one of its faces: in such strange and disturbing stories that rise, strong and dangerous as snakes, from some deep hollow within, refusing to be neatly contained or explained, but demanding to be reckoned. These stories seem indeed to be "before" or outside religion, not to be contained by its names and categories. Indeed, I would claim, they are products of some "unoriginal innocence," which may be another name for imagination, whose strongest claim is that it emerges from the very ground of being and of Being, which sometimes, in some of its manifold attributes, we call God.

Notes

1. Quoted in Stanley Romaine Hopper, *The Way of Transfiguration: Religious Imagination as Theopoiesis*, ed. R. Melvin Keiser and Tony Stoneburner (Louisville, Ky.: Westminster/John Knox, 1992), 125.

2. See Jeff Gundy, *Walker in the Fog: On Mennonite Writing* (Telford, Pa.: Cascadia, 2005), passim.

3. For recent explorations of the struggle to achieve religious tolerance in Europe, see Jeremy Dupuis Bangs, *Letters on Toleration: Dutch Aid to Persecuted Swiss and Palatine Mennonites 1615-1699* (Rockport, Maine: Picton, 2004); Benjamin J. Kaplan, *Divided by Faith: Religious Conflict and the Practice of Toleration in Early Modern Europe* (Cambridge: Harvard University Press, 2007); and Peter J. Klassen, *Mennonites in Early Modern Poland and Prussia* (Baltimore: Johns Hopkins University Press, 2009.

4. Hopper, *The Way*, 125-6.

5. Hopper, 155.

6. Gordon Kaufman, *In the Beginning . . . Creativity* (Minneapolis: Fortress, 2004), 54.

7. Hopper, *The Way*, 220.

8. Qtd. in Martin Heidegger, *Poetry, Language, Thought*, trans. Albert Hofstadter (New York: Harper, 1971), 128-9.

9. Martin Heidegger, *Existence and Being*, trans. Werner Brock (Chicago: Henry Regnery, 1949), 279-80.

10. John Keats, Letter of 21 Dec. 1817, *Selected Letters of John Keats*, ed. Grant F. Scott (Cambridge: Harvard University Press, 2002), 60-1.

11. Robert Bly, *Selected Poems* (New York: Harper & Row, 1986), 57.

12. Hopper, *The Way*, 70, 81.

13. John Howard Yoder, *The Priestly Kingdom: Social Ethics as Gospel* (Notre Dame: University of Notre Dame Press, 1984), 11.

14. John Howard Yoder, *Body Politics: Five Practices of the Christian Community Before the Watching World* (Scottdale, Pa.: Herald Press, 1992), 44.

15. Yoder, *Body Politics*, 53, emphasis added.

16. For a more detailed treatment of these issues in Yoder's thought, see Chapter 11.

17. Heidegger, *Existence and Being*, 300-01.

18. Anne Carson, *Eros the Bittersweet* (Princeton: Princeton University Press/Dalkey Archive, 1998), 108.

19. Carson, *Eros*, 107, 77.

20. Grace Jantzen, *Becoming Divine: Toward a Feminist Philosophy of Religion* (Bloomington, Ind.: Indiana University Press, 1997), 86-7.

21. William Blake, *Jerusalem*, plate 5, *Jerusalem, Selected Poems and Prose*, ed. Hazard Adams (New York: Holt, Rinehart, and Winston, 1970), 311.

22. Jantzen, *Becoming*, 311.

23. Jantzen, 44.

24. Jantzen, 43.

25. Jantzen, 124.

26. Cf. the critique of "binary dualisms" by Derrida, Foucault, and other post-modern theorists, almost two centuries later.

27. Jantzen, *Becoming*, 124.

28. Jantzen, 124-5.

29. Jantzen, 126.

30. Jantzen, 136.

31. Jantzen, 138.

32. T. S. Eliot, "Blake," *The Sacred Wood* (London: Methuen, 1920; Bartleby.com, 1996). http://www.bartleby.com/200/. 26 May 2006.

33. Harold C. Goddard, *Blake's Fourfold Vision* (Wallingford, Pa.: Pendle Hill, 1956), 35.

34. Goddard, 31.

35. Goddard, 31.

36. Blake, *Jerusalem*, 462.

37. Goddard, *Blake's Fourfold Vision*, 34.

38. Goddard, 34.

39. John D. Caputo, "On Being Clear About Faith: A Response to Stephen Williams." *Books & Culture: A Christian Review*. 11/01/2006. http://www.christianitytoday.com/bc/2006/novdec/18.40.html?start=1. 11 August 2009.

40. David L. Miller, *Hells & Holy Ghosts: A Theopoetics of Christian Belief* (Nashville: Abingdon, 1989), 158.

41. Julia Spicher Kasdorf, *The Body and the Book: Writing from a Mennonite Life* (Boston: Johns Hopkins, 2001), 35.

42. Julia Kasdorf, *Poetry in America*, Pitt Poetry Series (Pittsburgh: University of Pittsburgh Press, 2011), 6-7.

43. Jean Janzen, *Paper House* (Intercourse, Pa.: Good Books, 2008), 27.

44. Jantzen, 45.

45. Jeff Gundy, *Spoken among the Trees* (Akron: Akron University Press, 2007), xi-xii.

46. Donald Revell, *Invisible Green: Selected Prose of Donald Revell* (Richmond, Calif.: Omnidawn, 2005), 126.

47. Revell, 127.

Part Three
Poetry, Pedagogy, Peace

CHAPTER SEVEN

ADDING REAL BEINGS TO THE WORLD: TEACHING PEACE, WRITING, AND HUMAN EXCHANGE

"A poem is like a ghost seeking substantiality, a soul in search of a body more appealing than the bare bones mere verses rattle. It is consequently not the message in a bottle that Rilke previously thought it was, nor a young man's feelings raised like a flag."
—William Gass[1]

Two millennia have passed since the coming of the Prince of Peace, and for eight recent years the most powerful self-proclaimed Christian in the world was George W. Bush. In such a time, all of the talk that Anabaptists and others do about teaching and peace surely must confront a variation of the old utilitarian American question: "If you're so smart, why ain't you rich?" If we know so much about peace, why are wars and rumors of wars still everywhere, certainly during the Bush era yet also in various ways continuing on these years later? Why does the belief that violence can be both redemptive and effective persist, here and all around the world, despite so much evidence to the contrary? The recalcitrance of the human world, its resistance to being remade in our image, makes the ongoing meetings that Mennonites and other peace groups hold necessary, but also threatens to make them futile. How can real work for peace happen? What place do the arts have in that work? I propose to reflect here on some basic challenges of art-making and peacemaking, and

127

look briefly at some texts, artists and approaches that may suggest a way forward.

William Gass states concisely the problem for poetry that became clear to Rainer Maria Rilke during his relationship with the sculptor Rodin: even the strongest feelings and the most honorable opinions are insufficient to make art. "All of us have emotions urgently seeking release," Gass writes, "and many of us have opinions we think would do the world some good; however the poet must also be a maker, as the Greeks maintained."[2] A poem, no less than a sculpture, must be a "real being in the world," a thing in itself.

A famous dictum by William Butler Yeats offers another view of the tension between art and politics: "We make of the quarrel with others, rhetoric; but of the quarrel with ourselves, poetry."[3] Politics (national, international, and religious) may require both argument with others and the sort of contestatory rhetoric Yeats had in mind. Yet while much great art has political implications, the world is even more crowded with bad art that expresses worthy opinions.

Nonviolent educators surely face a parallel set of questions. Should education be rhetorical or poetic? Put more carefully, does a commitment to nonviolence in the Anabaptist tradition (or any other) resolve the important "quarrels with ourselves" well enough to allow or even require teachers to deal rhetorically with students, to argue them into acceptance of truths we already possess? Or must we acknowledge, even foreground, the dilemmas and difficulties we have not ourselves resolved? Should teachers deliver what we believe is truth to students, or engage them with our own interior quarrels and encourage them to share their own with us? The answers to these questions need not be absolute, but surely they are crucial.

One set of artists who confronted similar tensions particularly sharply were those associated with European Dada and Surrealism. These poets and artists emerged from the maelstrom of World War I, driven by a radical, iconoclastic resistance to conventional society and art. Patrick Wahlberg sums up the tension within this movement well:

> Surrealism was from start to finish a revolutionary movement. The surrealists had two passwords: "To change life" (Rimbaud) and "To transform the world" (Marx). To change life meant to modify feeling, to guide the spirit in new directions, to wean the individual away from a rational view of the world. To this poetic

requirement was added that of transforming the world on the social and moral level.[4]

The conflict between the rationalist materialism of Marxism and the irrationalist idealism of surrealism-as-aesthetic was never, and perhaps could never be resolved; thus "the entire history of [Surrealism] was marked by conflicts, self-contradictions, denunciations and exclusions."[5]

Surely these disparate goals—to change consciousness, and to change the world—apply to education as well As a peace educator I have often felt the somewhat unsettling tug of these two aims, and found myself drawn toward both the aesthetic and the pragmatic, intuition and reason, free imaginative exploration and the transmission of The Truth. And of course similar tensions exist among Mennonites and other religious groups as well. Calvin Redekop once went so far as to suggest that the only plausible position for Mennonite artists and intellectuals would be similar to that of "the artist intellectual under Soviet communism," because "[t]o be totally free to express oneself would lead to the forsaking of or, worse still, the undermining of the tradition."[6]

Despite (or because of?) his own long and distinguished career in Mennonite academia, Redekop suggests that left to their own devices, artists and intellectuals will naturally discover that their tradition is insufficient and must be abandoned or subverted—and that some sort of bureaucratic control is the only way to prevent such disasters. I am tempted to observe that any community that cannot withstand intellectual and aesthetic scrutiny deserves whatever fate it finds, but I will argue instead that free and open exploration, in the context of human exchange, actually enables the kind of exacting confrontations with the world that any vital community, educational or religious or both, needs to thrive over the long haul. If we want to teach peace, then, its practice must begin in our most basic interactions with each other and with the materials from which we seek to make art.

What *do* we value most as teachers, thinkers, and artists? A set of propositions about the way the world is and what we should/must do? A process by which new things of beauty and utility come into the world? A set of relations through which we serve each other, seek to provide the sustenance of all sorts that is needed to live well in this world and find hope for the next? No doubt recklessly, I would place these things in a rising hierarchy, at least pragmatically. After all, what do all our propositions add up to? Can we promise our students that signing on to what-ever noble vision we offer will make their lives easier, or equip them to transform the world in their first three years out of school, or even get them jobs? If we look at the history of Christianity we hardly see an un-broken skein of worldly triumphs.

What we can offer, surely, is at best a difficult and complicated—though also joyous—way forward. Education is, or should be, about the development of passionate and informed commitments. It means—or should mean—falling in love, even a series of loves: with teachers, with ideas, with words and texts, with images of a transformed world. But (I hope to persuade you) it is also about the ethics and the aesthetics of love. And to accomplish all this, I think careful attention to human ex-change is essential.

The sorts of love that true education requires and inspires are pow-erful, energizing, and dangerous, the sorts that can open our eyes or blind us. We *need* the passionate commitment that comes with love if we are to do anything, to be anything, to accomplish anything important. But the difficult work to do demands all our craftiness, insight, and in-telligence as well as our energy. Ask any mechanic, any carpenter: strength and commitment are vital, but without skill and knowledge, mere energy may well just make things worse.

How can we teach, and learn, to live in the world with skillful pas-sion, with smart love? Let us return to Wahlberg's formulation of the dual surrealist goals: "To change life" and "To transform the world."[7] To ask more carefully just what they mean is to enter a whole new maze of complications. The particular surrealist program, their attack on "rea-son," bourgeois morality, warfare, and conventional religion, seemed to suggest a sort of secular conversion that might even be salvific. In his *Manifesto of Surrealism* Andre Breton wonderfully envisioned "the fu-ture resolution of these two states, dream and reality, which are seem-ingly so contradictory, into a kind of absolute reality, a *surreality*, if one may so speak."[8] The dream of a new and renewed life, of transfiguration, of salvation, is surely central to all sorts of movements—political, reli-gious, artistic. The terms of this transformation, however, require more examination.

Let us stray from the surrealists and back to Rilke for a moment. Say that the young, poor, ambitious Rainer Maria Rilke, having learned from Rodin that art is not a matter of "expressing" feelings or ideas but of *making* things that would take their place in the world, makes of a rather ordinary experience a poem called "Eingang" or "Entrance," a thing made of words:

> Whoever you are: go out at evening,
> leaving your room, where everything's familiar;
> between you and the distance lies your house:
> whoever you are.
> With tired eyes, that scarcely pull themselves
> up and away from the worn-down threshold,
> you slowly lift up one black tree
> and place it against the sky: slim, alone.
> And you have made the world. And it is large
> and like a word that's ripening in silence.
> And as your will takes in the sense of it,
> your eyes can gently let it go. . . .[9]

Is what happens in this poem "spiritual" or "practical," "inner" or "outer"? Surely it invites a change in consciousness, and intimates that the right kind of attention actually remakes the world as we perceive it. Yet the process it describes, from observation to recognition to release, seems to me both deeply human and beautifully unassuming in its acceptance of limits: the poem invokes but does not pretend to own or even name the "word" that is the world, and while making the world might seem a rather grand gesture, the modesty of the title and the gentle relinquishment of the end bring the poem quickly back to a fundamental humility—and an aesthetic that I would argue is nonviolent in a quite deep sense.

Rilke was not a surrealist—though he shared their times and their interest in realms beyond naïve realism—nor a political poet, except in the most indirect ways. But the poets and artists of Dada and Surrealism, horrified almost beyond response by World War I and then by the run-up to an even more disastrous war, *were* political, though also often in quirky and indirect ways. When the first Dada meetings began in Zurich in 1916, the idea that Enlightenment rationality and conventional Christianity had failed spectacularly as pragmatic guides to human affairs must have seemed nearly self-evident.

Their response—both within Dada and in the Surrealist movement that soon emerged from it—was an all-out assault on reason, on religion, on propriety, on bourgeois values. Dada and Surrealist poets explored automatic writing, chance compositions, and other techniques for generating texts outside the control of the rational intellect. The results were often baffling, sometimes curiously entrancing; one famous result was the prophetic sentence "The exquisite corpse will drink new wine."

For all their diatribes against conventional religion, the Surrealists have some noteworthy (if partial) affinities with another group of anti-establishment, iconoclastic rebels who insisted that the principalities and powers of the world were corrupt almost beyond redemption, and pledged faithfulness to a creed that most found bizarre and foolish. Someone should do a careful, scholarly comparison of the *Schleitheim Brotherly Union*, adopted by a gathering of Swiss Anabaptists in 1527, and the various Dada and Surrealist manifestos. In one of the former, Tristan Tzara explained things this way:

> A manifesto is a communication made to the whole world, whose only pretension is to the discovery of an instant cure for political, astronomical, artistic, parliamentary, agronomical and literary syphilis. It may be pleasant, and good-natured, it's always right, it's strong, vigorous and logical. Apropos of logic, I consider myself very likeable.[10]

Dada poet Richard Huelsenbeck argued that the goal of the short-lived movement was "the liberation of the creative forces from the tutelage of the advocates of power." His poem "We Hardly" is a disorienting, sardonic narrative of war, a precursor to much later black humor such as *Catch-22* and *Slaughterhouse-5*. Here is just a glimpse of the poem:

> The Kaiser was only a young man, and he had the world
> on a string, and he wore the imperial orb as a jock-
> strap like the upright man that he was. . . .
>
> And we took hold of Freedom and we reasoned with her,
> while the boys hung around and lamented the
> general lot of mankind.[11]

Dada and Surrealism yielded many such brilliant fragments and glimpses, few sustained masterworks. As programs for art or politics, for inner or outer transformation, they fell short of bringing us to paradise—like all the other programs. Still, surrealist interest in creative sources outside the intentional and rational self and radical cultivation of the associative, whimsical, and marvelous into the realm of art remain as rich resources. There is much to learn from art that stretches our sense of what language is and can do, that offers *experience* as well as information, that make us think and feel in new ways about what we as human beings are capable of thinking and feeling and saying.

More and more, the aim of the transformed life consumes my attention. And yet I know that without the parallel dream of transformation of the world, as well as the individual life, the first dream is at best private, at worst narcissistic. I was pondering how to somehow draw the two together when my favorite folk station played an old, live recording of a song that clearly owes something to surrealism. It imagines a journey from this world into another one:

> Take me on a trip upon your magic swirlin' ship,
> My senses have been stripped, my hands can't feel to grip,
> My toes too numb to step, wait only for my boot heels
> To be wanderin'.
> I'm ready to go anywhere, I'm ready for to fade
> Into my own parade, cast your dancing spell my way,
> I promise to go under it. . . .[12]

The young Bob Dylan wrote "Mr. Tambourine Man" not long after he wrote "Blowin' in the Wind," "The Times They Are A-Changin'," and those other great, early protest songs that helped to galvanize the 1960s movement for social change and resistance to the Vietnam War. For Dylan, too, it seems, the dreams of inner and outer transformation were both active at the same time. But what exactly is the relation between these two kinds of activity? Is one merely a relief from the other, or are they more deeply connected? Is it possible that to hear what is blowing in the wind we need to spend a night or two with Mr. Tambourine Man?

At the very least, to do so helps to make clear that "the world" as described by those who claim to be "realists" is neither the entire nor the only world. One might then imagine another, or many other worlds, and begin to envision how these imagined worlds might become, if not "real," present enough among us to enable us to change the one we inhabit.

In this process, I think, the loving human connection, inevitably lost or perverted in acts of violence, is essential. Perhaps this is where the surrealists were unable to imagine their way forward—they wrote much, often beautifully, about sexual love, but were not very successful at imagining this other sort of love. Perhaps—I am speculating wildly here—the general revulsion with "the world" that both the surrealists and the first Anabaptists felt can become a source of interference, as it invites an objectification of others that makes it possible to regard them as less than human beings. Who would propose firing a revolver blindly into a crowd of one's children? Who, these days, can read the fifteen pages of the *Martyrs Mirror* that are devoted to excoriating the Catholic Church in the harshest possible terms without squirming?

As the poem must be a real thing in the real world, so the human exchange must be real, though it may be indirect. Pablo Neruda's compelling story of exchanging toys with an unseen child through the fence of his childhood home provides a glimpse of the kind of relation that must—and can—exist between writer and reader, teacher and student. "Maybe this small and mysterious exchange of gifts remained inside me also, deep and indestructible, giving my poetry light," he muses:

> To feel the love of people whom we love is a fire that feeds our life. But to feel the affection that comes from those whom we do not know, from those unknown to us, who are watching over our sleep and solitude, over our dangers and our weaknesses, that is something still greater and more beautiful because it widens out the boundaries of our being, and unites all living things.[13]

I love this story and Neruda's commentary, the mutual generosity of the gift and the hope it carries. As Neruda says, the anonymity of the exchange seems precious as well. This is a human exchange, but not a calculated contract nor a condescending act of pity. It emerges from a mutuality that requires only the most elementary recognition of shared humanity.

But of course more personal sorts of mutuality are also possible, and vital. Sometimes I look out over a roomful of faces and bodies and think I know them all too well. Other times I realize that what I know of them is just the tiniest shred of their whole beings, that they carry burdens and griefs, joys and preoccupations that I will never glimpse. I know that I create stress and difficulty, at a minimum, simply by expecting that these young beings show up for class, pay some attention, and complete what-ever semi-arbitrary tasks I assign. I know that often I have—more or less unwittingly—done worse by them than they deserve. I can only imagine the investment of time and attention it would take to be fully present for each of them; I fall short, again and again, of being all that I wish I could be for them in the time we share. But I believe that my work is to seek to be present, to be openly fallible and openly passionate about what I be-lieve and think, to give whatever small gifts I can and to receive those I am given. And I believe that whatever teaching about peace might hap-pen in that process, it depends upon somehow establishing this sense of primary, almost mute connection.

I know a lot of words, but I wish there were a more exact word for the kind of love that can exist between teacher and student. In a time when we know so well the perils of all love, all intimacy, it seems perilous even to speak of this love, and surely if not practiced with great care it can turn into something dangerous and destructive. But I would say what Paul says, that without it all our efforts are only clanging gongs and clashing cymbals. And I believe that learning and practicing this love, making it also a real being in the world, is the key to educating for peace, to breaking the coercion and oppression built into the academic process, to bringing together the drives toward interior and exterior transforma-tion.

Let me close with a recent prose poem, "Letter to Students Gone for Summer," which at least gestures toward the sort of teaching I have been talking about.

> In the sunny afternoon I walked home past the lagoon, thinking of our evening walks, how we would try to slow down, to be quiet, to see. The new leaves unfold everywhere now, almost hid-ing the trees the ice storm broke and the ruts we dug, dragging off the deadfalls.
>
> Tiny daisies bloom along the path, and new poison ivy grows below the steps down to the creek. I would have brought you here, but there wasn't room for us all. The water is low and as clear as it ever gets, slipping over its stones like a dancer.
>
> What else is new? The bastards and the unholy fools still run most of the world. My life is still calm and easy. It makes no kind of sense. Birds sing from every side, and two ducks zoom down-stream, climb through the trees like quiet fighter jets. For all they

know, this is the best of all the worlds. For all I know this is the world of all the best birds and God the great heron cares nothing about me, the ants, or the garlic mustard.

In that stuffy classroom, I would say *write now* and listen to the rustle of pens and pencils. It was like listening to birds invent new songs, like watching those films of flowers unfolding. Sometimes a face slipped so open that I had to turn away not to melt or go blind.

Wind tips the shadow of a young maple back and forth over my page, the fish strike at insects skimming the pool upstream, the mistuned pickup rackets away. We will never all be in the same room again, but I sit here with all of you in my mind, dreaming that the words that will save us are just two steps ahead.[14]

Notes

1. William Gass, "Rilke's Rodin," introduction to *Auguste Rodin* by Rainer Marie Rilke (Brooklyn: Archipelago Books, 2004), 17.

2. Gass, 22.

3. William Butler Yeats, *Per Amica Silentia Lunae* (New York: McMillan, 1918), 29.

4. Patrick Wahlberg, *Surrealism* (1965; reprint New York: Thames and Hudson, 1997), 18.

5. Wahlberg, 18.

6. Calvin Redekop, *Mennonite Society* (Baltimore: Johns Hopkins, 1989), 121. See my *Walker in the Fog*, 180-3, for a more extensive discussion of Redekop's argument.

7. Wahlberg, *Surrealism*, 18.

8. Andre Breton, "Manifesto of Surrealism: Three Excerpts," *Poems for the Millenium: The University of California Book of Modern and Postmodern Poetry*, ed. Jerome Rothenberg and Pierre Joris (Berkeley: University of California Press, 1995), 469.

9. Rainer Marie Rilke, *Selected Poems of Rainer Maria Rilke,* trans. David Young (Oberlin, Ohio: Field Translation Series 20, 1994), 19.

10. Tristan Tzara, "Dada Manifesto on Feeble and Bitter Love," *Poems for the Millenium: The University of California Book of Modern and Postmodern Poetry*, ed. Jerome Rothenberg and Pierre Joris (Berkeley: University of California Press, 1995), 299.

11. Hulsenbrock, "We Hardly," *Poems for the Millenium: The University of California Book of Modern and Postmodern Poetry*, ed. Jerome Rothenberg and Pierre Joris (Berkeley: University of California Press, 1995), 307.

12. Bob Dylan, "Mr. Tambourine Man," bobdylan.com. 25 May 2004.

13. Pablo Neruda, "Childhood and Poetry," *Neruda and Vallejo: Selected Poems,* ed. Robert Bly (Boston: Beacon, 1973), 13.

14. Jeff Gundy, *Spoken Among the Trees* (Akron: University of Akron Press, 2007), 74.

CHAPTER EIGHT

ON JESUS AND TEACHING

The purpose of art is to lay bare the questions which have been hidden by the answers.
—James Baldwin[1]

People won't leave Him alone.
I know He said, Wherever two or more
are gathered in my name...
but I'll bet some days He regrets it.
Cozily they tell you what He wants
and doesn't want as if they just got an e-mail. ...
—Naomi Shihab Nye, "I Feel Sorry for Jesus"[2]

Jesus is the great example for Christian teachers, the great resource, and (just as important) the great enigma. As Naomi Shihab Nye says, it is hard to resist thinking that we *know* what Jesus means and what he wants us to do. But as Baldwin suggests, a bit more obliquely, the notion that Jesus is the answer to all questions (especially in the minds of young students) can conceal important matters.

A student in my fiction class once wrote a dialogue between two voices, one a troubled young woman, the other a rather disembodied but reassuring, older, male presence. As we talked about it in class, the light dawned, and I found myself saying "Oh! It's only Jesus!"

"*Only* Jesus?" she quickly and understandably objected. "What do you mean, *only* Jesus?"

What I meant—and struggled to explain to her and the class—was that once Jesus entered her story its troubling, urgent exploration of her character's suffering and struggle drained away into the soothing, predictable platitudes that he uttered. His presence as an easy answer drained the life from her story by hiding the questions it needed to explore.

One challenge for teachers at Mennonite and Christian institutions, I think, is to resist making Jesus a quick and superficial answer to all questions. (If the question, for example, is "How do I shake this enormous, dark depression?" much testimony suggests that "You wouldn't be depressed if you really believed in Jesus" is a common but not a helpful answer.)

For those of us who have grown up steeped in Jesus-language and stories and images, it may seem that we know all we need to know—*more* than we need to know—and the remaining questions merely have to do with details. Personally, and I suspect this is also true for many of you, I know that I can't get *outside* of Christian rhetoric and assumptions in any but the thinnest and most speculative ways—they have been bred into my bones and every aspect of my being since before I can remember. Even my doubts and questions, though many, are *Christian* sorts of doubts and questions.

At the same time, the particulars of my experience are not identical to any of yours, and our students represent even wider ranges of experience. Another challenge, then, is to recognize the widely various figures of Jesus that they bring into the room, knowingly or not. One may bring the personal-assistant Jesus who helped get her into college and makes the stoplights turn green when she's in a hurry. Another carries the Jesus who inspires him to go on mission trips and do good things for the poor, unfortunate natives. Another brandishes a Jesus who forms an impenetrable force shield against any people or ideas that seem threatening or alien. Still another is flinching in the back corner, because the Jesus he knows is the one others have used like a club to beat *him* for his sexual orientation or his failure to achieve the right emotional response during a crusade.

As is obvious, I am not enamored of any of these versions of Jesus, and my discomfort with them has made me careful about laying my own Jesus—however much healthier and more appropriate I think he is—too heavily on students, or anyone else. Mainly, I try to imitate the Jesus who was a master of parabolic suggestion rather than the table-tossing Jesus of the temple. Even though some of those versions of Jesus seem naïve, misleading, or downright dangerous to me, I try, at least, to be respectful, to avoid slipping into my own self-righteousness as I question others', to leaven questions with humor, to plant seeds and water them rather than expecting sudden conversions.

And of course the authors and texts I teach, and those that have influenced my thinking and teaching, often have their own Jesus as well—some more or less orthodox, some decidedly not. The many voices and images in my head (Nye and Baldwin are just two) create a kind of constant choral commentary on my life, my daily encounters, and what I believe. I have learned something about Jesus, about God, about this blooming, buzzing world from more sources than I can count or name, but I cannot sum any of that up quickly, clearly, or completely. Still, we must say *something*. So let me make a few more assertive remarks.

Some things we think we know about Jesus are brief and powerful, although not simple. I come back over and over to the commandments to love God and love our neighbors "as ourselves." They seem clear, don't they? But when some student who has blown off my class for a month shows up at my office and wants to know if she's missed anything important, what does it mean to love her as my neighbor? When someone insists that God rejoices when "foreigners" die so Americans can feel safe, what does it mean to love that person, or the God he worships?

Other thoughts about Jesus are long, complicated, and challenging. Oscar Wilde suggested provocatively that the essence of his nature was not some sort of spiritual holiness but sympathetic imagination akin to that of the artist:

> the very basis of [Christ's] nature was the same as that of the nature of the artist—an intense and flamelike imagination. He realized in the entire sphere of human relations that imaginative sympathy which in the sphere of art is the sole secret of creation. He understood the leprosy of the leper, the darkness of the blind, the fierce misery of those who live for pleasure, the strange poverty of the rich. . . .
>
> Christ's place indeed is with the poets. His whole conception of Humanity sprang right out of the imagination and can only be realized by it.[3]

I think Wilde's suggestion that the sympathy necessary to loving our neighbors *requires* the imagination is vitally important, especially if we have tended to think that exercising the imagination is somehow *opposed* to following Jesus. When the late Jerry Falwell proclaimed that "God Is Pro-War" in the run-up to the Iraq War, I took it as a great slander on God and violation of the commandment that we love our neighbors. Still, I must admit that I also found it very difficult to love Jerry Falwell. How might I understand him well enough to love him? Only, I think, through an imaginative leap that might bring me, for a moment, to empathize with the feelings and belief structure that enable such pronouncements.

Let me close, then, by emphasizing this one of the many ways that Jesus might bear on our teaching: that he might inspire us to cultivate our own and our students' sympathetic imaginations, to widen and deepen our understanding of modes of life and thought that seem strange and forbidding and alien, to enable us to more fully love our neighbors. This imaginative sympathy, I believe, must extend not only to other people but to the whole of life and the universe. "God so loved the world," we are told, not "God so loved men and women." This may mean going far outside of our selves and deep within—for our inner beings are, often, as strange and unknown to us as the most distant "foreigners." To love our neighbors "as ourselves" we surely need to know how to love ourselves—which isn't easy either.

This is a bottomless topic, isn't it? We ought to talk for days. But let me end this little disquisition with a poem that may be a kind of illustration, and perhaps a small step on the way.

Second Morning Song from Oneonta
So early the black flies are still asleep.
A high scruff of rock where lovers

carved their names and then slipped back
into the soft needles under the trees.

Already the valley hums and crackles
and the last rolls of mist hang over

the smokestacks like those fine scratches
that pile up on your glasses. God said,

the places that please you will often
be difficult to find. God said, sweat

is a good sign but not reliable.
God said, hold this day like an egg,

hold and cherish it as you dream
of being touched yourself. Break the day

but gently as the great chef breaks eggs
for the dish you cannot name or afford.

God says all this has been given you,
the whine of the crane and the whir of engines

pulling tired women to their bad jobs
and the drumlin where the last glacier

gave up its journey and grumbled away.
God says remember, God says

don't give up. God says give up.[4]

Notes

1. James Baldwin, *Creative Process* (New York: Ridge Press, 1962), 17.

2. Naomi Shihab Nye, *You & Yours* (Rochester, N.Y.: BOA Editions, Ltd., 2005), 71-2.

3. Oscar Wilde, *Collected Works of Oscar Wilde*. Ware (Hertfordshire: Wordsworth Editions, 1997), 937.

4. Jeff Gundy, *Deerflies* (Cincinnati: WordTech Editions, 2004), 70-1.

NINE
CHAPTER NINE

TOWARD POST-PEACE POETRY: OR, WHAT TO DO WITH THE DRUNKEN SOLDIERS?

One of the emblematic events in William Blake's life took place in 1803, when a drunken soldier invaded the garden of Blake's little house in Felpham, England. When the soldier refused to leave, Blake forcibly evicted him. According to Alexander Gilchrist, "In the course of the scuffle, while blows were being exchanged, angry words passed of course; the red-coated bully vapouring that 'he was the king's soldier,' and so forth. 'Damn the king, and you too,' said Blake, with pardonable emphasis—a not unnatural reply, perhaps."[1] The soldier charged Blake with sedition for this recalcitrant outburst, and he was tried—but acquitted when it became clear at the trial that the soldier was not exactly a sober witness himself.

At the time, Blake was at work on his long poem *Milton,* with its famous preface asking "And was the holy Lamb of God / On England's pleasant pastures seen?" and "was Jerusalem builded here / Among these dark Satanic mills?" Blake resolves to resist the mechanization of English life, and its attendant violence, in any way he can:

Bring me my bow of burning gold!
Bring me my arrows of desire!
Bring me my spear! O clouds, unfold!
Bring me my chariot of fire!

I will not cease from mental fight,
Nor shall my sword sleep in my hand
Till we have built Jerusalem
In England's green and pleasant land.[2]

During the 1973 coup in Chile, when the leftist government of Salvador Allende was overthrown with the support of the United States, soldiers invaded the house of the dying poet Pablo Neruda, himself a famous leftist and a supporter of Allende. A poem by Martin Espada, "The Soldiers in the Garden," describes the incident and Neruda's indignant response: "*There is only one danger for you here: poetry.*" At least in Espada's telling, the lieutenant promptly apologizes and retreats, although (the poem concludes ruefully):

For thirty years
we have been searching
for another incantation
to make the soldiers
vanish from the garden.[3]

Several things are worth noting here. First, this officer actually respects Neruda's position as poet, apologizes, and leaves his house. Can we imagine any contemporary American poet being offered such respect? Certainly Blake's adversary felt no such qualms about invading the poet's space—though everyone agrees he was drunk.

Second, we must recognize that United States soldiers only rarely invade the homes of their fellow citizens—though the police do, quite often. The empire's troops are busy elsewhere, although even news of the wars is scarce, these days. Plenty of Americans are harassed, humiliated, threatened, and thrown into prison daily, by credit card companies, mortgage holders, and the police, but mostly for the offenses of being poor, of color, or undocumented.

Finally, while the dying Neruda's fame may have shielded his garden from the soldiers, in the end his support for Allende was not nearly enough to save that populist government from the authoritarian, corporate-friendly coup led by Augusto Pinochet.

Not only are the soldiers not in our gardens, in my area it is rare to spot them at all, except in airports. The curious absence of military personnel from my immediate life, even in a hyper-militarized society, came home to me last Christmas break when on a whim I watched the classic holiday movie *White Christmas*. The film's lead characters (portrayed by Bing Crosby and Danny Kaye) bonded in the army during World War II, and their former commander now owns the failing lodge where the main action takes place. At the crisis, the Old Man's former division turns up in full dress to sing a big production number in his praise ("We'll Follow the Old Man") and set up the happy ending, when a big snow restores the inn to fiscal health.

Fictional and commercial as it is, the movie reflects a midcentury America in which military experience was the norm for men, and civilian life more or less mirrored the military hierarchy. At the height of World War II, nearly one in every ten citizens was in one branch of the military or another. The resisters, including 12,000 men who served in Civilian Public Service, 25,000 in noncombatant roles, and 6,000 who went to prison, formed a very small puddle compared to the ocean of 10 million soldiers. As the movie demonstrates neatly, veterans who returned to civilian life shaped and even dominated American society for decades.[4] Only the turmoil of Vietnam and the end of the draft in 1973 truly shifted twentieth-century American society away from military service as a default experience for men.

The country is no less militarized today, in terms of the vast Pentagon budget (in recent eras typically over $600 billion) or the American forces scattered around the world in shooting wars and in more or less permanent bases.[5] Yet the United States now maintains its decaying empire with increased desperation but far fewer troops. About 1.5 million Americans are on active duty, and a similar number in the reserves—a large number, but less than one in a hundred Americans. Mainstream Americans avoid the military, including many who enthusiastically "support our troops." Even in my conservative, middle-class small town, few young men and women join up, unless they can wangle an appointment to a service academy or are driven into it by the poverty draft. The men who show up for the color guard on Memorial Day are older every year, and the veterans are mostly middle-aged or beyond. It's a far cry from *White Christmas*.

What can and should it mean to be a peace poet in the current context? The men in uniforms are mostly out of sight, the draft is but a fading memory, and the violence that most demands resistance takes multiple and complex forms. William Blake, though he stood against drunken soldiers, was even more outraged by the structural violence he saw in England during the rise of the "dark Satanic mills" and the "black'ning churches" that supported them. A soldier has never invaded my garden, but the wars go on, and other forms of violence (economic, environmental, and interpersonal) demand response as well—perhaps in even more pressing ways.[6]

This subject has been raised repeatedly by Mennonite writers and literary critics in recent years—usually to complain that poets are not producing enough "peace poetry." In an essay presented at the 2006 Mennonite/s Writing conference in Bluffton and later published in *The Mennonite Quarterly Review,* for example, John Fisher states with disappointment that "there is not much contemporary Mennonite peace poetry."[7] He notes the Japanese poet Yorifumi Yaguchi's comment at the same conference that North American Mennonite poets "do not generally write about global conflict" and quotes a review by Jill Pelaez Baumgartner of Ann Hostetler's 2003 anthology, *A Cappella: Mennonite Voices in Poetry,* suggesting that "one would expect more political statement" in it. While W. H. Auden's famous claim that "poetry makes nothing happen" has long been accepted in some circles, Fisher believes that Mennonite poets could indeed "make something happen" if they put their minds to it: "their moral-aesthetic sensibilities, technical skill with language and seriousness of purpose exhibit strong potential for a more effective witness for peace."[8]

Like Fisher, many in the broader literary community call for more peace-oriented and activist poetry. To mention just two recent examples, the poet David Wojahn argued vigorously for such work in a prominent 2007 article in *The Writer's Chronicle,* and in a recent issue of *Poetry* (May 2010), David Biespiel also complained that "America's poets have a minimal presence in American civic discourse and a minuscule public role in the life of American democracy."[9] I will comment further on both pieces below.

I am entirely in sympathy with Fisher's desire that Mennonite poets should write "peace poetry," and his argument that poets should try, in whatever ways they can, to "make something happen." Like him, I was pleased to discover, when I read John Paul Lederach's *The Moral Imagination,* that this experienced and successful peacemaker recommends poetry as a resource for conflict transformation. And like Fisher, I admire "The Baby Screaming in the Back Seat" by Julia Spicher Kasdorf, a poem he discusses at some length, and find the Irish poet Seamus Heaney's interest in poetry that creates "transformative moments" congenial and even inspirational.

Yet in what follows, while I will echo Fisher's argument that poems of resistance and reconciliation are still vital, I will also argue that current poets often work in ways both subtler and broader than those traditionally associated with "peace poetry"—as is only natural if their poems are to succeed as performative utterance in the contemporary world, far from both *White Christmas* and the Vietnam War. It has become widely accepted that the practice of active nonviolence cannot be limited to opposition to war, and so much of the work I will examine might be termed "post-peace" poetry—poems that also understand the pursuit of peace to mean much more than resistance to war.

The paucity of "peace" poems in *A Cappella* seems real, if one defines such poems as those dealing directly with military conflict. Still, although the anthology did not appear until 2003, the poems—five or six by each poet—were mainly chosen by editor Ann Hostetler well before 9-11. Most were written in the 1980s and 1990s, decades in which the United States and Canada were generally not involved in hot wars, except for the brief Gulf War and various smaller conflicts. One might even speculate that the dearth of peace poems in *A Cappella* indicates the relative success of the empire, for most of the late twentieth century, at keeping conflicts at a distance from its citizens. Few North American poets of this time, Mennonite or not, wrote poems of the sort that Yaguchi wrote out of his experience of the bombing of Japan during World War II and the American occupation.[10]

Must a poem deal directly with war to be a "peace poem"? When I asked Ann Hostetler to comment on this question and her editorial principles, she replied that in editing her anthology she was not "looking for poems that reified Mennonite positions—I was looking for what kinds of poems writers from Mennonite contexts were writing." On the other hand, she added, "I actually think that there are a lot of peace poems in this anthology, in the sense that many of the poets in *A Cappella* are confronting or articulating conflicts within the culture, or among various cultures, or even within the psyche, that stand in the way of peace." After listing a number of examples, she offered these redefinitions:

Poetry often grows out of dissonance and trying to resolve the dissonance within the poet's consciousness. "Peace" as an agenda is a good subject for essays, but not for poetry. When peace becomes incorporated into the interpersonal, into the interspecies, into relation with the environment, then I think it becomes a part of poetry. On the other hand, when the Mennonite ideology of peace is imposed, as Rudy Wiebe and others have pointed out, it can result in domestic and intrapsychic violence.[11]

My own explorations of Mennonite poetry convince me that many Mennonite poets share Hostetler's sense that true "peace poetry" may and should take many forms and address many issues—and that traditional Mennonite "peace" ideology can impose its own violence. A thorough reading of Mennonite poets' work shows a pervasive investment in peace issues, especially once one recognizes that poems that object to war are just one type of "peace poem."

Over twenty years ago I wrote an essay grappling with the problem of writing successful political poetry. In the late 1980s, there was not much serious "Mennonite poetry" to be found, and so I wrote mainly for a general audience of poets, many of whom I knew to be opposed to war.[12] Not unlike John Fisher, I complained about the general decline in "politically and socially charged" poetry since the days of Vietnam, and noted a turn toward irony and comedy and away from moral urgency. I singled out some exceptions among poets of that era, including David Ignatow and Carolyn Forché, well-known for her searing "The Colonel," written after a long visit to El Salvador, and her anthology *Against Forgetting: Twentieth Century Poetry of Witness,* a massive collection of poems from around the world marked by the violence of the last century.[13] And I argued, not especially originally, that successful political poems required both some level of engagement and "acceptance of complicity [and] refusal of easy moral superiority." The sermonic paragraph that ends the essay was not meant specifically for Mennonite poets (I hardly knew any then), nor is it framed in any sort of Mennonite or even Christian terms:

> The temptation to aestheticize our own suffering and peripheralize everyone else's is hard to resist. Subsumed in history as we are, we want to abandon it, to take refuge in the cheerful, comfortable rooms of the palace of art. But the time of kings is past, and so is the time of retainers. Auden's tyrant, like Forche's Colonel, pur-

sued "perfection of a kind"; we must remember that the impulses of life are not toward perfection but toward plenitude and diversity. The most perfect forms we have lie waiting in silos and submarines and hangers, dreaming of making everything in the world simple, hot, and pure. If their dreams do not trouble our waking, we have not yet awakened.[14]

Much in this essay seems dated now, but the argument that poets do too little to bring about social change can still be heard from many quarters. Poet David Wojahn, in his 2007 essay "Maggie's Farm No More: The Fate of Political Poetry," argues that after the mid-1960s American poets and artists in general turned away from socially engaged art. With the changing zeitgeist of the 1970s, Wojahn claims, "most American poets—regardless of whether they were writers of color or white, gay or straight, male or female—simply turned inward. . . . the direction American poetry has taken during the past three decades has been overwhelmingly subjective and hermetic."[15] His critique is sharp:

> American poets may choose to look up from their laptop screens and out their windows long enough to add a couple of snide observations about their neighbors' SUVs or to bemoan the latest example of Bush administration hubris, but their efforts at combining the personal and the political remain for the most part failures, plagued by reductive thinking, a clumsy shuffling between anemic anecdote and simplistic rhetoric, and a pervasive sense of futility—we know how marginal we are, but don't know how to change our status.[16]

Wojahn takes a long look at Sam Hamill's "Poets Against the War" effort, and grants it some value as a grassroots effort toward protest and consciousness-raising. But he finds most of the work gathered there simply bad as poetry. One problem, he notes (quoting a review by W. S. De-Piero), is a tendency to simplistic moralizing: "if poets suppress ambiguity, generative vagueness and destabilizing inquiry, they collude with the media circus we all criticize for its depredations on language."[17] Poets who claim to *know* the right from the wrong may quickly fall into the same black/white thinking that often issues from Washington, assign all blame to the other side, and fall into self-righteous rhetoric.

For all his interest in re-energizing a poetry of protest and engagement, however, Wojahn struggles to find his way toward one. He rightly insists that getting beyond "sentimental simplifications" is necessary:

> The poem will be sensitive thanks to its emotional complexity
> and dividedness rather than through its adherence to period style
> mannerisms and pc posturings. . . . It will combine social engage-
> ment with personal authenticity, yet it will not proceed from pre-
> determined definitions of the social or the personal. Neverthe-
> less, it will be intensely aware of how, as Kevin Stein puts it, "his-
> tory inscripts our lives in subtle and manifest ways."[18]

One major problem Wojahn does not resolve, or even address directly, is how such intense awareness and emotional complexity might
intersect with religious, ideological, and moral commitments and beliefs. This problem seems clearly relevant as well to Mennonite poets,
who are (perhaps) more accustomed than most to think that there are
indeed some "predetermined definitions" of right and wrong, and that
not killing even our enemies is primary among them.[19]

Yet his argument suggests some inherent possibilities as well, particularly if not uniquely available to poets who write out of Mennonite
identities and traditions. In response to Wojahn, I might suggest that
American poets lack not a sense of personal values or engagement (there
are the authors of those 20,000 poems posted on the Poets Against the
War web site, for starters) but an underlying sense of history and tradition that provides some sense of what to *do* with those values. Besides
"write a poem," there are plenty of Mennonite answers: go clean up after
the tornado, spend a year doing service somewhere, build a house for
someone, or even put some money in the offering plate. None of these is
sufficient, but all are concrete responses.

What Wojahn describes as "a rich and emotionally sustaining sense
of personal history"[20] seems to me a necessary but likely insufficient
context for writing effective, socially engaged poetry, unless such history
is connected to some larger sense of communal memory and purpose.[21]
Anabaptism, even the ambivalent identification with it that characterizes many contemporary Mennonite poets, provides an axis of orientation and purpose that can be highly generative. The sail of a poetic identity can be strung between two such poles, if the tension is sufficient but
not excessive—and as we shall see, many Mennonite poets have done so.

David Biespiel, in the opinion piece in *Poetry* mentioned earlier, argues that an individual poet can and should take on political issues in the

role of an "honest broker, one who possesses the poet's core values of il-lumination, imagination, reflection, and sincerity."[22] Also posted on the *Poetry* website, this piece generated vigorous discussion there. Some were enthusiastic; others noted that Biespiel's short list of activist poets omitted numerous other good candidates, especially poets of color, and failed to mention groups like Split This Rock, an organization that hosts a biannual festival of "poetry and activism" in Washington, D. C.

Groups of poet-activists *do* persist around the country, often deeply committed despite their small numbers. In spring 2009 I was invited to a peace symposium in Portland entitled "Another World Instead," after a collection of William Stafford's early poems,[23] many written while he was in CPS camps during World War II. Several of those at this event planned and presented a panel at the Split This Rock Festival in Wash-ington, D.C., in April 2010 on how we might stock the "peace shelves," if only our local bookshelves had such things. The second event also pro-vided a chance to mingle with and learn from diverse writers committed to peace and justice, many of them located in the Washington area but others from all over the country and the world.[24]

At the Portland symposium I met Philip Metres, a young Arab-American poet-critic whose book *Behind the Lines: War Resistance Poetry on the American Homefront Since 1941* is one of the few systematic treat-ments of its subject. Metres's broad survey of American resistance poetry of the last century suggests an ongoing debate between two approaches: "a poetry that favors the aesthetic, the formal, and the individual," on one hand, and on the other "a poetry that favors the political, the rhetor-ical, and the cultural-political movement." In the end, he argues that poets can and should play an important role in the peace movement, "by articulating, complicating, and sustaining war resistance—not only through poems but also through daily involvement in the forms and genres of activism: media press releases, flyers, placards, and songs."[25]

Metres specifically questions the general tendency to take those who have experienced war directly—especially soldiers—as those best equipped to speak of both war and peace. "The soldier-poet alone is still held up as the principal proprietor of viable antiwar poetry," he notes, offering a long list of such poets, from Wilfred Owen to Brian Turner. Why should this be, Metres asks, when total war affects us all? "[D]oes such poetry actually promote and idealize warfare *even as it protests* against its brutalities?"[26]

While he allows that "some Vietnam-era antiwar poetry was self-righteous, rhetorically clumsy, and tonally arrogant," Metres points out that such charges could be leveled against much antiwar poetry of any era. Resistance poets, he believes, must negotiate a difficult dance between art and conscience, and between two very different audiences: the peace movement and the nation at large. Despite these difficulties, Metres argues convincingly, poets and poetry have played a significant role in the American peace movement.[27]

Especially relevant here is Metres's analysis of the problems with writing peace poetry in the lyric mode that has dominated modern poetry. Because the lyric tends to privilege epiphany over narrative, subjective experience over knowledge and analysis, the individual and private over the public, it seems awkwardly suited to broad public purposes. Poets who seek to write poems of resistance face several problems, he suggests. First is the problem of authorial persona: "how does a war resistance poet project herself as a lyric subject when she is speaking from a position of dissent? How does the poet invite the reader into a position that the reader might not initially want to inhabit?" Second, resistance poets must contend with the "problematics of representation":

> [D]oes the poet approach the problem of describing or representing an event not witnessed with his own eyes, and if so, how? How does the poet deal with not only the unrepresentability of war but also the politics of representing other cultures, in light of Orientalism? And third, the problematic of poetic form. In other words, how does the poet engage the poetic tradition's forms and modes to articulate, question, and sustain war resistance culture?[28]

Contemporary American poets, Mennonites and otherwise, are experimenting with strategies to address these issues, to stretch the limits of the lyric and to produce genuinely engaged poems of resistance. In so doing, they find their own solutions to the problems of lyric subjectivity, representation, and poetic form that Metres describes. In the remaining pages of this essay I will briefly examine and evaluate some of these efforts more closely, beginning with a number of the poems posted by Mennonite poets at Poets Against the War.[29] In almost all cases, these poems deal with issues of military violence from a considerable distance—none of the poets are soldiers themselves, or in combat zones.

Through a variety of moves, they often engage those issues in terms of other forms of violence and oppression that are more immediate in the poet's own experience.

Jean Janzen's "No Stars for Me," posted at Poets Against the War on February 10, 2003, reaches back to World War II. She remembers radio news of the war, and stars posted in her third-grade classroom for the war bonds that her classmates had bought with their dimes and dollars:

> Other Mennonite names
> had stars, one for each ten dimes
> for War Bonds, one for each
> pound of scrap iron for tanks.
>
> Didn't their fathers tell them?
> Stars made war:
> a circle of blood on shirts,
> shrapnel, helmets
> with nothing in them [. . .]
>
> The admiral wears them on his coat.
> No stars for me.[30]

This poem suggests, in an understated but very clear way, the power of childhood learning, and what a tradition of war resistance can mean to a whole life. Janzen's memory of refusing to buy war bonds echoes all the way into the present: "no stars for me."

Keith Ratzlaff offers "July 4," posted on February 11, 2003, quite different from Janzen's poem but in a mode typical of much of his work: a small-scale, sharply focused meditation on territoriality and the male propensity for violence:

> Down the street a man has sued his neighbor
> over maple branches trespassing his yard's air.
> And the court has agreed, so now the trees
> are sheered and flattened like pears, like heads
> caught under the mower.

This seemingly quiet, small-town street teems with middle-class, covert conflict; even the narrator dreams of smashing the radio that "dumps / contemporary Christian rock over my fence." "Imagine us with baseball bats and chainsaws," he says:

> What we know about liberty you could scoop
> in a sack like kittens and throw into the river,
> but we'd go at it rev and thwack and whiff
> and keep going, until the sad playing out
> of democracy at work, of police blotters
> and sentences suspended. [...]
> The only moral is the one my cat knows:
> pissing on the dill is what makes it his.

Raylene Hinz-Penner's disquieting "Inside, After September 2001," posted on February 12, 2003, reflects on her experience teaching in a prison writing program. After 9-11 she speculates on how the men inside will react:

> I know they know, of course, know how they'll follow
>   this plot, slaves to routine and television, all that fresh
>   meat for their talk, banter, braggadacio—but more,
>   the way they'll feel it in the air: something changed—
> imagined possibility, for one thing—for us out here too.

Hinz-Penner remembers an inmate asking a guard, naively, a question to which he gets an unexpected response: "'So what happens in here / to us when the U.S. goes to war?' 'We kill you,' the guard says, 'so that we are free to go out there and fight.'"

The first parts of the poem are unsettling enough in their sketch of prison culture, where so many Americans live out large portions of their lives under guard, many for relatively minor offenses. The prisoners will find it much more difficult to "change [their] lives" than the free citizens Hinz-Penner speaks for in the middle of the poem. But the final anecdote turns positively chilling. Surely it's not true; and yet the guard's casual threat brings home just how completely the system controls the lives under its command. It doesn't even sound *entirely* implausible.

Todd Davis sets "Can We Remember?" in an open field where heavy machines are digging, making "the earth shudder"; where his thoughts turn to an uncomfortably prescient series of questions about the American response to 9-11: "Are our protests / like these ghosts, like the awkward / voices of the crows that accompany / them?"

> Heavy machinery clears the pit, makes
> way for more machinery. Wheels turn,
> metal clanks, the earth shudders: today
> there is the threat of war. There are also
> these asters and the dying grasses that lie
> down in strong winds. Can we remember
> what has fallen? Can we help what will grow?

Betsy Sholl offers "Back with the Quakers,"[31] a poem that perhaps references the venerable tradition of soldier-poets juxtaposing wartime memories with the experience of civilian life. Sholl, however, memorably transposes the poles of memory and experience: her memory is of training in nonviolence, her immediate experience of casual hostility and aggression in everyday America:

> All the driver has to say is, "Move it,
> Lady," and you're back with the Quakers,
>
> who trained you to lie down limp in the street.
> Three days they stepped on your hair,
> ground cigarettes half an inch from your nose,
> while you lay there, trying to be against
> violence, your fists tight as grenades
> and a payload of curses between your teeth,
>
> Oh woman, with a mind Picasso
> could have painted, giving you many cheeks,
> each one turned a different way.

My own poem, "Epiphany with Sirens and White-Tail," posted on February 9, 2003, was first published in the weekly Bluffton newspaper during the Christmas season of 2002, at the invitation of the editor. As I thought about this assignment, with the war clearly on the way, I found myself reflecting on the parallels between the biblical story of Herod's desperate effort to preserve his own security by killing all of the boy children who might threaten him, and the post-9-11 mood in the U. S., when the administration, with popular support, claimed the right to punish any number of innocents elsewhere for the sake of our own illusory security. Thus my poem parallels Herod's words with some of George Bush's ("*Our goal is to secure the peace,* / said the one who leads us, *voluntarily,* / *or by force,*" and the current scene with the young Jesus being carried off into exile:

> The white-tail floats through brush
> like a half moon set free,
> like a light on the path to Egypt
> where the boy child will live out his exile
> and return when the mad king is dead.

I got a few comments from friends after this poem appeared in the paper, and have read it in public a number of times, usually with a remark or two about my somewhat grim satisfaction in referring, however obliquely, to the (now former) leader of the free world as a mad king. I was somewhat disappointed to get no angry letters in response, no emails labeling me a traitor or communist for daring to raise such questions. Of course, it was just a poem, and very likely the people whose minds I would most have liked to change didn't bother to read it.

All of these poems are both "personal" and "public," and all display comparable yet distinctly individual resistance to nationalism and militarism. I have read too much recent critical theory to share entirely John Fisher's enthusiasm for "binary" thinking, but surely these poems are authentic and plausible efforts at writing genuine poems of peace. Examples of such poems can readily be multiplied from the published work of these poets and many others, as I found when I turned my attention to books already on my shelves—where I quickly found far too many examples to discuss more than a quick sampling here.

That reading also brought me back to questions of definitions, issues, and priorities. For every "war poem," I found two, three, or five that addressed violence and injustice on other scales and in other situations, from the personal and local to the global. It struck me, to offer one example, that addressing global climate change may be an even more important "peace issue" than ending the wars in Iraq and Afghanistan, given that environmental disruptions may well lead to greater violence to both people and the earth, as climate refugees multiply and countries compete for scarce resources and habitats. Are poems about loving the earth therefore "peace poems"? How are they not?[32] Issues of personal and interpersonal violence also demand attention, as Ann Hostetler notes in the passage quoted earlier, and as Rudy Wiebe pointed out in *Peace Shall Destroy Many*, nearly fifty years ago. Many Mennonite poets are exploring such themes; I can provide only a few examples here.

Though she is sometimes identified (superficially) as an "ethnic" poet, much of Julia Spicher Kasdorf's work has explored the effects of interpersonal and intercultural conflict and oppression, especially that driven by gender. For a compact overview of Kasdorf's intricate and substantial reflections on these issues, one might begin with her essay "Writing Like a Mennonite," which incorporates both prose and poems, weaves together personal and public history, and reflects on the act of writing and recording both personal and public events, in forms from the lyric poem to the *Martyrs Mirror*. "The tight-lipped survival strategy of my childhood is no longer useful," Kasdorf writes of her long silence about her sexual abuse by a neighbor man

> and in the martyr stories, I now see, not submission and silence, but men and women who spoke with their words and with their bodies, who refused to hold their tongues or keep the peace. . . . I write simply to remember and to bear witness.[33]

Kasdorf's newer book of poems, *Poetry in America,* continues to explore these themes, especially the intersections of gender and violence. One of the most powerful poems, "Bat Boy, Break a Leg," discussed at length in Chapter 6, interweaves two encounters with strangers and indeed bears witness to active (though unexpected) acts of local, interpersonal and even interspecies peacemaking. The poem begins by describing a tattooed, pierced student "who seems always ready to swoon / from bliss or despair," then describes an encounter with the bat of the title:

> I woke to black fluttering at my feet,
> and a mind fresh from the other side
> said *don't turn on the light, don't*
> *Wake the man, don't scream or speak.*
> *Go back to sleep.* [. . .]

In the morning, she finds a "big-eared mouse" at the screen, but lets him remain there until at dusk she realizes he is gone.

Pale boy dressed in black,
Maybe the best that can be said for any of us is that
once we were angelic enough to sleep with strangers.
He touched my cheek. I opened the screen.
He flew in his time. We did no harm.[34]

Most notably, this poem not only tests and reaffirms nonviolence, but also extends it to animals and other such strangers, and (in its most crucial line) resists waking "the man" who can be expected to react with an aggressive defense of his home against the intruder. Making peace with bats, *and* with tattooed rebels? Shocking.

Di Brandt's poetic career offers another salutary example of a poet whose work has consistently taken on wider and deeper engagements with violence, injustice, and conflict on many levels. Her poem "nonresistance, or love Mennonite style," reprinted in *A Cappella*, is a searing treatment of sexual abuse and its quasi-justification by appeal to "traditional" values: "you want to run away but you / can't because he's a man like your father" and "you love your enemy / deeply unwillingly & full of shame."[35] *Jerusalem, beloved,* a poetic response to a 1991 trip to the Holy City, was sufficiently sympathetic to the Palestinian cause to earn the ire of some Jewish critics.[36] Her 2003 book, *Now You Care,* reflects deep ecological concerns spurred by her years of residence in the polluted city of Windsor, Ontario:

Breathing yellow air
here, at the heart of the dream
of the new world,
the bones of old horses and dead Indians
and lush virgin land, dripping with fruit
and the promise of wheat [. . .]
Who shall be fisher king
over this poisoned country
whose borders have become
a mockery,
blowing the world to bits [. . .][37]

Brandt's rhetoric is white-hot at times, but her poems are also deftly controlled, often sardonic yet witty, inventive, and tender as well. "Interspecies Communication," to choose one more example, offers us the world from what might just be a bee's perspective:

And then everything goes bee,
sun exploding into green,
the mad sky dive
through shards of diamond light,
earth veering left, then right. . . . [38]

Todd Davis's "Migration" is dedicated to Brian Turner, whose *Here, Bullet* (2005) is one of the most acclaimed American books of poetry to come out of the Iraq War. Turner is very much in what Philip Metres calls the tradition of the soldier-poet, claiming the authority of direct experience and writing a great deal about combat and its lingering effects on the soldier's consciousness. Davis writes as one far removed from such scenes. He takes them to visit Gettysburg, and is disquieted by his sons' enthusiasm for "the idea / of war" and, it seems, by his own inability to frame any effective response:

At a souvenir shop my youngest
bought a snow globe of Little Round Top,
and on the trip home he kept shaking it,
telling me the snow was falling
on the wounded or dead. I can't shake
my friend's poems, or the absurdity
of selling any war, the fact the battle
of Gettysburg was fought in July,
no chance of snow except in the shiny
bauble my son now holds in his hands. [39]

The difficulty of resisting a culture that both glorifies and sanitizes violence troubles Davis, as it does Jean Janzen. Her recent collection, *Paper House,* repeatedly addresses types of violence that are at once distant and pervasive. The beautiful "Penitential Psalms" begins with memory of war that is both present and distant: "When the war began, we practiced / blackouts in our small Midwestern town, / listened in our beds for sirens." The bombers never come, but in the present Janzen again hears figures of war dead on the radio, sees police cruising her street, and knows that she is complicit:

Like the deep breath we take
and hold for the bad news to pass

in its persistent prowl, as now
I breathe at the ends of stanzas
confessing that I am visible,
that I am an accomplice in
the Falling bomb and the shivering
child without home or bed, one
who prays today to be found.[40]

The poem ends with a complex, fascinating release of (it seems) nearly everything, including her own words, a radical and innovative defenselessness:

I have nothing, then, to own
or guard, not even these words,
my hand loose on this pen,
which marks a trail on a white
field owned by no one, not even
you, reading this, you with your
borrowed breath, the stars far above.[41]

Keith Ratzlaff's "What Kind of Guy Are You?" seems to me representative of what may be the Mennonite peace poem of our moment. His encounter is at several removes from war—merely a phone call from a man who says he represents *"Vietnam Vets trying to help / disabled children."* The speaker's refusal is reflexive, the response predictably aggressive and familiarly moralistic:

You don't want to help disabled children?
Someone's voice was hiking in the jungle,
up some indignant hill, the pack full
of draft papers, the pictures of his wife asleep,
one bowl to cook in and eat out of.
What kind of guy doesn't want to help
disabled children—you . . . and I hung up.

This question/accusation triggers remarkable, quirky answers:

I'm the kind of guy who sits so quietly
that yesterday in the park

a squirrel nearly ran up my leg.
I don't stand up even for the national anthem,
but I stood up then—for the squirrel –
to save him some embarrassment.
And I'm the kind of guy who listens
when an old women with an ugly dog
says, *It's been a long rain,* then walks away [...]
And I'm the kind of guy who wants to be
like my cat Dudley, how every night
he claims the pillow at my wife's head—
as he has for fifteen years—sleeping there,
touching her hair, as all my passive,
crippled life I've wished I could.[42]

There is no heroism here, no grand call to action, no claim to a moral high ground—unless it is in the speaker's gentle recognition of all those small, lonesome lives outside his own, his letting those lives go on undisturbed. How useful is that? I mean this as a very serious question, as I think Ratzlaff does. Notice just how much humility there is in these closing lines—not the usual, stagy Mennonite humility, which desires above all to be recognized as virtuous, praised, and rewarded for its good behavior, but the deeper humility that grows out of genuine recognition that one is a flawed, incomplete, guilty, irrevocably human being.

The drunken soldier is still trampling the gardens of this earth, befuddled and destructive, confusing shallow nationalism with fidelity to God's creation, spreading bad information and outright lies, fracking and selling short and arguing that we cannot afford to tax the rich or to help the poor. Are poems going to change all this? Of course not. No poem stopped the Iraq War, any more than the marches, letters, petition drives, and prayers for peace did. But that did not keep their authors from writing them, or seeking to post and publish them.

Whether or not they believe they will "work," Mennonite poets have persisted in writing poems that might have some kind of resistant resonance in the cacophonous echo chamber of contemporary culture. While many of these poets use various strategies to soften or dissipate the lyric/narrative "I" or to place the speaker in a context that is more than merely personal, their concern (I would argue) is less with literary experimentation for its own sake than with reckoning with the postmodern world in which we are all embedded inextricably in multiple layers of information and affiliation, within which claims of a confident authorial persona are at best difficult and "dubious," to use Keith Ratzlaff's term. The best poetry, I would argue, has always resisted and complicated such easy egotism; the problem, now and always, is to find readers for the best poetry. I hope that this chapter will send many readers in search of the poems, books, and authors mentioned here, and many more that I have not managed to fit in.

We all know how little good it does merely to curse the soldier or the powers that he serves. But we must continue to resist, in every way we can manage, small and large, in poetry and prose, in action and thought and imagination and prayer. Mennonite poets have not done enough, surely, to bring peace to the world. Mennonites have not done enough, or Americans, or white people, or plain people, or people of color, or people with advanced degrees. No one has done enough, and very likely none of us ever will. But that must not stop us from doing whatever we can, and from looking where we can for help. Insufficient and minor as all we do has been and seems destined to remain, who is to say how much worse things would be without it?

Notes

1. Alexander Gilchrist, *Life and Works of William Blake,* 2nd. ed. (London, 1880. Reissued Cambridge University Press, 2009), 173.

2. William Blake, *Jerusalem, Selected Poems and Prose*, ed. Hazard Adams (New York: Holt, Rinehart, and Winston, 1970), 272-274.

3. Martin Espada, *The Republic of Poetry* (New York: Norton, 1006), 12-13.

4. After Teddy Roosevelt, the U. S. had six consecutive presidents with *no* military service record in the early part of the century: Taft, Wilson, Harding, Coolidge, Hoover, and Franklin Roosevelt. The next nine, from Truman through George H.W. Bush, were all veterans, although their level of involvement and experience varied considerably. (It seems only fair to add that the political and other views of these veterans also varied widely.)

5. I hope I may simply stipulate the many dismal effects of all this, since they are not my subject here. Recent studies suggest, for example, that current veterans have even higher rates of post-traumatic stress disorder and other negative effects than occurred in earlier wars, probably because so many are serving multiple tours of duty.

6. Some years ago, a man stole a pickup truck in Georgia, headed north on I-75, filled up at a gas station at the next town south, and left without paying. With the local police in hot pursuit, he pulled off and drove into Bluffton, crashed his truck into a garage in an alley and abandoned it to flee on foot. He was apprehended in our back yard, in the shadow of the young dogwood bushes we had brought home from

church not long before. There is no escaping the world.

7. John Fisher, "Making Something Happen: Toward Transformative Mennonite Peace Poetry," *The Mennonite Quarterly Review* 82 (Jan. 2008), 27.

8. Fisher, 29. For one account of a poet's attempt to use his poems for peace, see Yorifumi Yaguchi's essay "The Movement for Non-Defended Localities in Sapporo, Japan," *Center for Mennonite Writing Journal* 1.2 (2009), http://www.mennon-itewriting.org/jour-nal/1/2/movement/#all. Yaguchi and others in Sapporo, Japan, attempted to have their city declared a "Non-Defended Locality," but despite the eloquence of the poems about World War II Japan that he read to the city council, only one member supported the movement.

9. David Biespiel, "This Land Is Our Land." *Poetry* (May 2010), http://www.po-etryfoundation.org/journal/article.html?id=239284. n.p. 26 July 2010.

10. In a recent advanced poetry writing class, I assigned the excellent international anthology *The Poetry of Our World*, ed. Ed Paine, and read through most of it with the students. We were all struck with the multitude of poets for whom history—often brutal and tragic history—was a major theme of their work, and the differences in texture as well as subject matter from the American poets we had read earlier.

11. Ann Hostetler, personal email to Jeff Gundy, July 28, 2010.

12. I suspect that the percentage of committed pacifists and peace activists among poets is probably at least as high as it is among Mennonites, though I have no hard evidence for this claim. In a recent review of Yaguchi's memoir, *The Wing-Beaten Air*, Di Brandt remarks, "It's edifying to see contemporary poets listed with their pacifist commitments and vision (Stafford, yes; Gary Snyder, yes; Denise Levertov, yes; Kenneth Rexroth, yes) . . . . Nor do I have the impression that the links between pacifism and poetry are talked about all that much in Mennonite churches or academic conferences."—*The Mennonite Quarterly Review* 84 (July 2010): 462-464. See also *Come Together: Imagine Peace*, ed. Ann Smith, Philip Metres, and Larry Smith (Huron, Ohio: Bottom Dog, 2008). This collection of peace poems by 100 poets, mostly contemporary, includes poems by two Mennonites, Jeff Gundy and Todd Davis, but mainly because both have also published books with Bottom Dog Press.

13. "The Colonel" is in Carolyn Forché, *The Country Between Us* (New York: Harper & Row, 1981), 16. See also Carolyn Forché, *Against Forgetting: Twentieth-Century Poetry of Witness* (New York: Norton, 1993).

14. Jeff Gundy, "Arrogant Humility and Aristocratic Torpor," in *World, Self, Poem: Essays on Contemporary Poetry from the "Jubilation of Poets,"* ed. Leonard Trawick (Kent, Ohio: Kent State University Press, 1990), 20-27.

15. David Wojahn, "Maggie's Farm No More: The Fate of Political Poetry," *The Writer's Chronicle* 39 (May/Summer 2007): 27.

16. Wojahn, 24.

17. Wojahn, 26.

18. Wojahn, 27.

19. I am thinking here especially of John Ruth's long poem "Lecture for a Limited Audience," *Mennonite Life*, March 1983, 24-26. It begins with an assertion: "There

are two kinds of people in the world": by this Ruth means those willing to kill other human beings and those who refuse. He develops the theme at considerable length, and much to the advantage of those who refuse to kill.

20. Wojahn, "Maggie's Farm," 23.

21. It would be interesting here to compare Robert Lowell and William Stafford—both poets who were conscientious objectors in World War II. Stafford's engagement with C.P.S. communities in Arkansas and California deeply influenced his life and his poetry, while Lowell pursued a much more individualistic trajectory. Lowell also remained involved with peace efforts, notably during the Vietnam War, but his poems only rarely engage peace issues, and seem to become more and more skeptical of the possibility of meaningful communal effort toward peace. Stafford continued to write inventive and engaged "peace" poems throughout his long career. Today Stafford's work remains a significant resource for peace activists; see, for example, the 2009 documentary film *Every War Has Two Losers*, dir. Haydn Reiss.

22. Biespiel, "This Land," n. p.

23. William Stafford, *Another World Instead*, ed. Frederick Marchant (Minneapolis: Graywolf, 2008). After the war Stafford worked for a time in the Church of the Brethren offices in Elgin, Ill., and taught for a year at Manchester College in Indiana.

24. The name "Split This Rock" comes from a poem by Langston Hughes. The group's website and blog now offer a weekly poem as well as other information and links. Other members of the "Peace Shelves" panel were the poets Frederick Marchant, Sarah Gridley, and Philip Metres, all of whose work I recommend to you.

25. Philip Metres, *Behind the Lines: War Resistance Poetry on the American Homefront since 1941* (Iowa City: University of Iowa Press, 2007), 23, 24.

26. Metres, 5, 4.

27. See Metres, p. 10 and passim, for Metres's rationale for preferring the term "war resistance" and a more detailed analysis of these issues.

28. Metres, 15.

29. For an exploration of the efforts of two current Mennonite poets (one the author of this essay) to revise and redefine the conventional lyric "I," see Ami Regier, "Experiments in Sociolyric Voicing: Dubious Narrators in the Recent Work of Jeff Gundy and Keith Ratzlaff," *The Mennonite Quarterly Review* 82 (Jan. 2008), 84. John Fisher reads Julia Spicher Kasdorf's "The Baby Screaming in the Back Seat" (included in the Poets Against the War archive) carefully in his essay. The poems I consider in the rest of this essay virtually all engage in some version of what Fisher, following a statement by Kasdorf, calls a "binary mode," juxtaposing private and public concerns. I am not so sanguine as Fisher, though, about the "transformation" that he claims occurs in the final lines of "The Baby Screaming . . .," which read "and still the baby screams because she can't believe / anyone is driving this machine." Yes, the mother (who clearly has close connections to the poet herself) *is* driving, but her inability to quiet the child suggests to me a considerable skepticism about the degree of control the mother really has over the child, much less the world.

30. The full text of this poem, and the others in this section, were found using the author search function at Poets Against War. As noted above, I regret that the site is no longer available.

31. Why Quakers rather than Mennonites? Sholl's husband was an interim pastor at a Mennonite church for a time, and as this poem suggests, her values are clearly pacifist and she is a sympathetic fellow traveler. But while she is included in *A Cappella* and has taken part in panel discussions on Mennonite writing, she does not identify as Mennonite in any thorough-going sense.

32. My first book, *Inquiries* (Huron, Ohio: Bottom Dog, 1992), begins with a long prose poem written during the drought summer of 1988, when for the first time it became clear to me, in a physical way, that the world I had grown up in, fickle as its weather could be, was quite likely not the one that my children would inhabit.

33. Julia Kasdorf, *The Body and the Book*, 188-189.

34. Julia Kasdorf, *Poetry in America* (Pittsburgh: Pittsburgh University Press, 2011): 6-7.

35. Ann Hostetler, ed., *A Cappella: Mennonite Voices in Poetry* (Iowa City: University of Iowa Press, 2003), 81.

36. In an online review tellingly titled "Poetry or Propaganda," Judith Fitzgerald is entirely hostile: "Ms. Brandt, evidently a graduate of the Sacred Ego School of Composition, gives neither intrinsic nor extrinsic poetic justification for this loose and lazy see-me-seeing-that-squalor-or-this-tragedy-or-that-movie attitude which infects and defeats the book's edifying intentions; hence, the opening sequence—a political exercise filtered through a *CNN* haze—never delivers on its implied promise to offer readers an unmediated experience of a solid self situated in the Holy City." *M&C Books*, Dec. 17, 2008. http://www.monstersandcritics.com/books/features/article_1448811.php/Propaganda_or_Poetry_by_Judith_Fitzgerald. May 13, 2011.

37. Di Brandt, "Zone: <le Détroit>," *Now You Care* (Toronto: Coach House, 2003), 13.

38. Brandt, 48.

39. Todd Davis, *The Least of These* (East Lansing: Michigan State University Press, 2010), 71.

40. Jean Janzen, *Paper House* (Intercourse, Pa.: Good Books, 2008), 22.

41. Janzen, 24.

42. Ratzlaff, *Then, a Thousand Crows* (Tallahassee, Fla.: Anhinga, 2009), 34; 35.

Part Four
Music, Metaphor, Martyrs, Mystery

CHAPTER TEN

SOUND AND THE SIXTIES: SEX, GOD, ROCK AND ROLL, AND FLOURISHING

Suzanne takes you down to her place near the river
You can hear the boats go by
You can spend the night beside her [. . .]
—Leonard Cohen[1]

"So what did we *get* from the Sixties?" the Canadian Mennonite poet Di Brandt demanded at a dinner table not too long ago. The things uppermost on her mind were the wreckage—"free love" that meant divorce, disease, and smashed hopes of all sorts. Leonard Cohen's 1966 novel *Beautiful Losers,* which she had just been teaching, is a kind of surrealist inventory of this wreckage from the middle of it.

Personally, I was lucky enough to skate through the Sixties on places where the ice was just thick enough to hold me up. Born in the farmlands of Illinois, I missed most of the grand adventures, including the "free love" and the more serious drugs, thanks to relative isolation and enough religious pressure to keep me from complete submersion in hippie culture. The times were a-changin' in Flanagan and Goshen, Indiana, certainly, but not quite so abruptly as elsewhere.

I'm well aware of my good fortune, and make no claims of moral or any other kind of superiority. But I told Di that from the Sixties *I* got a

sense that in "the world," along with all sorts of tedious, tawdry, dangerous, and even lethal junk, there *were* some glints of gold, some genuine
glimpses of peace and hope and truth and love. Many of them were connected with music: songs by Dylan and Hendrix and Joplin and Neil
Young, Simon and Garfunkel and Joni Mitchell, Peter, Paul and Mary
and the Grateful Dead and Jefferson Airplane, so much earnest, angry
and lyrical sound, woven deeply into the movements for civil rights,
peace, and justice. There was the dream of a gathering of tribes who
would sing and dance together, stardust and golden, when the moon
was in the seventh house. . . .

Yes, much of it was silly and naive, some of it was cynical and ma-
nipulative—and then we got disco, and I had to flee to bluegrass. Most
of popular culture has always been mediocre-to-awful, and always will
be. Yet some of those Sixties songs and poems which struck me at the
time as among the truest and most beautiful things I had ever encountered hold up surprisingly well.

Cohen's "Suzanne," with its muttery, atmospheric eloquence, places
together things that I had learned were opposed, if not opposites: minds
and bodies, women and Jesus, the spiritual and the sensual. Cohen intimates that women, even half-crazy ones, may be sources of wisdom, that
the unknown and exotic are not always to be feared, that Salvation Army
counters may hold treasures. Such ideas were rarely found in the hymns
we sang or the sermons I heard at Waldo Mennonite Church, though
the hymns had their own sorts of beauty. But this was also decidedly not
the slick, smug, overtly "worldly," often macho music that I still associ-
ate, perhaps unfairly, with Frank Sinatra, tuxedos, and glasses clinking
with ice and whisky. "I did it my way." Please.

"Suzanne" draws together the guitar and the singing voice, the
image of a beautiful, half-crazy but wise woman, Jesus, and the possibility of trusting *both* the body and the mind. This was a religious and aesthetic sensibility radically at odds from the stark, plain, and patriarchal
one of my youth in some ways—yet in its earnest seeking after the truth
of things and simple, unadorned arrangement of voice and guitar, in
other ways it felt surprisingly familiar. I found myself, indeed, trusting
it. Material like this opened up not only that exotic (to me) urban territory of strange encounters with mysterious, eccentric women—which I
sensed from the start was a kind of extreme—but all sorts of territory in
between. I've been exploring such ground ever since.

But beyond songs like this one, I want to testify to and explore another point: that music changes us, changes the way our brains work and the way we perceive the world at a deep, experiential, phenomenological level. For me, this effect has been especially connected with playing the guitar. Like many poets, I hoped to be a rock star or at least a folksinger, but I soon found that I didn't have the patience to play songs over and over with other people until we could actually do them just right. (Nor the skill, but that's another question.) Yet I kept playing, occasionally for and with others, but more often just when I felt down, or tired, or stale. I still regularly pick and sing my way through a batch of my current favorites—mostly sad love songs with plenty of minor chords. The experience of playing that music is hard to describe clearly, but I'm convinced that it has taught me things about how sounds and words and meaning are connected that have enriched my writing considerably.

One summer I learned a new guitar tuning, euphoniously called "DADGAD," to play some songs by Richard Shindell (who spent some time in seminary before becoming a full-time singer/songwriter). His "Reunion Hill" and "The Ballad of Mary Magdalene" both connect erotic and religious desire, and both have lovely melodies and arrangements that adapt well enough to a single guitar. "Reunion Hill" is a Civil War ballad in the voice of a woman whose husband has not returned. She remembers nursing other soldiers, "dousing for [her] husband's face," and describes finding their "glasses, coins, and golden rings" in the field where they camped. The last verse is the key:

Alone there in a sea of blue, it circles every afternoon,
A single hawk in God's great sky, looking down with God's own
    eyes.
He soars above Reunion Hill, I pray he spiral higher still—
As if from such an altitude, he might just keep my love in view.[2]

Such a gorgeous rendering of absence, longing, distance, and the yearning for restoration. And the hawk, as a kind of avatar for God, is equally beautiful in its ambiguous, suggestive presence—if its eyes really are "God's own," we can hardly help asking, why does God only watch?

"The Ballad of Mary Magdalene" is even more provocative. Also written from a woman's point of view, well before *The Da Vinci Code,* it takes up the old legend that Mary Magdalene and Jesus were lovers.

And I remember nights we spent, whispering our creed.
Our rituals, our sacrament, the stars our canopy.
And there beneath an olive tree we'd offer up our plea
God's creation, innocent, his arms surrounding me.
Jesus loved me, this I know. Why on earth did he ever have to go?
He was always faithful, he was always kind,
But he walked off with this heart of mine.[3]

Shindell knows that he is flirting with heresy—his Mary uses the word—but in his treatment, Jesus seems not at all less holy for having known his beloved in the biblical sense. Again, though, the sharpest poignance of the story is in its sense of loss. And as in "Reunion Hill," when the singing stops the background instruments pick up with a lyrical variation on the melody, suggesting that words cannot fully express the singer's feeling.

Curiously, both of these songs are spoken by women who lament lost men, inverting Edgar Allen Poe's famous dictum that the death of a beautiful woman is "the most poetical subject possible." But I am even more interested in their mingling of the erotic and the religious. Anne Carson's brilliant study *Eros the Bittersweet* examines erotic love from the Greeks to the present. Strikingly, however, almost everything Carson says about Eros is congruent with the longing for closure with God that is religious desire as well. One key point: both erotic and religious desire are extremely powerful, but neither is an especially *comfortable* sort of experience—both, as Carson documents generously, are "bittersweet" and not for those who seek placid, conventional happiness. In both, desire is concentrated upon an external object that is unattainable but which, in fantasy, would complete and satisfy the self. "Who ever desires what is not gone?" Carson asks. "No one. The Greeks were clear on this. They invented eros to express it."[4]

"Desire for knowledge is the mark of the beast," Carson writes. "The unplucked apple, the beloved just out of touch, the meaning not quite attained, are desirable objects of knowledge. It is the enterprise of eros to keep them so. The unknown must remain unknown or the novel ends."[5] So, she suggests, the very structure of desire *requires* that God be unknown. What sort of known or knowable God is worth worshipping?

Carson's account of desire and imagination is not just private, but it is not necessarily communal either. If Eros is merely a matter of a relation between two lovers, or a writer and a reader, or a singular soul and God, we are stuck with one or another variety of a dangerous binary, a loop that threatens to exclude all else in the intensity of its emotions. Carson traces awareness of these dangers of desire far back, noting that Plato discusses the "damage done by lovers in the name of desire" and "the damage done by writing and reading in the name of communication" in the same passage: "Plato appears to believe that they act on the soul in analogous ways and violate reality by the same kind of misapprehension." This harm, Carson thinks, has to do with "determination to freeze the beloved in time" or to "fix words permanently outside the stream of time." The written word is fixed, Plato thinks, but *logos* is "a living changing, unique process of thought."[6]

But the real secret of Eros, Carson argues, is that no binary relationship, even the most powerful, is really enough to satisfy completely over time—and that's why it is "bittersweet." Is it going too far to say that ultimately no satisfaction available to human beings can satisfy us in an absolute, permanent way? Desire has no upper limit, while what takes place in the physical universe is innately limited.

Perhaps the closest we can come, then, is some network of relationships, none of them having to bear the weight of unlimited expectation. The imagination that is desire leads us outward, but what if its object is not singular but multiple? "What is the grass?" said Whitman. "Love calls us to the things of this world," said St. Augustine.

If this is so, then surely desire must be educated, drawn out of narrow obsession with a single beloved, or with a preoccupation with sexual satisfaction (as "Suzanne" hints) if it is to be useful rather than destructive to the human community—not domesticated exactly, but attuned to the complicated web of wish, need, and outcome that enfolds us all. And this necessarily complicated task is the work of the poet, the work of religion, the work of the tribe. The absolute selfishness of infant desire must be trained to understand and acknowledge its place in the web of things, in which nobody can have everything. Robinson Jeffers spoke of drawing the child's attention to the wider world, of which he/she is only a part, as analogous to a larger need to "inhumanize" our views away from a narrow concentration on the human as the measure of all things. Stephen Crane's little poem had it just about right: when a man says to the universe, "Sir I exist," the universe replies coolly, "The fact has not created in me / A sense of obligation."[7]

Yet for all its difficulties, Carson recognizes, desire is hardly dispensable. *Eros the Bittersweet* ends with a vision of a dystopian city "where there is no desire" and also no imagination: "Here people think only what they already know. Fiction is simply falsification. Delight is beside the point. . . ." Socrates' resistance to such a life, Carson argues, that which "constitutes [his] wisdom and motivated his searching life," is his "power to see the difference between what is know and what is unknown." His key realization is "In this one small thing at least it seems I am wiser—that I do not think I know what I do not know."[8]

This dystopian vision has some resemblance to the strictest versions of Anabaptist community, in which the imagination is consigned to the Devil and anything new is received with suspicion. But many small communities fit this description at least in part, having been somehow drained of the vital desires and the imaginative energy on which they were founded. Few things are stranger, it seems to me, than the common claim that opposition to change can be justified by an appeal to history and tradition—as though history is not the record of the inconstant but ongoing struggle to do better, as though what we receive as tradition was not arrived at through the passionate pursuit of more truth, more knowledge, deeper understanding of the real nature of things.[9]

Certainly both the Anabaptist movement and the European-American experiment began in yearnings for freshness, renewal and rebirth driven by the imagination of communities far different from the status quo. "[D]esire is a movement," Carson says, "that carries yearning hearts from over here to over there, launching the mind on a story":

> In the city without desire such flights are unimaginable. . . . To reach for something else than the facts will carry you beyond this city and perhaps, as for Sokrates, beyond this world. It is a high-risk proposition, as Sokrates saw quite clearly, to reach for the difference between known and unknown. He thought the risk worthwhile, because he was in love with the wooing itself. And who is not?[10]

Negotiating the best forms of communal desire and communal imagination, then, becomes crucial. The sorting of known and unknown, good and evil, life-giving and destructive, will continue. The preservation of the communal lore, the arduous nurturing of children, remain crucial. But as there is nothing closed in desire, nothing final about the imagination, so in communal life there is nothing so fixed or precious that it cannot, must not, be re-imagined, renewed, or re-vised as we travel the way.

Feminist theologian Grace Jantzen devoted her career to re-imagining such matters in a series of striking recent books. Most relevant to my purposes is her *Becoming Divine: Towards a Feminist Philosophy of Religion*. Jantzen has very little use for most philosophy of religion, which she regards as "masculinist" and preoccupied with seeking answers to all the wrong questions: the existence and nature of God, the salvation of the isolated individual, abstracted truth-claims, the problems of "belief" and "evil," and the defense of Christendom. The usual notions of "the divine," she argues, valorize disembodied power, rationality, and meaning, and preclude women from becoming subjects at all.[11] In working toward an alternate "feminist symbolic" within which it would be possible to "think differently," Jantzen pays careful attention to desire. She notes that in Jacques Lacan's influential theory, desire is a "remainder" which (as Carson also says) can never be entirely satisfied:

> But since what is really at stake is a desire for absolute love, goodness, and certainty, such complete fulfillment is impossible. Lacan refers to it as the Other (with a capital O), the fantasized (m)other. . . . The development of desire also the development of language: desire constitutes the entry into the symbolic. . . . desire here is that which structures the subject who makes these choices, constitutes the subject (36) by its entry into language, and at the same time ensures repression and fragmentation, the creation of the unconscious.[12]

If desire is "that which structures the subject," then its importance can hardly be overstated. Jantzen argues that this understanding radically undermines "the rational self of modern philosophy." Perhaps even more radically, she suggests that given this understanding of desire, God also must be either fractured, as human subjects are, or not so much like human subjects as has been claimed.[13]

Following Foucault, Jantzen suggests that it *is* possible to develop alternatives to conventional thinking, to "use and destabilize the dominant symbolic about God, religion, and religious language . . . showing up its investment in violence and death." Such an effort would deconstruct the standard binary dualism of theism and atheism, and the centrality of "belief":

What is taken to be of overwhelming importance is intellectual subscription, whichever of the positions is adhered to. Hence also the centrality of evidence, argument, counter-argument, and so on. But once we note that this is the case for either pole of the binary, then a gap opens up, a possibility of thinking differently, and asking whether, instead of this insistence on belief, we might focus on other possibilities—love, for example, or longing, or desire? . . . [W]hat if instead we were to explore . . . the opening of desire that interrupts this emphasis on belief with longing for the divine horizon?[14]

Like Carson, Jantzen notices the connection between religious and erotic desire, and that both involve "desire for the unattainable, the lost primordial unity. . . . God is the Ultimate Other. But then, so is woman—at least to male fantasy." Jantzen also points out, astutely, a considerable irony: that the focus in conventional theology on belief, the will, and rational discourse concerning God stems precisely from an "intense *desire* to be rational":

It is often overlooked that unless the God of classical theism were *desired* by contemporary philosophers of religion, unless they wanted this God and no other, they would hardly spend their energy seeking out arguments and evidence justifying their beliefs about "him"—again, this God, and no other.[15]

For Jantzen, it is the *education* of desire that is crucial, not blindly obeying or ruthlessly suppressing it. She shows that medieval mystics had "much to say about the education or training of desires . . . they certainly did not treat desires as emotional or volitional tempests that come from nowhere and must be passively accepted or violently resisted . . . It will be a great day when philosophers of religion pay as much attention to desires as to beliefs."[16]

The constructive element of Jantzen's project is a turn toward "transformative suggestions for a new symbolic" based on what she calls "natality" in place of the dominant "masculinist necrophilic imaginary." In contrast, natality is *this*-worldly; rather than defining life in terms of death, over against death, or in denial of death, it celebrates "life, birth, and material bodies,"[17] recognizing the uniqueness of each individual life *and* the web of connections that bind us to each other and to the entire biosphere. Birth is even more fundamental than death, after all.

Why do we argue so much about salvation of immortal souls when many of those "souls" need food, water, and basic health care?

In place of salvation, Jantzen proposes "flourishing" within community as a more desirable goal, this-worldly and interconnected. She points out that both are metaphors: "Whereas with the metaphor of salvation God is seen as the saviour who intervenes from outside the calamitous situation to bring about a rescue, the metaphor of flourishing would lead instead to an idea of the divine source and ground, an immanent divine incarnated within us and between us." The God Jantzen imagines would be a "less deistic" one: "God could not be thought of as a being external to the world, but rather its source and well-spring. Jesus could not be envisaged as the heroic saviour entering human history from outside, but rather one who manifests what it may mean to live fully and naturally in the creative justice of God."[18]

Jantzen's ideas here seem strikingly similar to Gordon Kaufman's proposal that God is best understood as the "serendipitous creativity" that undergirds the universe, and Jesus as the pre-eminent agent of that creativity. "Jesus could be seen as the one who manifests what human flourishing can be," Jantzen says. "Becoming divine," then, means not some transgressive, arrogant assumption of God's powers, but something much more modest, pragmatic, and this-worldly:

> If our understanding of the divine is constructed from our deliberate projections, and if this is done so that we can then reclaim those attributes and become divine, then it is indeed the intention that "all God's attributes" become "my attributes."

Such a project would not be selfish or individualistic, given its underpinnings:

> [B]ecoming divine is inseparable from solidarity with human suffering; a symbolic of the divine is a symbolic of outrage, imagination and desire, and compassionate action, not the detached and objective intellectual stance which traditional philosophers of religion assume.[19]

I find Jantzen's analysis and proposals both inspiring and (somewhat) disturbing—not her bold ideas about God, but her critique of the "masculinist necrophiliac imaginary," with its conflation of love, desire, and death. In many of my favorite texts and songs, indeed, violence and death cast long shadows. Are even antiwar pieces and pacifist theology

overly preoccupied with violence? Do they reinforce the hegemony of
force even in seeking to resist or refute it?

Charles Frazier's Civil War novel *Cold Mountain* weaves together
concerns with violence, male and female roles, and music in a compelling way. A subplot concerns a rather no-account man named Stobrod, a heavy drinker and lackadaisical fiddle player whose life is transformed after he plays for and talks with a badly burned, dying girl. This
confrontation shocks Stobrod into a whole new way of thinking and acting in the world. He begins to seek out talented musicians, learning
from them, paying attention to technique and to lyrics: "he began listening to the words of the songs the niggers sang, admiring how they
chanted out every desire and fear in their lives as clear and proud as
could be." Soon he discovers he is learning things about himself as well:

> One thing he discovered with a great deal of astonishment was
> that music held more for him than just pleasure. There was meat
> to it. The grouping of sounds, their forms in the air as they rang
> out and faded, said something comforting to him about the rule
> of creation. What the music said was that there is a right way for
> things to be ordered so that life might not always be just tangle
> and drift but have a shape, an aim. It was a powerful argument
> against the notion that things just happen.[20]

Stobrod's conversion is not "religious" in conventional terms, but it
takes him down a path that I think Grace Jantzen would recognize and
approve. Along with learning things about himself, he learns about the
world, and his new sense that "there is a right way for things to be ordered" transforms his behavior as well as his fiddle-playing. He had essentially abandoned his daughter, but he returns to heal his relationship
with her, and becomes more attentive and respectful of everyone he encounters; he even quits drinking. In Jantzen's terms, he begins to live as
one who values communal "flourishing" rather than mere drifting.

Frazier suggests, then, that aesthetic, imaginative experience can be
ethically transformative. Is it necessary that this experience be connected with violence and death, as Stobrod's is linked to the dying girl? I
want to resist this notion, but not only men have thought so. I cannot
help but think here of Flannery O'Connor's fiction, especially the famous ending of her story "A Good Man Is Hard to Find," in which the
smug main character, a superficially pious grandmother, is jolted into

awareness of her need for grace by her family's murder and her own impending death. After carrying on a speculative theological conversation that culminates in his shooting her, the outlaw Misfit ruminates, "She'd of been a good woman if it had been somebody there to shoot her every day of her life."[21]

Even the early Anabaptists composed and sang hymns to sustain themselves while locked up in prison. Consumed by the desire to be faithful, threatened with torture and death, they responded by making song. The simplicity and conviction of the hymns in the *Ausbund* is of the same order, I think, as "This Train" or "We Shall Overcome" or "Blowin' in the Wind." Truth and the urgent desire for what is just and right have close traveling companions and allies in beauty, rhythm, and song.

I think Jantzen is right that the drive for justice, community, and imaginative worship must be disentangled from our collective fascination with violence and death—although while we inhabit this earth I can envision no way of evading those realities entirely. The longer I try to write poems, the more I find myself reaching for the music that lies within language, and for language that acknowledges the brokenness of the world without yielding to it entirely. I find myself trying to write poems in which the sense is so entangled with the sounds that they are, somehow, their own accompaniment, that what they are as things made of words and sounds is as important as "what they say."

Perhaps music—literal or figurative—is what bears the meaning, the way water lifts and holds the boat, the way the air holds the heron in flight. You can push a boat along a dry creek bed, and a heron can walk on a path made by people, but it's not the way that either travels best.

There is a moment in many songs when the verse or chorus ends and the instruments pick up with some slightly or radically altered version of the melody. That sequence often forms the emotional climax—and often the effect is as though words have carried us as far as they can, and it's necessary now to leave them behind to travel any further into something we can experience but not fully understand or explain.

So poems may be openings, devices to generate possibilities that they do not fully contain or constrain, made of the mysterious stuff of language, itself made of sound and shape, of breath and image pressed into the tangible world from that other one which is also real, which we enter and depart from constantly as we breathe in and out. Here is one, a sort of oblique autobiography and register of some of my own desires, obscure and otherwise, as a sort of ending.

Autobiography with Blonde on Blonde

The ragman drew circles on everything, but St. John dragged
his feet through them all, saying *In the beginning was the Word!*

until time shuddered like a bus with bad brakes and my dad
rubbed his face and sat down at the kitchen table, his farmer tan

glowing. It had been a windy day, and the brutal stench
of Hillman's hogs wafted through the screens. I whacked Kathy

on the back of the head just to hear her howl. It worked.
Then they drove me off to college, where I learned

that the not-yet has already happened, if you squint at it
just right. *I am, I said,* said Neil Diamond, and we had

to agree with that. Then the president explained that those
unwilling to kill for peace might once have been good people,

but godless communist drugs had made them into trolls
and orcs. We knew he was an idiot—we were elves and hobbits—

and decided to set off for Mordor to destroy the Ring
right after dinner. But somebody put on *Blonde on Blonde* again,

and it was just like the night to play tricks, and we could hardly
root out the fascist pigs while Louise and her lover were so en-
    twined.

We walked down beside the dam instead, tried to lose ourselves
in the scant woods. I never got to Memphis or to Mobile.

The hard rain was already falling, but the sun still shone like glory
some of those afternoons, with classes over and the long night
    ahead

and water roaring down the spillway like the great I AM.[22]

Notes

1. Leonard Cohen, "Susanne," *Songs of Leonard Cohen* (Columbia Records, 1967).

2. Richard Shindell, "Reunion Hill," *Reunion Hill* (Shanachie Records, 1997) .

3. Shindell, "The Ballad of Mary Magdalene," *Blue Divide* (Shanachie Records, 1994).

4. Anne Carson, *Eros the Bittersweet* (Princeton: Princeton University Press/Dalkey Archive, 1998), 11.

5. Carson, *Eros,* 109.

6. Carson, *Eros,* 130; 132.

7. Stephen Crane, *War Is Kind and Other Lines.* 1899. About.com. 27 July 2010.

8. Carson, *Eros,* 168; 172.

9. Among many other things, Kathleen Norris's *Dakota: A Spiritual Journey* (New York: Houghton Mifflin, 1993) describes this curious phenomenon in declining Midwestern towns, where people yearn for growth and prosperity yet respond to newcomers with suspicion and hostility. See esp. the chapters "Gatsby on the Plains," 45-64, and "Can You Tell the Truth in a Small Town," 79-88.

10. Carson, *Eros,* 173.

11. Grace Jantzen, *Becoming Divine: Toward a Feminist Philosophy of Religion* (Bloomington, Ind.: Indiana University Press, 1007), 10, 18-19.

12. Jantzen, *Becoming,* 36-7.

13. Jantzen, *Becoming,* 38.

14. Jantzen, *Becoming,* 57; 65.

15. Jantzen, *Becoming,* 50; 87.

16. Jantzen, *Becoming,* 87.

17. Jantzen, *Becoming,* 137.

18. Jantzen, *Becoming,* 161; 162.

19. Jantzen, *Becoming,* 163; 91; 263.

20. Charles Frazier, *Cold Mountain* (New York: Vintage, 1997), 294-6.

21. Flannery O'Connor, *A Good Man Is Hard to Find and Other Stories* (New York: Mariner Books, 1977), 23.

22. Jeff Gundy, "Autobiography with *Blonde on Blonde,*" *Center for Mennonite Writing Journal* 2.4 (July 2010). http:www.mennonitewriting.org/journal/2/4/. 2 August 2010.

CHAPTER ELEVEN

THE RULE OF GOD AND THE RUBY: THE THEOPOET TALKS BACK

Several years ago, when the contours of this book were only dim shapes in my mind, I determined to learn more about John Howard Yoder. My friends in theology and religious studies were always referring to Yoder, without question the most influential Mennonite theologian of the last half-century; many had known him personally, and several had been deeply influenced by his work. But while I had read his classic *The Politics of Jesus* as a rather surly college student, and some bits and pieces since, I had never really warmed much to Yoder. Still, I had learned much from other theologians, Mennonite and otherwise, and figured that at the least I could offer a semi-magnanimous reconciliation, as Ezra Pound does to Walt Whitman when he says, "I come to you as a grown child / who has had a pig-headed father."

So I read a good deal of Yoder—though certainly not all—and dabbled in the voluminous commentary and criticism on his work. When I showed one of my expert friends my first version of this chapter, though, he was dismayed, and insisted over lunch that I was getting Yoder all wrong, reading him like an ignorant poet. More or less the same thing happened with other readers. "You've got to read this," they kept saying, as they offered generous explanations and glosses on the great man. I am pig-headed enough myself, but I did keep reading, and my view of Yoder did keep evolving,. This chapter did too—although I also want to highlight that despite largely bracketing off the sexual offenses to which Yoder admitted, I grieve along with those he offended. I recognize that their stories need to be remembered, and that we have only begun to create and maintain healthy sexual boundaries.

My first reading of Yoder led to an effort to sort out and state briefly, as much for myself as for anyone else, his central ideas that made sense to me. That led to these paragraphs, which I still stand by, though with considerable supplementation and hedging to follow:

1. Yoder makes bold statements about the essential meaning of the universe with a minimum of mystery or mystification. Though the body of his thought is large and intricate, his essential claims can be stated fairly simply: that the Rule of God as seen in Jesus Christ is the ultimate (though not yet fully realized) reality, that this rule requires certain behaviors of human beings, and that these behaviors include nonviolence, community, mutual aid, and care for the poor. All these claims derive from Yoder's Anabaptist commitments, but he insists that they are not merely sectarian views, and that all Christians ought to take them seriously.

2. Yoder recognizes that these imperatives depend on, and follow from, confessing Jesus as Lord. That does not lessen their breadth and depth, but it does mean that the work of faithful Christians is *not* to take charge of the social world and make it into some version of paradise. Those who have tried, he points out, have always compromised Jesus' call to nonviolence and rationalized their use of violence in various ways, none of which Yoder finds persuasive. Yoder argues that we can never precisely predict the results of our actions, and that there is no point in obsessing over making things "turn out right" or, to follow the title of an influential essay, seeking to be in charge. We must try to be faithful, but we can determine to contribute to society without thinking that we can or must *control* it. As an example, Yoder offers the early Quakers who founded Pennsylvania. Such groups, he says, "can . . . and do in fact, discharge social responsibilities when such are entrusted to them without demanding that they betray their truth-telling, nonviolent ethos."[1]

3. Yoder shows the advantages of disentangling a particular narrative thread from history and claiming it as one's own. In "Armaments and Eschatology," a key essay, he adroitly traces a possible tradition of alternate community within Judaism after the Diaspora. Small and scattered communities, living in exile among (often hostile) strangers, man-

aged to survive and even prosper around the synagogue (community), Torah (sacred text), and the rabbinate (nonviolent leadership). They persisted without seeking to "be in charge" of their larger locales, yet were able to "seek the peace of the city" and contribute in positive ways without violating their principles. This, he suggests, is the basic structure that the first Christian communities adapted, and others would do well to take it as a model.

All this is well and good, I think. I have no better version of a broad, social vision. Yet reading *The Politics of Jesus, The Priestly Kingdom, Body Politics,* and some individual essays really only confirmed my earlier sense of Yoder as an earnest, even dour definer of The Way We Must Follow. This Way, it seemed, involved not only peace and justice, but lots of small groups that would sip their grape juice and nibble their crackers while planning their next witness to the State. There seemed little space for poetry or art in these communities; I searched Yoder's work for an appreciation of the depths and complications of language and human experience, or the importance of subjective experience to creating and maintaining healthy communities, without much success. Thus I must, however reluctantly, devote much of this essay to quibbling with him.

When Yoder does bring up those who take a special interest in language, in a section of *The Priestly Kingdom* devoted to "Agents of Linguistic Self-Consciousness," it is only to hedge them around with warnings and suspicions. He notes of this role as "*didaskalos* or teacher" that it "is said of this function that it is a dangerous one because the tongue is hard to govern. Not many people should be in this office, the epistle of James says . . . because like the small bit turning a horse around . . . language has a dangerously determining function":

> It is a significant anthropological insight to say that language can steer the community with a power disproportionate to other kinds of leadership. The demagogue, the poet, also the journalist, the novelist, the grammarian, all are engaged in steering society with the rudder of language. This applies both to rhetoric as a skill and also to the place of any set of concepts in predisposing what kinds of thoughts the members of a given community are capable of having. . . . There should not be many *didaskaloi,* not many articulators in the church, because not many of those who use language are aware of its temptations.[2]

Where do the poet and the demagogue rub elbows in the same dire list, outside this stern directive? It reminded me of Plato's famous edict that the poets must be banished from the Republic lest they contaminate it with their wild, ungovernable thoughts and stories. How can a poet-teacher not read this as a transparent power play, meant to validate some kinds of discourse and dismiss others? Surely Yoder's own enterprise also involves seeking to "steer society with the rudder of language," whether that language is instrumentalist, hortatory, or didactic, to "predispose what kinds of thoughts the members of a given community are capable of having." And the poets I know, constantly engaged with problems of language, are generally far more "aware of its temptations" and snares than most people.

Granted, here and elsewhere Yoder worries about unnecessary hair-splitting and quibbling over trivia. Still, he seems to find a few verses in James reason enough to deny any role for those specially attuned to language beyond a minor, negative one as a censor of certain kinds of discussion, one who "will denounce the diversion of attention from what must be done to debate about how to say it. . . . Metaethical analysis will be made accountable at the bar of common commitment, not the other way around."[3]

This passage only strengthened my sense of Yoder as another, if idiosyncratic, member of the guild of lofty theologian/ethicists, eager to keep the troublemakers quiet and the other guilds subservient. Where was all the concern for patience, for careful listening, that I kept hearing was at the heart of his ethics? Why mistrust those who use language with the most care and attention to its nuances and possibilities?

The New(er) Yoder

I will let that question go for now, because when I read some recent commentary on Yoder I found a figure that I barely recognized. The proponents of the "New Yoder" (the title of a recent collection of essays edited by younger Mennonite scholars Peter Dula and Chris K. Huebner) make him out indeed to be an advocate of radical patience and the embrace of uncertainty, a kind of postmodern Anabaptist hero with nearly supernatural powers. In the introduction to his own book of "Yoderian explorations," *A Precarious Peace*, Chris Huebner describes Yoder as one who "does not develop positions": "Yoder's work is not a self-generated and self-standing theological enterprise. It does not reflect the dominating presence of an authorial 'I,' let alone the stance of a professional theologian, even though many mistakenly approach it as though it does."[4] We should not treat Yoder as someone whose voice can be "established, owned, and located," Huebner argues, though he does not explain clearly how else he imagines Yoder's voice coming to us . . . perhaps as a disembodied whisper? or a series of runes inscribed on a mountain? or a text unrolling into space, a la *Star Wars*?

However Yoder might achieve this oracular status, it is taken largely as given in *The New Yoder*. Huebner and Peter Dula note in their introduction that, at least in terms of Yoder's insistence on particularity, their gathered critics "simply start with the assumption that Yoder is right and build from there," having learned from Foucault, Deleuze, or Nietzsche of the inevitable particularity of knowledge.[5] To create an edifice of thought that is without "I," that cannot be "established, owned, and located" and yet is taken by a whole cadre of followers as simply "right"— now there is an accomplishment.

Still, I do not mean to mock these claims, however extravagant they seem, because this disestablished, decentered Yoder is far more intriguing and appealing to me than the authoritarian figure of my own early readings. The New Yoder, I learned, refuses the Will to Power. He does not urge us to quiet the tongues of others or to avoid pointless discussion but questions the motives of all religious/ethical argument:

> We want what we say not only to be understandable, credible, meaningful. . . . We hanker for patterns of argument which will not be subject to reasonable doubt. . . . To say it another way, *the hunger for validation is a hunger for power.* We want people to *have* to believe what we say.[6]

This Yoder, Peter Blum argues, insists that we have no *proof* we are correct, nor can we *demand* that anyone believe as we do. In this he aligns well with postmodern favorites like Nietzsche, Foucault, and Derrida, unlikely as these linkages might seem. Furthermore, this Yoder argues that if our truth-claims stand on no absolute ground, neither do anyone else's—and, therefore, we are free and indeed obligated to witness with conviction, if not certainty: "Instead of seeking to escape particular identity, what we need, then, is a better way to restate the meaning of a truth claim from within particular identity."[7]

When I returned to Yoder's crucial essay "'But We Do See Jesus': The Particularity of incarnation and the Universality of Truth" with these ideas in mind, I saw much that I had missed, especially his acceptance that "Reality always was pluralistic and relativistic, that is historical. The idea that it could be otherwise was itself an illusion laid on us by Greek ontology language, Roman sovereignty language, and other borrowings from the Germans, the Moors, and the other rulers of Europe."[8] "We still do not *see* that the world has been set straight. We still have no *proof* that it is right," Yoder acknowledges, but then quotes Hebrews 2:9: "But we do see Jesus, revealing the grace of God by tasting death for everyone."[9]

Romand Coles, whose essay in *The New Yoder* is devoted to the problem of "how people might live well amid others who are radically different from themselves," finds in Yoder a "vision of dialogical communities that brings forth very particular and powerful practices of generous solidarity."[10] As Huebner and Dula suggest, Coles assumes from the start that Yoder is right about such matters, and reads his work with an emphasis on its most dialogic and undefended threads. He finds a Yoder who praises "receptive engagements with outsiders who contest hegemonic practices" and "enable new light to break forth."[11]

This is pretty good, I think . . . until I try to place myself in this scheme. Am I inside, part of "the church"? Many would say so; I'm a birthright Mennonite, have been a member in good standing of one Mennonite church or another since I was baptized, and have been educated at or employed by Mennonite institutions for all my adult life except for a four-year expedition into the secular wilds of graduate school.

And yet . . . as readers of this book know by now, my own affinities, my sense of tribal identity, are at least as Romantic and Transcendentalist and poetic as they are Anabaptist. I would take Whitman, Thoreau, and Blake to a desert island; if I had room, I would take Mennonite poets Julia Spicher Kasdorf and Keith Ratzlaff and Jean Janzen. Would I take Menno or Marpeck or Yoder? Only if I had a big, big suitcase, and well after Rumi, Kabir, Machado, Akhmatova, Mary Oliver, Kafka, Rilke, Borges, Garcia Marquez. . . .

So—what to do when the "Other" is not just outside the boundaries of the visible church, but inside as well, and less clearly marked than a good Yoderian might prefer? Might we need categories like "semi-Other"?[12]

I'm happy enough to agree with Yoder that the "Christ vs. Culture" dualism of the Troeltsches and Niebuhrs is mistaken, pleased to follow him into the realm of particularity and allegiances chosen from a multitude of particular locations. But I suspect my interior map of those locations is considerably different from his. In the world I inhabit, patient listening to voices outside the Visible Church has shifted my sense of the borders of both the Holy and the Sensible quite drastically. A host of others, however "worldly," are no longer "outsiders" in my personal geography, not "others" whose "Insights which are not contradictory to the truth of the Word incarnate" can be "not denied but affirmed and subsumed within the confession of Christ."[13] They are for me trusted advisers, sources, confidants whose wisdom and knowledge seems to me closer to truth than I have yet moved. How then am I to "affirm and subsume" them within anything of my own?

So I would not so much challenge Yoder's own "missionary arrogance" (carefully hedged around with patience as it may be) as confess that my own sorting, affirming, and subsuming has led me to much less confidence that my own particular sect, fond of it as I am, has special access to the truth of the Word, incarnate or otherwise.

A Side Note: On Rook and High Christology

The card game Rook, long popular among Mennonites seeking to avoid the "worldly" deck with its kings, queens, jacks, and jokers, has numbered cards of four colors and one wild card—the Rook, of course. Its rules resemble bridge, but some cards have number values, and the game is won and lost on points rather than tricks taken. The Rook is always trump in whatever suit is called during the bidding. There are two main ways to play: "Rook high," which means that whoever draws the Rook always has the highest card, and "Rook low," which places the Rook between the 10 and 11 of trump—a valuable card, but one that you might lose if you don't play your cards right, or even if the draw just happens to fall the wrong way.

"Rook low" always seemed to me the only way to play. If the Rook always already wins, there's not enough suspense to keep the game interesting for long. If the Rook is uniquely valuable (it's worth more points than any other card) but under certain circumstances can be captured by another, then the negotiations become vastly more interesting, and possibly more productive, because nobody has an omnipotent trump card.

This analogy is already on the brink of collapse, but you can see where I'm going. In theopoetic negotiations—at least in mine—the Rook is always low, because true nonviolence requires giving up the high position that is based merely on authority-claims. Yes, the Rook is the most valuable card, but not the "strongest" one, because (like the crow, like Coyote) the Rook is not a warrior; he refuses the sword and even rhetorical violence. He chooses the way of parable, of indirection, of cunning and wit, of compassion and solidarity with the weak and the poor.

Yoder and "The World"

Do you want to improve the world?
I don't think it can be done.

The world is sacred.
It can't be improved.
If you tamper with it, you'll ruin it.
If you treat it like an object, you'll lose it.
—Lao Tzu, *Tao Te Ching* 29[14]

During my first reading of Yoder, I stumbled hard over a passage from his essay "But We Do See Jesus." It comes at the end of a summary of five New Testament passages that all make bold claims for the victory of Christ over the powers of the world. Here is his synthesis of what these passages show operating:

> A handful of messianic Jews, moving beyond the defenses of their somewhat separate society to attack the intellectual bastions of majority culture, refused to contextualize their message by cloth-ing it in the categories the world held ready. Instead, they seized the categories, hammered them into other shapes, and turned the cosmology on its head, with Jesus both at the bottom, crucified as a common criminal, and at the top, preexistent Son and creator, and the church his instrument in today's battle.
>
> It is not the world, culture, civilization, which is the defini-tional category, which the church comes along to join up with,

approve, and embellish with some correctives and complements. The Rule of God is the basic category. The rebellious but already (in principle) defeated cosmos is being brought to its knees by the Lamb. The development of a high Christology is the natural cultural ricochet of a missionary ecclesiology when it collides as it must with whatever cosmology explains and governs the world it invades.[15]

Yoder means here, I think, mainly to describe what these sources claim, yet the difference between the bold and even violent rhetoric of these paragraphs and the patience and existential modesty he advocates elsewhere (even in the same essay) is striking. "Attack the intellectual bastions of majority culture" and "the church his instrument in today's battle"? Overtly military metaphors. "Seized the categories, hammered them into other shapes"? Even if only categories are being seized and hammered, this sounds rather brutal. "The rebellious but already (in principle) defeated cosmos is being brought to its knees by the Lamb"? A "missionary ecclesiology" that is "invading" the world, like an army or, at the least, a foreign species?

Here I found myself stopped short. I simply do not share the view, popular among Christians (and some Gnostics, though few enough of those are left) that the physical, material cosmos is somehow fallen, let alone rebellious. Human beings may indeed be in rebellion against the Lamb; evidence of that is plentiful, even overwhelming. But the robins and the oak trees, the oceans and the stars, surely are innocent of any such failing, and to speak of defeating them is surely to slip into an anthropomorphism that borders on the absurd.[16]

What would the cosmos do differently, after the surrender? Would the robins sing hymns and shun the starlings? Would the squirrels cross themselves before biting into the next walnut? Would the heavens proclaim the glory of God? Oh, yes. But they did so across unimaginable reaches of space and time long before the tribes of Israel invented the name Yahweh in our minor backwater of the Milky Way, long before the miracle of Bethlehem and the Sermon on the Mount.

It may well be that Yoder does not have the physical universe in mind—that he is mainly arguing with reductionists who find no room for God in a materialist cosmos. Even if this is so, however, I see no reason to let Yoder off the hook here. His language betrays a lack of attention to the world, and a lamentably pinched dualism. In choosing a cosmology, we have other choices than vacant materialism and a grand war between a sinful universe and the eventually triumphant Lamb.

One of many poets and thinkers who resist viewing the world as "fallen" is the maverick priest Matthew Fox, whose *Original Blessing* traces an alternate tradition of "creation-centered spirituality" that is "open, seeking, and explorative of the cosmos within the human person and all creatures and of the cosmos without, the spaces between creatures that unite us all. . . . It is all a blessing, an ongoing and fertile blessing with a holy, salvific history of about twenty billion years."[17] Fox argues vigorously against the "fall/redemption tradition" that he traces to St. Augustine and to authoritarian, patriarchal politics. "In the New Testament and the earliest hymns of the Christian community and in medieval, creation-centered spirituality, the cosmos is present," Fox argues, but "the condemnation of Meister Eckhart's creation-centered spirituality was one example of a threatened ecclesial establishment trying to suggest that life is bigger than controls, that life is cosmic for everyone."[18]

Yoder slips into this mode again, if in a more modest way, at the end of "But We Do See Jesus." The "ordinariness" of Jesus (not here, apparently, the Lamb who can wrestle the cosmos to its knees) he describes as "the low road to general validity," which "frees us to use any language, to enter any world in which people eat bread and pursue debtors, hope for power and execute subversives."[19] Is the sum total of the world outside of the Church, then, food, money, power and violence?

Well, maybe. To the theopoet, however, this seems a paltry and ungenerous accounting of the myriad lives that spin on around the planet, the vast majority of them entirely outside the realm of human language and categories—indeed, of anything identifiable as "religion" except in the largest, vaguest sense. Do the dogs and eagles, the fish and the bacteria, know Jesus in their own ways? Do not the atheists and Hindus and Buddhists and Muslims also love their spouses, kiss their children, care sacrificially for their old ones?

Yoder is right, surely, that all human stances are particular and contingent, and that we must choose one or another. But this theopoet remains skeptical that "The nonterritorial particularity of [Jesus'] Jewishness defends us against selling out to *any* wider world's claim to be really wider, or to be self-validating."[20] Yes, we can claim that Jesus gives human beings meaning and purpose within the cosmos; still, the cosmos remains, its enormous and brilliant body sprawling far beyond our most distant conceptions and intimations, to say nothing of our instruments and our knowledge. Surely, whatever truth-claims we make within our little human realm, we must recognize that as the galaxies retreat in all directions from us we can say less and less about them, and about the larger purposes of God within those arcs and grains of the universe that very likely have nothing to do with human beings at all.

This recognition, it seems to me, is a variation on patience and respect for the other that is entirely consistent with Yoder's own anti-foundationalist position—and I wish that he had been more willing to follow out what seem to me the implications of his own precepts. I do not presume to say where the edge of human revelation might be, or what form God's body might take for beings whose own bodies we can imagine only with the near-certainty that we will be wrong, or what grace God brings to the souls of Fomalhaut or the Lesser Magellanic Cloud—who will, of course, have their own names for their own places.[21]

Language and the World

"How could we ever have become so *deaf* to these other voices that nonhuman nature now seems to stand mute and dumb, devoid of any meaning besides that which we choose to give it?" —David Abram[22]

When I wrote my long-ago dissertation, the poet Robert Pinsky had just published *The Situation of Poetry,* an influential book of literary criticism. Pinsky accused Keats's "Ode to a Nightingale" of sentimentalizing and anthropomorphizing the bird and its song. Any claim that the natural world might communicate with a human being, Pinsky, was simply naïve:

The Romantic poet is attracted, through intense perception, to dimness. The more actively he perceives the natural world he loves, the more alienated he is from it, for its quality is to perceive nothing. The more closely and lovingly he enumerates its separate details, the further he grows away from it, for its attribute is not to enumerate. Above all, the more he knows it or tries to perfect that knowledge in his writing, the more he widens the gap between himself and it, because its essence is not to be conscious at all.[23]

This seemed absurdly overstated to me, even then; a few minutes with any dog or cat puts the lie to the notion that animals "perceive nothing" or that they are not "conscious at all." The recent work of David Abram provides a more thorough rebuttal to Pinsky's dismissals, and a further challenge to Yoder's inattention to the physical world.

Abram argues that human language, far from being a unique production that sets us apart from other animals and beings, emerges from the matrix of the physical world, and that we must give up the claim that language is an exclusively human property.

> If language is always, in its depths, physically and sensorially resonant, then it can never be definitively separated from the evident expressiveness of bird-song, or the evocative howl of a wolf late at night. . . . Language as a bodily phenomenon accrues to *all* expressive bodies, not just to the human. Our own speaking, then, does not set us outside of the animate landscape but—whether or not we are aware of it—inscribes us more fully in its chattering, whispering, soundful depths.[24]

Linguistic meaning, Abram claims, is "primarily expressive, gestural, and poetic," and the notion that language sets humans apart from all other forms of life—common at least since Aristotle—must be reexamined. Following the phenomenologist Maurice Merleau-Ponty, Abram urges that we "acknowledge the life of the body," "affirm our solidarity with this physical form," and "acknowledge our existence as one of the earth's animals" (47). Being and perception then may be recognized not as the activities of some sort of ethereal consciousness embedded in a corporeal body, but as animate interactions: "Our most immediate experience of things, according to Merleau-Ponty, is necessarily an experience of reciprocal encounter—of tension, communication, and commingling" (56). Such reorientation might also yield a rediscovery of the earth and the cosmos as not a vacant, silent realm of mere matter but as the very ground of our being and, if we are believers, the very being of God.

"Ode to a Nightingale" describes something very like this "reciprocal encounter" as Keats listens "darkling" to the bird's song, conscious of his brother's recent death from tuberculosis and aware that his own may also be approaching:

> Now more than ever seems it rich to die,
>   To cease upon the midnight with no pain,
>   While thou art pouring forth thy soul abroad
>   In such an ecstasy!
>   Still wouldst thou sing, and I have ears in vain—
>   To thy high requiem become a sod.[25]

"The human mind is not some otherworldly essence that comes to house itself inside our physiology," Abram insists. "Intelligence is no longer ours alone but is a property of the earth; we are in it, of it, immersed in its depths." This shift in understanding affects much else, including our most basic notions of truth, meaning, and value: "Ecologically considered it is not primarily our verbal statements that are 'true' or 'false,' but rather the kind of relations that we sustain with the rest of nature. A human community that live in a mutually beneficial relation with the surrounding earth is a community, we might say, that lives in truth."[26]

This peaceable community, I would suggest, looks a lot like Grace Jantzen's gathering of "natals" dedicated to "flourishing," and a good deal like Yoder's witnessing church—except that to both Abram and Jantzen, such communities are to be judged not for the abstract belief systems they espouse, but by the human and cosmic relations they maintain.

Further Adventures in Language and the So-Called Real World

In "Armaments and Eschatology" Yoder asks a series of pointedly rhetorical questions about what he calls "an 'ordinary' or 'reasonable' modern view of things":

> Would a normal world-view know for sure that the cosmos is unspoiled? That it is closed, with no intervention from beyond, no radical change in its structures, and no division within it being conceivable? That human action can control history's outcome? That a uniform ethos for all kinds of people is possible and desirable? That the language of divine agency is meaningless?[27]

I would answer all these questions with "No," although with some quibbles. But surely they set up something of a straw man. Certainly it is right to doubt "modern" confidence about the nature of things, but at most these questions fling us back into the realm of multiple, competing truth-claims and perspectives; to point out that there is no "self-evident rational base line cosmology" takes us only so far, and as I have argued throughout this book, a strong case can be made for treating the cosmos with more respect than Yoder allows.

Let us look once more at the visionary conclusion of "Armaments and Eschatology":

> The point that apocalyptic makes is not only that people who wear crowns and who claim to foster justice by the sword are not as strong as they think—true as that is: we still sing, "O where are Kings and Empires now of old that went and came?" It is that people who bear crosses are working with the grain of the universe.[28]

Notice how much imagery, metaphor, and even lyricism this passage contains: crowns and swords, the singing of hymns, bearing crosses, and then the striking closing metaphor. The *didaskalos* must ask, again: what does it mean, exactly, "working with the grain of the universe"? And how does it square with a cosmos that is, earlier to this same essay, described as "spoiled"? Yoder's phrase resonates with one often associated with Martin Luther King Jr., "the universe bends toward justice"; King's 1965 version was itself drawn from a much earlier statement by Universalist preacher and abolitionist Theodore Parker, who said in an 1853 sermon, "I do not pretend to understand the moral universe; the arc is a long one . . . And from what I see I am sure it bends toward justice."[29]

I was pleased to find such a passage in Yoder and to learn that it is often cited and quoted. It seems a rare but crucial instance in Yoder of what Keats famously called "Negative Capability"—a relinquishing of the "irritable reaching after fact and reason" that all too often rule us. So rather than explaining away this figure as merely one of conventional apocalyptic expectation, or a casual lapse into figurative language, let us take Yoder at his word here, and explore his metaphor a bit further.

The grain of wood, we know, is not separable from the wood itself, but a visible aspect of its very structure. There is such a "grain" to the universe, the metaphor asserts, however fallen or spoiled it may be, and that grain leads toward justice and truth. Such a grain, then, can only be that of a God deeply interpenetrated into the universe, perhaps even an indivisible part of creation, a ground of being like the river bed from which (as we will see shortly) Rumi's reed flute is torn. I do not claim that Yoder would agree with this reading, but I would suggest that at times the language says things through us that we do not intend nor even think we believe, and that at times these things are truer than we know. This is the nature of metaphor.

I love working with wood, smoothing the surface, cutting and fitting pieces closely. I love especially to dip a rag into the stain and spread it across a fresh surface of oak or birch, to see the grain leap into a new, darker, more beautiful relief at the touch of my hand.

In Which Jelaluddin Rumi Dances with, or around, John Howard Yoder

When I walk down the sloping sidewalk past the art building on my campus on a clear summer day, I see how the leaves catch most of the sunlight but let what they cannot contain shine right through them. I come down to the creek and look both ways to see the particular path, never the same from day to day or moment to moment, that the water is finding across and around the limestone and pebbles of the creek bed. When I watch the creek I do not find that the church precedes the world, epistemologically or any other way. When I encounter strong poets, musicians, artists, their claims on my attention, my allegiance, my very construction of the world will not be subordinated to anything.

The great Sufi poet and teacher Jelaluddin Rumi is one such strong poet. Born in Persia in 1207, he has become one of the best-selling poets in contemporary America, especially in translations by Coleman Barks. At the heart of Rumi's teaching is his sense of the human predicament, which he often speaks of using the imagery of a reed flute. Torn from the mud of the riverbed, pierced with nine holes and pressed into sound by a breath not its own, the reed is like human beings, conscious of having been deprived of a primal unity that we yearn to regain:

Since I was cut from the reedbed,
I have made this crying sound.

Anyone apart from someone he loves
understands what I say.[30]

But as Coleman Barks notes, separation and yearning are only the
start of this line of imagery:

> Rumi has a whole theory of language based on the reed flute
> (*ney*). Beneath everything we say, and within each note of the reed
> flute, lies a nostalgia for the reed bed. Language and music are
> possible only because we're empty, hollow, and separated from
> the source. All language is a longing for home. Why is there not a
> second tonality, he muses, a note in praise of the craftsman's skill,
> which fashioned the bare cylinder into a *ney*, the intricate human
> form with its nine holes?[31]

Rumi weaves from this simple imagery a sophisticated understanding of human existence and the nature of language, the origins of longing and desire, and ways melancholy and joy mingle as we recognize our
situation. Far from mistrusting those who use language and seeking to
limit their numbers in the community, he views language (in a way that
postmodernists will recognize) as the very ground of identity, as he says
in this prose discourse: "Human beings are discourse. That flowing
moves through you whether you say anything or not. Everything that
happens is filled with pleasure and warmth because of the delight of the
discourse that's always going on."[32]

Like many mystics, Rumi insists that the great world is *inside* of us
as well as outside:

> There is a light seed grain inside.
> You fill it with yourself, or it dies.
>
> I'm caught in this curling energy! Your hair!
>
> Whoever's calm and sensible is insane![33]

Rumi resists sectarian identification as persistently as Yoder insists
on it; his poems allude freely and sympathetically to Moses, Jesus, Mo-
hammed, and many other religious figures. "Only Breath" outlines a
sense of identity and location quite different from Yoder:

Not Christian or Jew or Muslim, not Hindu,
Buddhist, Sufi, or zen.

Not any religion or cultural system.
I am not from the East or the West,

not out of the ocean or up from the ground,
not natural or ethereal, not composed of elements at all.

I do not exist, am not an entity of this world or next,
did not descend from Adam and Eve or any

origin story. My place is placeless, a trace
of the traceless. Neither body or soul.

I belong to the beloved, have seen the two
worlds as one and that one call to and know,

first, last, outer, inner, only that
breath breathing human being.[34]

The difference of tone and stance between "I belong to the beloved"
and "The rebellious but already (in principle) defeated cosmos is being
brought to its knees by the Lamb" suggests why I find Rumi such a necessary supplement to Yoder. As much as I love the particularity of the
Anabaptist narrative, so much else seems equally lovely and sound; must
it all be dismissed or subsumed? Rumi's embrace of multiplicity, experience, and wonder means that his claims take an entirely different form,
sometimes questioning even their own relation to language: "Thoughts
take form with words, / but this daylight is beyond and before / thinking
and imagining," he writes. "The rest of this poem is too blurry / for
them to read."[35]

Still, Rumi's awareness of the limits of knowing dovetails in unexpected ways with Yoder. This passage on the apparent discontinuities
and transformation of the natural world fits quite neatly with Yoder's argument that "being in charge" is not necessary or appropriate:

A branch of blossoms does not look like seed.
A man does not resemble semen. Jesus came

from Gabriel's breath, but he is not in that form.
The grape doesn't look like the vine.
Loving actions are the seed of something
completely different, a living-place.
No origin is like where it leads to.
We can't know where our pain is from.
We don't know all that we've done.
Perhaps it's best that we don't.
Nevertheless we suffer for it.[36]

Neither the world nor our lives, Rumi suggests, are fully knowable nor predictable; we cannot control the world or make things happen exactly as we wish—a point on which he and Yoder agree. Hope as well as suffering lies in the recognition that what we do may be transformative in some completely unexpected way, as vines produce grapes, as the blossom produces seed, as egg and semen produce a new human being.

In the conclusion of *Body Politics*, Yoder insists again that "Sacraments" are "human actions in which God acts."[37] Those he has mentioned, he repeats, are all quite everyday human practices, with nothing of the mystical about them. He does note, very briefly, that there also exists "another set of terms" like "prayer, meditation, counseling, devotional practices, and spiritual direction" (a curiously assorted list) and says brusquely "These activities are like the ones we have been studying here, in that they make the Christian life a matter of direct attention and intention. Such disciplines certainly will support and be supported by the 'five practices'; they differ in their interpersonal, even institutional concreteness."[38]

This passage raises many questions, but it ends here, quite abruptly. By "intention," Yoder clearly means something opposed to mystery, desire, emotion, and the like. But does he means simply to oppose religious mystification because it allows us to rationalize inaction (or bad action), or to dismiss everything except concrete practice as mere "mysticism"?

Whatever the answer to that question, reading Yoder and Rumi together made me think of the famous literary/religious conversation in Dostoyevsky's *Brothers Karamozov*, often excerpted under the title "The Grand Inquisitor." Nearly all of this dialogue is in fact a monologue by the inquisitor, who has found Jesus himself in his harsh care. The inquisitor accuses Jesus of offering human beings more freedom than they can cope with:

> You came to them with words that were unfamiliar, vague, and indefinite; You offered them something that was quite beyond them; it even looked as if You didn't love them. . . . Instead of ridding men of their freedom, You increased their freedom, and You imposed everlasting torment on man's soul. You wanted to gain man's love so that he would follow You of his own free will, fascinated and captivated by You. In place of the clear and rigid ancient law, You made man decide about good and evil for himself, with no other guidance than your example.[39]

What people really need, the Inquisitor claims, are "miracle, mystery, and authority," and Jesus rejected them all when he refused to free himself from the cross. Jesus has no verbal response to any of these charges; only, after hearing them all carefully,

> He suddenly goes over to the old man and kisses him gently on his old, bloodless lips. And that is His only answer. The old man is startled and shudders. The corners of his lips seem to quiver slightly. He walks to the door, opens it, and says to Him, "Go now, and do not come back . . . ever. You must never, never come again!" And he lets the prisoner out into the dark streets of the city. The prisoner leaves.[40]

Now Yoder is no Inquisitor, and Rumi left behind many thousands of words. Certainly Yoder's project is unlike that of the Inquisitor's insistence on ruling the weak masses through "miracle, mystery, and authority." Indeed, Yoder seems at times ready to dispense with miracle and mystery altogether, ready to make obedience to key passages of the New Testament the sole authority, and cast all else to the wayside. Still, however benevolent Yoder's Rule may be compared to the Inquisitor's, there seems a certain distant but real affinity between Yoder's effort to bring all the untidiness of human existence under the authority of a precisely defined, highly intellectual conception of the Rule of God, and the Inquisitor's more brutal edifice.

I love the gentle gesture of Jesus' kiss in this story, and I feel sure Rumi would have loved it as well. The kiss makes the Inquisitor's grand structure of order collapse into dust. In it is recognition that love is central but that it cannot be commanded or enforced; that besides the ostentatious miracles of the Inquisitor's violent imagination (the same sort of miraculous triumphs-through-violence that clot our national imagination) there are other kinds of miracles entirely, including the sort that transform the everyday water of experience into the wine of human kinship. It is a reminder of the mystery of forgiveness, of grace, of our fallen and lost condition and the strange, persistent hope that we may be restored one day to full communion with the blessed mud of the riverbed. And it is a reminder that while language is the best we have, it is neither a transparent nor a complete means of communication; God dances and shines and hides beyond all our words, until that great day when we see face to face.

> Inside the Kaaba
> it doesn't matter which direction you point
> your prayer rug!
> 			The ocean diver doesn't need snowshoes!
> The love-religion has no code or doctrine.
> 				Only God.
> So the ruby has nothing engraved on it!
> It doesn't need markings.[41]

Notes

1. John Howard Yoder, "On Not Being in Charge," *War and Its Discontents: Pacifism and Quietism in the Abrahamic Traditions*, ed. J. Patout Burns (Washington: Georgetown University Press, 1996), 83.

2. John Howard Yoder, *The Priestly Kingdom* (Notre Dame: University of Notre Dame Press, 1984), 32-3.

3. Yoder, *Priestly Kingdom*, 33.

4. Chris K. Huebner, *A Precarious Peace: Yoderian Explorations on Theology, Knowledge, and Identity* (Scottdale, Pa.: Herald Press, 2006), 22. In a foreword to this book, Stanley Hauerwas (for many years the main disseminator of Yoder's work to the larger Christian theological community) says that, as is true of Wittgenstein, we find after reading Yoder that "we cannot help but see the world differently" (9). I cannot help but think of Rilke's "Archaic Torso of Apollo," which ends with a similar pronouncement: "You must change your life."

5. Peter Dula and Chris K. Huebner, *The New Yoder* (Cambridge, UK: Lutterworth, 2011), xiv.

6. Qtd. in Peter C. Blum, "Foucault, Genealogy, Anabaptism: Confessions of an Errant Postmodernist," *The New Yoder*, 96.

7. Blum, 98.

8. Yoder, *The Priestly Kingdom*, 59.

9. Yoder, *The Priestly Kingdom*, 61.

10. Romand Coles, "The Wild Patience of John Howard Yoder: 'Outsiders' and the 'Otherness of the Church,'" *The New Yoder*, 217.

11. Coles, 232.

12. I still remember my teacher Mary Oyer telling the class about the old names for half-notes, quarter-notes, etc.: semi-quaver, demi-semi-quaver, hemi-demi-semi-quaver....

13. Yoder, *The Priestly Kingdom*, 11.

14. Lao Tzu, *Tao Te Ching*, trans. Stephen Mitchell (New York: Harper Perennial, 1992). http://academic.brooklyn.cuny.edu/core9/phalsall/texts/taote-v3.html#29. 31 May 2012.

15. Yoder, *The Priestly Kingdom*, 53-4.

16. In the typescript of a presentation from which "But We Do See Jesus" evolved, Yoder puts things even more strongly:

When the early witnesses make Messiah Lord of the cosmos, they reclaim what can be reclaimed of the original creation vision, precisely by denying that there exists an autonomous creaturely world needing to be served *in its own terms*. They confess instead that the claim of the cosmos to autonomy is its rebelliousness, and that its subordination to the Lord Yahweh has begun with the kenosis of the incarnation, with the cross, and moved forward with the resurrection and the ascension. ("Postscript" to John Howard Yoder, "That Household We Are," Typescript of presentation at Bluffton Conference, 1980, p. 8.)

17. Matthew Fox, *Original Blessing* (New York: Tarcher/Putnam, 1983, 2000), 69.

18. Fox, *Original Blessing*, 75. His account of the "loss of the cosmos" has striking parallels with Yoder's discussion of the "Constantinian shift" in which Christianity went from a pacifist, minority sect to a "universal" church that embraced both empire and violence.

19. Yoder, *The Priestly Kingdom*, 62.

20. Yoder, *The Priestly Kingdom*, 62.

21. Presumptuously, I might suggest that raising such questions about Yoder's rhetoric is one useful function of the *didaskalos*. I would love to ask him such questions in person.

22. David Abram, *The Spell of the Sensuous: Perception and Language in a More-Than-Human World* (New York: Vintage, 1977), 91.

23. Robert Pinsky, *The Situation of Poetry: Contemporary Poetry and Its Traditions* (Princeton: Princeton University Press, 1976).

24. David Abram, *The Spell of the Sensuous: Perception and Language in a More-Than-Human World* (New York: Vintage, 1977), 80.

25. John Keats, "Ode to a Nightingale," *The Oxford Book of English Verse*, ed. Arthur Quiller-Couch (1919). http://www.bartleby.com/101/624.html. 31 May 2012.

26. Abram, *The Spell*, 263, 264.

27. John Howard Yoder, "Armaments and Eschatology," *Studies in Christian Ethics* 1.1 (1988): 51.

28. Yoder, "Armaments," 58.

29. Arthur Howe, "The Arc of the Universe Is Long But It Bends Toward Justice," *Slate* (Jan. 9, 2009). http://open.salon.com/blog/arthur_howe/2009/01/18/the_arc_of_the_universe_is_long_but_it_bends_towards_justice. 31 May 2012.

30. Jelaluddin Rumi, *The Essential Rumi*, trans. Coleman Barks (New York: HarperSanFrancisco, 1995), 17.

31. Rumi, 17.

32. Rumi, 76.

33. Rumi, 16.

34. Rumi, 32.

35. Rumi, 41-2.

36. Rumi, 60.

37. Yoder, *Body Politics*, 71.

38. Yoder, *Body Politics*, 73.

39. Fyodor Dostoyevsky, *The Brothers Karamazov*, trans. Andrew R. MacAndrew (New York: Bantam, 1970), 307.

40. Dostoyevsky, 316.

41. Rumi, 167.

TWELVE

THE FARM BOY'S THOUGHTS TURN TOWARD BEAUTY

"The soul's natural inclination to love beauty is the trap God most frequently uses to win it and open it to the breath from on high."
—Simone Weil[1]

It is no secret among Mennonites that for a long time we have been suspicious about beauty, sought to domesticate and tame it, to manage it, if not to deny and thwart altogether its wilder and more dangerous forms. For a long time and for various reasons, my people sought almost to do without beauty, or to seek it only in its plainest, simplest manifestations—the quilt, the ornamented texts called Fraktur, the bedframe or dresser of sturdy wood, practical as well as pleasing to the eye.

This austerity made for difficulties, because beauty is the province and the respite and the rescue of the soul. I have come to think, with others, that beauty is the call of the world to the soul, a faithful and authentic call. Its presence in our lives is not a luxury nor a sin, but something as essential as food, something that teaches and enlarges the soul and enables it to live and to work and to rejoice in this world.

The hunger for beauty led me to the desire to make beautiful things out of words, and to send them out from shore like paper boats bearing lit candles. I wanted them to mean something, hoped they would be of some use, but I could never remember what they meant or should mean for very long, and that became almost secondary, just as we experience a good meal not for its nutritional value but for the pleasures of taste and consumption, especially in the company of others we cherish. Even sending poems into the world is often less satisfying, subjectively, than the act of making them—an unsettling thing to admit.

"He's been trying to surrender to the real things but can't find the right flag," I wrote in a poem long ago, not knowing exactly what I meant. "I'll let you be in my dream if I can be in your dream," sang Bob Dylan, and "I accept chaos. I am not sure whether it accepts me."

Yes, this desire for beauty is romantic and individualistic, in its immediate impulse. So are the maple trees, in some of their moods, and among their other layers of function. Yet as the yearning for beauty leans us toward leafy things, and flowering things, and all those things (some of them human beings) whose orders are harmonious and lovely, to enjoy and praise the beautiful things of this world is in the end an act of solidarity and generosity.

"Romantic" is not a pejorative, as far as I am concerned. Blake, Keats, and Whitman are surely better spiritual guides than many we might name. The poets have many things to say about beauty, many of them beautiful, some of them perhaps even true. They link beauty over and over to other great themes and realities, both light and dark. "Beauty is truth, truth beauty," Keats famously has his Grecian urn say; his long poem "Endymion" begins with a slightly different, perhaps more plausible claim: "A thing of beauty is a joy forever." "Beauty is the sole legitimate province of the poem," said E. A. Poe, that brilliant crackpot, in his essay "The Philosophy of Composition." In the same essay he wrote that the death of a beautiful woman is "unquestionably the most poetical topic in the world"—for in this beauty and melancholy are linked. Whitman's great shore ode "Out of the Cradle Endlessly Rocking" makes the same equation in a less clinical fashion; his young self listens to the shore-bird whistling mournfully for its lost mate, then hears the "low and delicious word" of death whispered by the breaking waves, and awakens to a sense of vocation: "Now in a moment I know what I am for."

Early in the twentieth century, Wallace Stevens returned to the theme in "Sunday Morning": "Death is the mother of beauty." "All the new thinking is about loss," writes Robert Hass a half-century later in "Meditation at Lagunitas." "In this it resembles all the old thinking." And Dean Young's heart-breakingly beautiful "Rothko's Yellow" brings the lament for the lost beloved (in this poem she is "only" estranged, not dead, which may be even worse for the poet) into the current idiom. "What I don't understand is the beauty," the poem opens:

Sometimes it's horrible, the things said
outright. But nothing explains the beauty,
not weeping and shivering on that stone bench,
not kneeling by the basement drain.
Not remembering otherwise, that scarf she wore,
the early snow, her opening the door
in the bathing light. She must have tried
and tried. What I don't understand is the beauty.[2]

Beauty is inseparable from desire, absence, and incompletion, as well as from joy and truth. It is not to be understood. And it seems irrevocably intertwined as well with the melancholy that seems a permanent feature of human life. Rubem Alves suggests that this meeting of beauty and sadness results from the essential isolation of the artist, who "is surrounded by a great solitude. This is why beauty is always mixed with sadness":

[I]f one wants the supreme joy of beauty, one must be prepared to cry. Sadness is not an intruder in beauty's domains. It is rather the air without which it dies. Artists are always sad. [. . .] Beauty is sad because beauty is longing. The soul returns to one's lost home. And the return to the 'no longer there' is always painful. The sunset, the blue skies, the sonata: they are there, but they are not our possession. Elusive like the sunset, the blue skies, the sonata, beauty touches us and quickly goes leaving only nostalgia in its place. Like God. . . .[3]

Simone Weil, though hardly a romantic, was another remarkable, iconoclastic outsider with some startling ideas about beauty. In her essay "Love of the Order of the World," she argues for a love of the world (and of beauty) which seems quite at odds with the hostility toward the human order, and even the natural world, too often found in Anabaptist and other Christian polemics: "By loving the order of the world we imitate the divine love which created this universe of which we are a part."[4]

This love, Weil says, finds issue in praise for the beauty of things, although "the beauty of the world is almost absent from the Christian tradition. This is strange. It leaves a terrible gap. How can Christianity call itself catholic if the universe itself is left out?"[5] Such attention to the beauty of the created order is, if not entirely missing, rarely emphasized in the sort of theology that is preoccupied with resisting and lamenting "the world" as the fallen habitation of the ungodly. And because it is love of beauty that yields inwardness, that is often missing too, as well as patience *in* the world. Even more often, perhaps, genuine inwardness, which is always a challenge to the established order and often revolutionary, gets confused with a kind of piety that is not only conservative but reactionary. Put another way, the inwardness that believes in a domesticated, intelligible God often gets confused with the genuine, wild sort—which is always aware of how little we really know about God.

Perhaps, Weil suggests, God plants beauty in the world to "trap" souls, to open them to grace: "The soul's natural inclination to love beauty is the trap God most frequently uses to win it and open it to the breath from on high." This beauty is, by its nature, distinct, amoral, not to be understood but only beheld, and it is thus free, wonder-ful, and open to the sort of contemplation that need not seek closure or direct purpose: "It is because absence of any finality or intention is the essence of the beauty of the world that Christ told us to behold the rain and the light of the sun, as they fall without discrimination upon the just and the unjust."[6]

Here's something I wrote long ago, at the end of a poem musing on beauty and poetry:

> In one bank's shadow, trees and sky
> and clouds laid their colors down
> full and gentle on water only a crawdad
> could love. The man thought: I am sad
> because I meant to write today, and now
> I have. Because of the cats. Because
> beauty is not truth, or justice, or love.
> Because it is something to love.[7]

I had not read Weil's essay then, but was groping after something very much like what she said here: "It is because it can be loved by us, it is because it is beautiful, that the universe is a country. It is our only country here below."[8]

One metaphor, then: beauty is a country that we may inhabit. But this takes us only so far. What do we *do* with it, and what does beauty *allow* us to do? "Beauty is full of love," Rubem Alves suggests, "but void of power. The artist's hands are empty. [. . .] The poem is a wingless arrow which wants to fly":

> Every poem is an incantation, a prayer, an invocation of power. The poet waits for the One who will have beauty in his heart and power in his hands: gracious power . . . The biblical tradition calls him by the name of Messiah. The Messiah is the symbol for this miraculous event: the ephemeral coincident between love and power: when the Lion, as in Zarathustra's parable, makes room for the Child, and disappears. Ephemeral because it is grace. It cannot be institutionalized as a party, a state, a church. It takes on visible form as a people.[9]

This is the problem, or one of the problems, for Mennonites and any other people who seek to carry their communal memory and history forward through time: institutions, by their nature, cannot capture this grace, the merger of love and power that happens only in ephemeral moments. How to form a "people" rather than a church or a party? We can only remember, and point forward, and try to endure in the times between, and seek to create the conditions where the fantastic feast will once again occur, where the arrow will find the bow. In the meantime, even would-be mystics like me must decide how to live, day by day, where to spend my petty and distractable attention, my feeble energy.

Alves ends his chapter on "Beauty and Politics" with a description of "the Warrior" as one born of visions of beauty, seeing darkness and pain with one eye, but with the other light and joy. "The warrior is a body who has heard the voice of the poet, has been possessed by beauty, and flies like the arrow into the future by virtue of the bow of power."[10] The martyrs are the closest thing to Anabaptist warriors: our images of those possessed by something great enough to lead them into death, without defense except for their words and the offering of their bodies. Such bravery, such zeal—the vision that had seized them must have been very beautiful.

Today disagreements over the right time for baptism and the doctrine of transubstantiation rarely lead to martyrdom, partly because the freedom of conscience and religion the martyrs struggled for has won at least modest acceptance in the parts of the world we like to consider enlightened. But when obedience to the ruling powers is at stake, the danger is still real. Alves is right, surely, that it was power they sought, even in their odd, seemingly perverse refusal to fight, even if it was only the power to opt out, to say "Not me" when the prince came around to sign up his next army.

But must this power be merely worldly, merely practical? Is beauty void of power, and the love of beauty then merely for the idle and the privileged? This common bit of Anabaptist folk wisdom especially troubles artists and poets: the notion that ethics is primary, that "following Jesus" means, above all, doing the right things and not doing the wrong ones, that the pursuit of beauty is frivolous at best and a harmful distraction at worst. The familiar dualisms follow: soul and body, sacred and profane, on and on.

Yet surely the love of beauty can and does lead to action—in fact, Alves specifically resists the conventional view that puts the ethical over the aesthetic, Agape against Eros.

> But is not the purpose of Agape the restoration of Eros, that the whole universe be loved *because of its beauty* and not *despite its ugliness?* The artist loves the formless stone because his eyes see the Pieta which lies dormant inside it. When Agape finishes his work, Eros explodes, triumphant. The ethical is not an end; it is only a means. The goal of all heroic struggles for the creation of a just and free world is the opening of spaces for the blossoming of the garden.[11]

Here Alves' thought closes strikingly on Grace Jantzen's work toward a theology of "natality," based on life rather than death, which I discussed at some length in Chapter 10. Jantzen's ideas on pursuing the beloved community rather than straining over questions of belief and dogmatics are worth another look in this context:

> The central contention of this book has been that it is urgently necessary for feminists [and everyone else, I would add] to work toward a new religious symbolic focused on natality and flourishing rather than on death, a symbolic which will lovingly enable natals, women and men, to become subjects, and the earth on which we live to bloom, to be 'faithful to the process of the divine which passes through' us and through the earth itself. . . . Divin-

ity in the face of natals is a horizon of becoming, a process of divinity ever new, just as natality is the possibility of new beginnings. And it can never be immune from response to suffering in the face of the natals and of the earth.[12]

The love of the beauty of the created order is the beginning of wisdom—could it be? Is the beginning of this revolutionary aesthetics and ethics in deeper attention to the Resurrection, and to the created world that we inhabit in its aftermath? Late in *Becoming Divine,* Jantzen quotes Luce Irigaray, who argues that beauty overcomes the dualism of the real and the ideal, the immanent and the transcendent: "The person would have attained what I shall call a *sensible transcendental,* the material texture of beauty. . . . beauty itself is seen as that which confounds the opposition between immanence and transcendence. As an always already sensible horizon on the basis of which everything would appear."[13]

Jantzen notes that her vision of "natality" requires not assent to a particular set of abstract beliefs nor the working out of theological issues, but a focus on bringing the beloved community into being:

> The issue is not so much "how can a good God permit evil" as it is "how are the resources of religion, particularly Christendom, used by those who inflict evil on others?" and "what does the face of the Other require of me, and how can I best respond for love of the world?"[14]

More lyrically, Alves suggests that

> The Christian churches have become notable for the beauty of their aesthetics of death. And the believers sing: the body must be denied for the soul to live. But the prophet loves life. In his soul there lives a child. And, as we know, children don't like burials. They would rather play in the gardens.[15]

"Beauty will save the world," reads a t-shirt I picked up recently. The quote is attributed to Dostoyevsky, but he actually offers it in a rather filtered, mediated way, attributed to the hero/fool Prince Myshkin, the central character of his novel *The Idiot,* by a more skeptical character:

> Is it true, prince, that you once declared that 'beauty would save the world'? Great Heaven! The prince says that beauty saves the world! And I declare that he only has such playful ideas because he's in love! Gentlemen, the prince is in love. I guessed it the mo-

ment he came in. Don't blush, prince; you make me sorry for you. What beauty saves the world? Colia told me that you are a zealous Christian; is it so[16]

As Dostoyevsky knew well, the skeptics will always be with us, demanding order and reason above all, scoffing at love, beauty, human solidarity, and the sort of worship that acknowledges where our knowledge grays out into mystery. His prince tries to love unreservedly and wholly, but is defeated by a corrupt and worldly society. So often this has been the case—for what does "worldly" society (see, I have slipped into this usage myself) care for the world? The drunken soldier, if he notices the beauty of the garden at all, sees it only as a site for plunder and carousing. So perhaps the work of the artist, having been opened to the beauty of the world, having felt the presence of the divine within and without, is to draw others into that presence, through whatever craft, guile and art may suffice.

Not only artists recognize this beauty and the presence of God in the world, of course. A number of years ago, an uncle read me a letter my grandfather wrote to him not long before his death. I tried to capture something of the moment my grandfather described in this poem. Only as I drafted this essay, nearly twenty years after writing the poem, did I realize that it is, precisely and entirely, about beauty, melancholy, death, and God.

His Name Was Gerdon and He Ran a Hatchery in Graymont, Illinois

He was alone that day, the letter said,
and Sunday after church he stopped
by a cornfield, the sun warm and the wind
stirring up the crisp blank sounds
that rise when stiff leaves meet.
But those are my words. What my grandfather
wrote to my uncle was nothing so literary
and self-conscious. Once my uncle read
the letter to me, and said he'd send a copy.
He hasn't, though he wrote to say he'd tried,
but it was faint, in pencil, hard to copy.

It was my grandfather's last year, and
the death music ran under the words like
a muddy prairie creek. His heart was bad.
He knew. But he stood there, his hands
in the pockets of his baggy pants, and felt
the hand of God was moving in the wind.
You can really feel him there, he said,
on a hot Sunday in the country, with nothing
for miles but you and the corn and the hot earth.
He said it better than I have, though
I can't remember how. I lived
ten miles away, and saw him every week,
but never knew he had such thoughts.

He died in his sleep, in October.
I came home from college with my hair long,
and didn't cry, and went back. And now
I am settled in Ohio and his letter
is still with my uncle in Bakersfield,
too faint and faded to copy well. And so
I put this down, to claim what I can,
to hoard for some cold day to come
my uncle's hoarse voice reading
the shaky pencil on cheap blue-lined paper.
My uncle's name is Gerdon, too.
And out in the country between us
a road lies between fields, a ditch
on either side, and above it moves
something like a music, like a birth.[17]

Notes

1. Simone Weil, *Waiting for God*, trans. Emma Craufurd (New York: Harper-Collins, 1951, 2001), 103.

2. Dean Young, *Beloved Infidel* (Middletown, Conn.: Wesleyan University Press, 1992), 55. The other poems mentioned can all be easily found through an Internet author/title search.

3. Rubem Alves, *The Poet, The Warrior, the Prophet: The Edward Cadbury Lectures 1990* (London: SCM Press, 1990), 114.

4. Weil, *Waiting for God*, 99. Far from subsuming her will into that of the collective like a good Anabaptist, Weil refused ever to join a church or be baptized, saying

that she belonged on the outside, where she could serve the search for truth with her intellect, which "requires total liberty." Weil accepted that the Church should punish disobedient individuals, even ones such as she, even as she noted the perennial uneasy relations between the collective and the creative individual: "A collective body is the guardian of dogma; and dogma is an object of contemplation for love, faith, and intelligence, three strictly individual faculties. Hence, almost since the beginning, the individual has been ill at ease in Christianity, and this uneasiness has been notably one of the intelligence. This cannot be denied" (34). Weil was also determinedly non-sectarian, insisting on the need to recognize the glimmer of God everywhere: "I came to feel that Plato was a mystic, that all the *Iliad* is bathed in a Christian light, and that Dionysus and Osiris are in a certain sense Christ himself; and my love was therefore redoubled" (28).

5. Weil, *Waiting for God*, 101.

6. Weil, *Waiting for God*, 103;,114.

7. Jeff Gundy, *Inquiries* (Huron, Ohio: Bottom Dog, 1992), 58.

8. Weil, *Waiting for God*, 114.

9. Alves, *The Poet*, 115-6.

10. Alves, *The Poet*, 120.

11. Alves, *The Poet*, 128.

12. Grace Jantzen, *Becoming Divine: Toward a Feminist Philosophy of Religion* (Bloomington, Ind.: Indiana University Press, 1997), 254.

13. Jantzen, *Becoming Divine*, 272.

14. Jantzen, *Becoming Divine*, 264.

15. Alves, *The Poet*, 137.

16. Fyodor Dostoyevsky, *The Idiot*, trans. Eva Martin (Project Gutenberg, 2012), part III chapter 5. http://www.gutenberg.org/files/2638/2638-h/2638-h.htm. 17 July 2010. Cf. Alves, who quotes Berdyaev here: "Beauty has its own dialectics, and Dostoievski has something to say about it. He thought that beauty would save the world. But he also says: 'Beauty is not only a terrible but a mysterious thing. Here the devil struggles with God, and the battlefield is the human heart.' The Devil wants to use beauty for his own end" (137).

17. Jeff Gundy, *Flatlands* (Cleveland: CSU Poetry Center, 1995), 74-5.

THIRTEEN

THE BAPTISM IN DARK WATER: APOPHASIS AND MYSTERY

Let us sing together. Knowing? Nothing we know.
From hidden sea we came, to unknown sea we go.
—Antonio Machado, "Proverbs and Songs"[1]

To point out how little we know, and call for singing instead, is hardly a new move. The trope of limits was famously expressed in Pascal's image of the "two infinities" of the very large and the very small: "For, in fact, what is man in nature? A Nothing in comparison with the Infinite, an All in comparison with the Nothing, a mean between nothing and everything. . . . equally incapable of seeing the Nothing from which he was made, and the Infinite in which he is swallowed up."[2] What Chekhov said of illness—"When a disease has many treatments, one can be sure there is no cure"—surely applies to what we know of ultimate things and the ultimate being as well. If we really *knew,* there would be no need for so much talk. The claims from certain circles that "just believing" in Jesus is enough perhaps *ought* to satisfy those of us doomed to keep asking the old questions, but those claims ring hollow while those who offer them, like all the rest of us, feel compelled to continually produce new explanations, embroideries, commentaries, and midrashes on just what it all means.

The situation is difficult but exhilarating as well. Just as language emerges, constantly and astonishingly, from silence, art's roots are in the fertile ground of unknowing. Poems, stories, paintings, and all the rest emerge out of chaos and old night not only by will but by chance, supposition, and (yes) whatever we mean when we say "imagination." Throughout this book, I have been exploring the edges and boundaries where knowledge blurs into faith, conjecture, and doubt—always with the faith that honest exploration is of more value in the end than reaching too soon for illusory certainties, and that the art that results from such explorations, while itself hardly final, has much to offer even in its uncertainties.

Over several years of work on this project, I have found myself returning repeatedly, even obsessively, to particular authors and texts. One is James Baldwin's elegant but hardly simple maxim: "Art lays bare the questions that have been concealed by the answers." Another is Donald Barthelme's brilliant essay "Not-Knowing," with its playfully serious account of a writer proceeding by inventing characters, plot details, and incidents as he goes. "Writing is a process of dealing with not-knowing, a forcing of what and how," Barthelme proclaims. "Art is not difficult because it wishes to be difficult, rather because it wishes to be art."[3]

One of these "difficulties" involves the renewal and refreshing of perception and experience, especially our experience of those things that through habit and routine have become dull, ordinary, predictable. As the literary critic Viktor Shklovsky pointed out in a well-known formulation, art often proceeds through "defamiliarization," or "making strange" those things and occasions that we have become so familiar with that we no longer perceive them with freshness or immediacy:

> The purpose of art is to impart the sensation of things as they are perceived and not as they are known. The technique of art is to make objects 'unfamiliar,' to make forms difficult to increase the difficulty and length of perception because the process of perception is an aesthetic end in itself and must be prolonged.[4]

Art, poetry, and theopoetics dwell on this ground of making strange, bringing us back to the uncertainty and oddity of the most familiar things, and within the frightening, liberating awareness that language is always already metaphorical, useful but incomplete, endlessly suggestive but incapable of any absolute or final precision. We must use it—must recognize the gift that it is—but with care and subtlety, recognizing that naming something is not the same as owning it, and that there is always a gap between the name and the named, the signifier and the signified.

The basic mistake of fundamentalisms of all sorts is not so much in their particular truth-claims, harsh and bizarre as those may be. It is in trusting too much not in God but in the capacity of human language and human thought to capture and define God. Such religion (and the same goes, surely, for politics and any system that claims detailed and complete Truth) is inevitably hostile to the imagination, because the imagination is always questioning the received order and seeking further revelation, and fundamentalists believe they have a full revelation already—or at least enough of one to judge those who fail to meet its standards.[5]

The awareness that our knowledge of God remains incomplete is not new to Christian thought, of course. The tradition of "apophatic" or negative theology goes back at least to Tertullian in the second century, who wrote in his *Apologeticus* "That which is infinite is known only to itself," and to Pseudo-Dionysius. Throughout Christian history those with mystical leanings, such as Meister Eckhart and St. John of the Cross, particularly emphasized the *via negative*, the path of un-knowing. Among theologians it has long been common to speak of a God "beyond all discursive knowing," although it has been equally common to circle rather quickly back toward radical confidence in just what God meant for human affairs and, especially, who God meant to be in charge of worldly power structures.

A full account of the disputes and positions of these worthy clerics is not my purpose here, but it may be illustrative to cite one early dispute, that between Barlaam of Calabria and St. Gregory of Nyssa in the fourth century. According to M. C. Steenburg (who takes Gregory's side in the dispute), "Barlaam's model seems to have been almost wholly negative—to the point of bordering on a certain agnosticism. God is transcendent, he taught, and thus to ascend to purer knowledge we must espouse negative theology and transcend our own perceptive reason; yet ultimately the Transcendent cannot be truly known, even with apophaticism used to its utmost."[6] Gregory, on the other hand, believed that people could actually *know* God, though only through grace: "Thus Gregory viewed natural knowledge, in all its philosophical forms, as a tool leading to something greater, yet every bit as real as that very knowledge: the divine grace which brings about *union,* the true source of contemplative knowing."[7]

For this Gregory, then, apophasis was merely a through-a-glass-darkly phase of life in this world, to be transcended sooner or later. Nearly a millennium later, another Gregory (of Palamas) held out for a fuller sense of mystery, according to David K. Goodin:

> Orthodoxy, on the other hand, has always upheld the belief that the cataphatic can only lead so far. While knowledge can add profound reverence to deepen belief through contemplation of created reality, the uncreated God is always met in the darkness of apophasis (negative theognosis). Gregory Palamas (1296-1359) states it this way, "for to God pertains both incomprehensibility and comprehensibility, though He Himself is one. The same God is incomprehensible in His essence, but is comprehensible from what He creates according to His divine energies" (The Philokalia IV, p. 384). The cataphatic and apophatic form a single antinomic whole; mere language shall always remain inadequate to encapsulate the entirety of this ineffable mystery.[8]

Even while allowing for a God who is "incomprehensible in His essence," however, Gregory offers a neatly rationalized domestication of the mystery, a dualistic division of the essence and evidence that drains the mystery of its energy and force by putting it into a tidy frame. "Mere language shall always remain inadequate," he allows, but even this language seems quite confident that it knows a great deal, even about the evidence of "divine energies" that we see in the creation.

Of late the apophatic tradition has drawn renewed interest in relation to postmodern and deconstructive interrogations of the nature of knowledge, including at least two anthologies and more books.[9] Melvin Laird describes this tradition, colorfully, as speaking of a God who is not only "beyond all discursive knowing" but also "beyond the dreaded clench of ontotheological fists." "The impression that God is situated at the end of a ratiocinative search," Laird argues, "is generated by the discursive mind and, according to Evagrius, marks the victory of the demons' attempts to distract the contemplative from the open space of pure prayer."[10]

My concern here is for an apophatic approach through poetry rather than contemplation or theologizing, but clearly these have many parallels. As contemplation emphasizes experience over discourse and intuition over reason, the poetry that interests me most takes place in a discursive space in which symbols remain symbols and metaphor remain metaphor, the tension between tenor and vehicle does not collapse into identity, and the relations between the narrative and detail of the poem and the order of things remain inherently fluid and not fully determinate.

This approach does not mean abandoning meaning and purpose altogether—but it does mean grasping such things less tightly, with a looser sense of what is accomplished through direct intention and what sort of knowledge is directly accessible to the intellect. Poet William Stafford mused in an interview on the compass as a useful image of knowledge and its limits:

> You know, the strange thing, I was thinking about a compass. Security of character would be like a compass, you know? Other people may say that this way is north, or this way might be north. But the compass just says—north. That's what we count on. [. . .]
>
> I can remember taking a compass to class, when I was teaching. And I'd put it on the desk and get the kids to look at it, and sort of spin it around, and it would go north. And I would say, "There's something in this room that we're not aware of, that the compass knows. We're surrounded by these things. Why should we assume that our senses are bringing us what's happening?"[11]

The compass offers information not available to our ordinary senses, but it doesn't make demands. If you know which way is north, you can go wherever you need to go—but the decision is still yours: "The compass just says—north." Poetry similarly offers information and guidance that is authoritative but not authoritarian.

Other useful images may be found in Gabriel Garcia Lorca's famous essay on the *Duende*. He suggests that its "black sounds" are "the mystery, the roots that probe through the mire that we all know of, and do not understand, but which furnishes us with whatever is sustaining in art." The Muse and the Angel have their place in art, Lorca believes, but the *Duende* is essential as well, and its place is radically different, as he memorably suggests in his final paragraphs:

> The Muse keeps silent; she may wear the tunic of little folds, or great cow-eyes gazing toward Pompeii, or the monstrous, four-featured nose with which her great painter, Picasso, has painted

her. The Angel may be stirring the hair of Antonello da Messina, the tunic of Lippi, and the violin of Masolino or Rousseau.

But the *Duende*—where is the *Duende*? Through the empty arch enters a mental air blowing insistently over the heads of the dead, seeking new landscapes and unfamiliar accents; an air bearing the odor of child's spittle, crushed grass, and the veil of Medusa announcing the unending baptism of all newly created things.[12]

The *Duende* is connected to death, to things spat out and crushed, yet also to baptism and creation. It springs from the deep mud of Rumi's reed-bed, perhaps. And it dwells in those moments when beauty and sorrow, joy and pain seem irretrievably mingled. Consider this recent poem by Mary Oliver, "At the Pond." The poem describes a gaggle of young geese, five of which grow "heavy of chest and / bold of wing" while the sixth fails to thrive:

> And then it was fall.
>
> And this is what I think
>   everything is about:
>   the way
>   I was glad
>
> for those five and two
>   that flew away,
>   and the way I hold in my heart the wingless one
>   that had to stay.[13]

The craft of this poem, its success as art, surely lies in its refusal of the usual explanations, glib or otherwise, about why such things must happen, about the inscrutable ways of God, about the Beautiful Necessity. Five who fly away (plus the parents), Oliver suggests, may really be pretty good, and something to celebrate; yet it is the wingless, doomed one who remains in her heart, and who makes the poem—a new gift of language, inadequate yet sweet in its own way—necessary and itself beautiful. Death and life, mortality and natality, are both held in the same grasp.

Much of Oliver's recent volume *Evidence,* as the title suggests, investigates traces of God in the natural world. Natural theology has a long history, of course, as practiced both by churchmen and poets. But Oliver's approach is fresh, and although through most of her long career she has shied away from using Christian terms directly, she is freer with that language now. "Spring" begins with a claim that might almost come from Cotton Mather or Jonathan Edwards, fellow New Englanders, but Oliver has a different, less dogmatic sort of instruction in mind; her thoughts turn quickly to her love of the world, and a quick catalog of grass, leaves, sun, and rushes. And her mysterious teacher, though he owns an "incomparable voice," does not speak, but suddenly leaves the room:

> and I follow,
> obedient and happy.
>
> Of course I am thinking
> the Lord was once young
> and will never be old.
>
> And who else could this be, who goes off
> down the green path,
> carrying his sandals, and singing?[14]

Oliver is acutely aware that poems like this can easily tip the merely maudlin or the pathetic fallacy of attributing human emotions to the natural world. Yet she also constantly tests that boundary, eager to find as much "evidence" as she can. The long poem "At the River Clarion," an extended observation and meditation on the nature of God, begins with the admission "I don't know who God is exactly." It then proceeds to describe an afternoon at the river, listening to the water striking the stone until

> slowly, very slowly, it became clear to me
> what they were saying.
> Said the river: I am part of holiness.
> And I too, said the stone. And I too, whispered
> the moss beneath the water.[15]

This holiness is not all "butter and good luck," Oliver adds quickly; God must also be "the tick that killed my wonderful dog Luke." He is everything, she insists, offering a Whitmanian catalog that includes forests, deserts, dying ice caps, Robert Motherwell and "the many desperate hands, cleaning and preparing their weapons."[16] The daily life continues, she suggests, and it is right that we give thanks even within its losses and our doubts and hesitations. The poem ends with a lyrical invocation of the river as an image of holiness and persistence, an image perhaps of a God who is inscrutable yet present:

> And still, pressed deep into my mind, the river
> keeps coming, touching me, passing by on its
> long journey, its pale, infallible voice
> singing.[17]

We might spend much longer exploring the details of Oliver's intricate natural theopoetics, but must stop with one more brief and lucid passage from "Mysteries, Yes":

> Let me keep my distance, always, from those
> who think they have the answers.
>
> Let me keep company always with those who say
> 'Look!' and laugh in astonishment,
> and bow their heads.[18]

Beauty, Truth, and Truth Claims

I have long brooded on some lines from Wallace Stevens' "On the Road Home": "There are many truths, / but they are not parts of a truth."[19] Shocking, yes? I memorized the verse from the gospel of John, along with everybody else in my Sunday School class: "I am the way, the truth and the life. No man comes to the Father but by me." I learned as well that to be a Christian is to turn away from all the other gods, who are all false gods, who are dangerous because they are false and might be more powerful than we think, who are all really Satan, who used to be an angel but rebelled . . . who said "I myself am hell," which Robert Lowell repeated in his poem "Skunk Hour," in a moment of either ironic confession or narcissistic grandiosity. I could never make all these warnings fit together, somehow, into a single truth.

I learned another verse about truth as well, and when I began teaching at Bluffton College I learned that a slightly condensed version of it was the college motto: "The Truth Makes Free." That still seems pretty good to me, though (as my attraction to the Stevens poem suggests) my sense that there is a single, particular, universal truth that we small and feeble human beings can access and express has been seriously shaken by postmodernism, deconstruction, poetry, and raising three rambunctious boys.

But back to Stevens. Notice how he embeds the most radical claims in the poem, puts them in the voice of a "you" who says something perhaps even more radical:

> You . . . You said,
> 'There are many truths,
> But they are not parts of a truth."
> Then the tree, at night, began to change [. . .]
>
> It was at that time, that the silence was largest
> And longest, the night was roundest,
> The fragrance of the autumn warmest,
> Closest and strongest.[20]

Though the speaker begins by saying "There is no such thing as the truth," the poem does not really attempt to defend or even to explain that claim. The emphasis is all on the *saying*, the speaking of an idea that seems to liberate and enrich experience. It only claims that life *feels* better, more intense and rich, once the speaker and his friend give up on idealistic monism and begin to measure the world by eye, to experience one thing at a time, to pay attention to its beautiful particulars. Against this particularity is set an idolatry associated with "poverty, / Snakes and gold and lice": or, we might say, most of western civilization, including institutional Christianity.

Among Stevens' major ideas was his notion of a "supreme fiction," the construction of an idea that might serve—in the way religion once served—to provide a sense of meaning and belonging in the world. In the late poem "Final Soliloquy of the Interior Paramour" he returns to this idea, suggesting that indeed God and the imagination might "be one":

Here, now, we forget each other and ourselves.
We feel the obscurity of an order, a whole,
A knowledge, that which arranged the rendezvous,

Within its vital boundary, in the mind.
We say God and the imagination are one . . .
How high that highest candle lights the dark.[21]

This is still not exactly "God loves you and has a wonderful plan for your life." But consider how different it is to say "God does not exist" and "God and the imagination are one." Stevens insists on abandoning God as the bearded guy in the sky, but while he can be brutal in his dismissals, he is much less so when he recognizes that some elusive excess, some otherness, refuses to be dismissed, though its precise location and qualities resist definition. Wordsworth referred with grandiose vagueness to "an obscure sense of possible sublimity"; Stevens has intimations that may be even more obscure and austere, couched here, again, in a tentative way, as something spoken for consideration, a product of the imagination rather than an objective Truth.

Unlike the theoretician of theopoetics Stanley Hopper, Gordon Kaufman never to my knowledge quotes Wallace Stevens. Yet as I have discussed in earlier chapters, Kaufman's theology offers a similarly austere and dehumanized version of God, emphasizing that theology is a "human construction" which can go only so far toward clear definition of its unknowable subject. We must beware, he argues in *In Face of Mystery*, what Kant described as "treating our thoughts as things":

taking the content of a symbol . . . to be a proper description or exact representation of a particular reality or being. . . . We reify the symbols "creator" and "lord" and "father" when we take them to mean that God *really is* a creator/lord/father. [. . .]

This religious symbolism has had repressive and oppressive power . . . not so much because of its particular content as because that content was reified: God was taken to be *in actual fact* a kind of creator/lord/father "out there" who really established—consciously willed and deliberately created—the patterns of order governing life here on earth.[22]

I will confess that notions like these still give me a kind of edgy thrill, as though I am treading close to some edge and may be snatched up or thrown down by the Lord Himself at any moment, simply for daring to think so recklessly. Can it be that we must give up on all these comforting metaphors, so deeply engrained into the minds and spirits of those of us who grew up in the church? What will we do without God the Father?

Most Anabaptists and most people of faith, theologians or not, have quite understandably been reluctant to follow Kaufman's austere path. Intellectually, we may be able to imagine God as the "serendipitous creativity" in the universe, but how do we ask Serendipitous Creativity for the favors and comforts, some trivial and others not, for which we pray? It seems unlikely that Serendipitous Creativity will help me catch the stoplights when I'm in a hurry, much less with making sure *my* child gets the job he needs or my aging parents find relief for their pains, no matter how many other children of God need the same job and the same relief. I certainly yearn for the presence of a Great Being who will comfort and protect me and those I love. But in other respects Kaufman's notions come as something of a relief. I have long found difficult to envision a God who has precise and particular opinions about matters such as the size of the ribbons on a woman's prayer covering and whether preaching should be done from a table or behind a pulpit—much less on how well or poorly some well-muscled athlete performs in a particular contest.[23]

Forgive me. I don't mean to mock. Or, if I do, at least I know it's bad of me. Like Dickinson, I have always felt that I was one of the bad ones, one of those God must surely see through. I'm quite willing to entertain the idea that my plain brothers and sisters are the truly faithful ones, that there's something wrong with those of us who can't quit asking questions and heading out over the mountains that border the valley. But here we are, anyway, compelled to keep at it. Who is to say that what drives us to invent, to explore, to imagine is not as deep a communal impulse as that other impulse toward order and conformity?

Rubem Alves, in his marvelous *The Poet, The Warrior, The Prophet*, muses on the strange reversals of poetry and of Pentecost: "Pentecost is madness, non-sense, the breaking of the familiar rules of understanding, the revelation of a knowledge which had remained hidden. Wisdom emerges from foolishness. What we call by the name of 'reality' is 'bewitchment.'" He cites a saying from Hegel that resembles Shklovsky on "making strange": "In Hegel's words, 'what is familiarly known is not really known, for the reason that it is familiar.' Truth appears when the world we familiarly know is subverted, when its etiquette is no longer able to maintain the farce."[24]

Alves sees no real conflict between religion and imagination, because both are means of seeking truth that has been only partly revealed. Neither offers certainty, dogmatics, or the tidy maps of the good teacher: "my reading is a non-reading, my texts, pre-texts: empty word-cages with open doors, with the purpose of creating the void for the Word which cannot be said, but only heard. What matters is not what I say but the words that you hear, coming out of your forgotten depths." "One must be reborn, by the power of the unpredictable Wind, to enter the kingdom. One must become a child again. . . ."[25]

Familiar words, but how often do we drain them of their meaning, demanding that the followers of Jesus be calm, orderly, obedient, and reasonable? The children I know have all of these qualities at times, but rarely any of them for long.

Cartesian rationalism, Alves thinks, gets the nature of things wrong, placing too much value on disembodied rationality and self-awareness, too little on sensation, intuition, and bodily awareness:

> Our bodies dwell in oblivion, like the Sleeping Beauty. We no longer know how to play the tune which is written in our flesh. The reflections, ten thousand, we know. But the depth of the lake is beyond our reason. We learned that we are where we think: "I think, therefore I am." Now, the reversed theme: "Where I think, there I am not."[26]

Anabaptists have been mostly followers of the Light, of Erasmus, of the dream that the Word has been revealed once for all, and that we can now follow Jesus if only our desire to do so is strong and pure enough. Reason, the will, and the Holy Spirit—in what proportions is not exactly clear—must be enough to enable us to surrender to it. So we try to read our sacred books as if their stories are clear, sensible, and straightforward, not filled with wild energies and contradictory demands. *Go get yourself thrown in jail,* the *Martyrs Mirror* whispers, *otherwise you must not really love Jesus like the martyrs did. The one time you do something selfless will get you a horrible, fiery death,* says the story of Dirk Willems, *if you're lucky. If you're a really faithful woman, they'll burn you at the stake for it, and screw your tongue down to keep you quiet as you burn. Your children will search in desolation through your ashes for the tongue screw. And that's how it should be,* says the tale of Anna Joris and her children.[27]

Some Anabaptists continue to enthusiastically recommend these stories to their children, though few can be found seeking martyrdom for themselves. Others regard the stories as merely obsolete, gruesome, or unsettling, but in any case of no further use. They trouble the children and the adults too. They refuse to mesh neatly with any narrative of progress or mutual respect or acceptance of diverse beliefs.[28]

But the martyr stories, like the story of Jesus himself, persist *because* they mean more than can be said about them, because they are echoes of the great mystery. The examples they offer cannot be taken as tidy roadmaps for living, no more than we can read the story of David and Bathsheba and conclude that it is *good* to lust after the comely wife of our neighbor and send her husband off to die in battle so that we can have her for ourselves. Alves argues that "Stories are not windows; they are mirrors. The story of the incarnation is my own story, my forgotten past and my hidden future. Christology is anthropology, Christology is biography. The mystery of God is the mystery of our own bodies." Trying to bring this mystery entirely into the light is a mistake, Alves thinks: love demands darkness, "depth, penetration, something that light is incapable of doing." Real knowledge is more spoken and heard than seen; the Word was born in the mouth, which was and is the place of eating long before speaking, as every child rediscovers:

> The mouth of the "infans" already knows the fundamental metaphysics: reality is not made up of "thought" and "matter" as we have been taught. Reality is made up of "hunger" and of an "obscure object of desire," which will satisfy it. Even before having ever touched the mother's breast, the mouth sucks the void, confident that it exists.[29]

Here, Alves' imagery suddenly resonates with a well-known passage from Simone Weil that I quoted earlier:

> The soul knows for certain only that it is hungry. The important thing is that it announces its hunger by crying. A child does not stop crying if we suggest to it that perhaps there is no such thing as bread. It goes on crying just the same. The danger is not lest the soul should doubt whether there is bread, but lest, by a lie, it should persuade itself that it is not hungry.[30]

Alves, like Weil, finds this language of spiritual hunger, of desire as a physical craving for the right kind of food, a rich and generative metaphor. He speaks of cooking and eating together as sites of ritual that move us back toward the primal satisfaction of mouth suckling breast.

> Pleasure cannot be described. It is not an object for the kind of knowledge which lives in the classroom. The end of epistemology. . . . But when the eyes are closed and unable to see, and the mouth tastes the food, all doubts are gone. "I eat, therefore I am." "Taste and see that the Lord is good" (Psalm 34.8): put the Lord inside your mouth (God is to be eaten!) and you will know how good his/her/its taste is. Again, a poetic violence: one sees through the mouth. . . .[31]

Perhaps, then, our stories need to be *consumed*, not observed and dissected; to be told and pondered, without claims of mastery. Alves offers an extended example of this sort of reading. His meditation on Gabriel Garcia Marquez' short story "The Handsomest Drowned Man in the World" runs through his book, as he describes how the discovery of a dead man transforms the life of a depressed village: "[E]verything would be different from then on." Yes, Esteban is a sort of Christ figure, but not a conventional one; he does not come back to life, he says nothing, his body is merely washes up on the beach, large, beautiful, and compelling contemplation.

Perplexingly, Alves repeatedly returns to this story without ever actually mentioning its title, and it is not listed in his extensive bibliography. Is this as an illustration of the need to resist undue clarity and rational identifications? Were there copyright issues? Or did he just lose track of the story and not manage to look it up? He offers only this explanation, on page 23: "I first read it in one of Gabriel Garcia Marquez' books. But it happened a long time ago . . . I really don't know if the story I tell is the same. Stories, indeed, are never the same, once retold."

It might be fruitful—or frightening—to ponder our stories of Jesus in this context. Surely no narrative in history is so encrusted with human accretions, so difficult to disentangle from the human purposes that have motivated its many versions. Even the efforts to recover the pure, true story are multiple and contradictory. Rather than take on that daunting task once again, then, I will try something more modest in the next chapter: to look again at stories that Anabaptists have been telling for centuries. There, again, I will seek not for clear and definite knowledge but for the shrouded and clouded outlines of stories and histories that (blessedly) can never be brought fully into the clear light of day.

Notes

1. Antonio Machado, *Border of a Dream: Selected Poems*, trans. Willis Barnstone (Port Townsend, Wash.: Copper Canyon, 2004), 277.

2. Blaise Pascal, *Penseés*, trans. W. F. Trotter (New York: Dutton, 1958). http://oregonstate.edu/instruct/phl302/texts/pascal/pensees-contents.html. 26 July 2010. #72.

3. Donald Barthelme, "Not-Knowing," *The Art of the Essay*, ed. Lydia Fakundiny (New York: Houghton Mifflin, 1991), 486, 489.

4. Victor Shklovsky, *Art as Device*, trans. Benjamin Sher (Normal, Ill.: Dalkey Archive Press, 1990), 16.

5. As I labored over this paragraph, a friend sent me this quote: "If it be true that God is a circle whose center is everywhere, the saint goes to the center, the poet and artist to the rings where everything comes round again." W. B. Yeats, *Essays and Introductions* (London & New York: Methuen, 1961), 287.

6. M. C. Steenberg, "Gregory Palamas: Knowledge, Prayer, and Vision," *Monachos.net: Orthodoxy through Patristic, Monastic, and Liturgical Study.* 15 May 1999. http://www.monachos.net/content/patristics/studies-fathers/62. 3 June 2011.

7. Steenburg, n.p.

8. David K. Goodin, "Sinners, Satan and the Insubstantial Substance of Evil: Theodicy within Orthodox Redemptive Economy," *Theandros—An Online Journal of Orthodox Christian Theology and Philosophy* 6.1 (Fall 2008). 3 June 2011.

9. See Harold Coward and Toby Foshay, Eds., *Derrida and Negative Theology* (Albany: SUNY Press, 1992), Chris Boesel and Catherine Keller, Eds., *Apophatic Bodies: Negative Theology, Incarnation, and Relationality* (New York: Fordham University Press, 2010), and John D. Caputo, *The Weakness of God: A Theology of the Event* (Bloomington: Indiana University Press, 2006).

10. Martin Laird, "The 'Open Country Whose Name Is Prayer': Apophasis, Deconstruction, and Contemplative Practice," *Modern Theology* 21.1 (January 2005): 147.

11. Jeff Gundy, "A Certain Courtesy of the Heart: A Conversation with William Stafford," *Artful Dodge* 18/19 (1990), 5.

12. Federico Garcia Lorca, "The Duende: Theory and Divertissement," *Margin: Exploring Magical Realism*, ed. Tamara Kaye Sellman. http://www.angelfire.com/wa2/margin/LorcaDuende.html. 17 July 2010.

13. Mary Oliver, *Evidence* (Boston: Beacon, 2009), 34-5.

14. Oliver, 14-15.

15. Oliver, 51.

16. Oliver, 51, 52.

17. Oliver, 54.

18. Oliver, 62.

19. Wallace Stevens, *The Palm at the End of the Mind: Selected Poems and a Play,* ed. Holly Stevens (New York: Vintage, 1972), 203.

20. Stevens, 203-04.

21. Stevens, 368.

22. Gordon Kaufman, *In Face of Mystery: A Constructive Theology* (Cambridge: Harvard University Press, 2006), 330, 334.

23. Kaufman does insist that Jesus remains the crucial instance of God's presence in this world, and that Christians should follow his teachings and nonviolent example. See especially his *Jesus and Creativity* (Minneapolis: Fortress, 2006), which begins with this comment on John 3:16: "Though [it] may be lovely poetry, whether [it tells] us anything about the real world with which we must come to terms every day may seem dubious. The metaphors get so thick and heavy in this sentence that it is hard to know just what they convey" (ix). His own project, he indicates, will be to "think through and make intelligible for our modern/postmodern time and world the story of Jesus. At many points we will be using quite different language and metaphors and ways of thinking than we find in the traditional texts" (x-xi), Though I regret Kaufman's condescending use of "lovely poetry," even this brief excerpt may suggest why I find his overall project intriguing and attractive.

24. Rubem Alves, *The Poet, The Warrior, The Prophet: The Edward Cadbury Lectures 1990* (London: SCM Press, 1990), 14-15.

25. Alves, 17, 19. Ellipses in original.

26. Alves, 55.

27. As I hope is obvious, these are not direct quotes, but see Van Braght, *Martyrs Mirror.*

28. See Kirsten Beachy, ed., *Tongue Screws and Testimonies: Poems, Stories, and Essays Inspired by the Martyrs Mirror* (Scottdale, Pa.: Herald Press, 2010), for a wide range of views of the martyr tradition. In the next chapter, I will consider a number of these views, and Mennonite martyr stories, in more detail.

29. Alves, *The Poet,* 75, 76, 77.

30. Weil, *Waiting for God,* trans. Emma Craufurd (New York: HarperCollins, 1951, 2001), 162.

31. Alves, *The Poet,* 86. Last ellipsis in text.

FOURTEEN

LOOKING IN THE *MIRROR*

Theology wants to be science, a discourse without interstices...
It wants to have its birds in cages...
Theopoetics *instead,*
empty cages,
words which are uttered out of and before the void.
—Rubem Alves[1]

If there is an Anabaptist Esteban for our time, a single figure who stands as an emblem for the whole community, it is surely Dirk Willems, martyr of Asperen, whose image (even more than his story) has become iconic, both metaphorically and literally.[2] There he is, on the cracked and fragile ice of the pond, turning back to pull the slave-catcher who was pursuing him from the water—only to be recaptured and burned at the stake for his generous gesture.

To me the truly fascinating moment is Dirk's turn to see his foe in the water, forcing a decision. This moment stands outside all of the theological controversies and religious disputes, even as it becomes the true test of practice. A moment like this one, when the power of life and death is suddenly, capriciously placed in one's hands, can hardly be precisely anticipated; given the climate of Palestine, Jesus never dealt with frozen ponds, melting or otherwise.

For all the Anabaptists' dedication to following the example of Jesus, turning the other cheek, and loving their enemies, they also repeatedly imagined their enemies thwarted and brought low—even if by God rather than by men. In fact, while the admonitions in the *Martyrs Mirror* routinely urge general Christian charity, they also often speculate with some relish on the vengeance God will wreak upon those who torment His faithful servants. The Willems narrative itself is harsh in its description of his opponents, especially the burgomaster who insists Dirk be returned to captivity:

> The thiefcatcher wanted to let him go, but the burgomaster, very sternly called to him to consider his oath, and thus he was again seized by the thief-catcher, and, at said place, after severe imprisonment and great trials proceeding from the deceitful papists, put to death at a lingering fire by these bloodthirsty, ravening wolves.[3]

The moment when Dirk Willems turns back, then, is the silent gap of the narrative, the moment of mystery. After all, Dirk *was* running away, having accorded to local tradition knotted together his bedclothes to make a rope. He *planned* to escape, he sought to be free; to avoid a horrible death in the flames, he ran for his life.[4] Why *did* he make his marvelous turn, then? No one will ever know, but I imagine that it might have been an immediate, uncalculated human impulse, rather than a sober decision based on rational contemplation of the situation and his belief system. If another man falls through the ice, you pull him out, even if he hates you, even if you fear and loath him. How can you do otherwise?

The thiefcatcher's response is likewise human and humane. Ideology is less important than human feeling; neither the Church nor the State will collapse if this one man runs off.

The second gap, however, is in the burgomaster's response, which suggests the opposite impulse from Dirk's turning. The crucial difference, I think, is that he can merely issue an order rather than acting himself. It is hard to kill a man, consciously and deliberately, at close quarters. But if you have been bound to a higher authority, and have a man bound to obey you in his turn, and can command him to do the will of the state, it is not so difficult to put the killing down to duty and necessity. If the burgomasters of this world had to do with their own hands all the murders and atrocities they distribute to their underlings, surely there would still be bad deeds, but not so many.

The third gap—and the most difficult one—has to do with the place of God in all of this. On this point the narrative is conspicuously silent, though elsewhere in the *Martyrs Mirror* there are plentiful references to Providence. Might we read Dirk's story in parallel to the frightening Old Testament stories of Job and of Abraham and Isaac? In both of these, Yahweh is a vigorous presence, pulling strings and issuing orders, testing his servants to their limits, by turns angry and magnanimous.[5] Here, though, there is no explicit suggestion of divine presence—and there is also no relenting, no last-minute reprieve, no celebration at faith rewarded.

It is hard to me to chew on this story for long without the taste turning slightly bitter, at least from a human perspective—for Dirk's bold turning does not receive its just reward, and its greatest mystery, in the end, is in this gap between gesture and reward. Who is redeemed? What is revealed? Dirk does the right thing, and the bloodthirsty Papists kill him anyway, just because they can, just because they are too stubborn to yield to the most basic human feelings, just because.... If this is the way the world works, what should we do when the enemy falls into the icy pond? If we tell this story to the young ones, what do we hope they will learn from it? That good deeds may well be not merely unrewarded but punished? Plausible, certainly, but not exactly inspirational, except in a particularly gnarly and difficult way.

Unlike many of the martyrs, Dirk Willems has almost nothing to say himself: he issues no elaborate testimonies, no eloquent contestations with the authorities over baptism or the sacraments, no heart-wrenching letters to his spouse or pious exhortations to the faithful. His only words recorded in the *Martyrs Mirror* account are spoken during his execution, and they are hardly a comfort:

> a strong east wind blowing that day, the kindled fire was much driven away from the upper part of his body, as he stood at the stake; in consequence of which this good man suffered a lingering death, insomuch that in the town of Leerdam, toward which the wind was blowing, he was heard to exclaim over seventy times, "O my Lord; my God," etc., for which cause the judge or bailiff, who was present on horseback, filled with sorrow and regret at the man's sufferings, wheeled about his horse, turning his back toward the place of execution, and said to the executioner, "Dispatch the man with a quick death."[6]

There is no answer to these cries of pain, as there was no quick answer to Jesus' agonized cry on the cross, when (the gospel tells us) he demanded to know why God had forsaken him. There is no miraculous in-
tervention for Dirk, only the belated and gruff mercy ordered by the
judge. The narrative ends with no great clarity:

> But how or in what manner the executioner then dealt with this
> pious witness of Jesus, I have not been able to learn, except only,
> that his life was consumed by the fire, and that he passed through
> the conflict with great steadfastness, having commended his soul
> into the hands of God.

Here's what I think: Dirk Willem's story moves us, seizes us, because
it is one of those stories that defies our categories and expectations. It
provides very little comfort, and the more we ponder it the stranger and
less profitable it seems. It holds the irreducible strangeness of the world
before us, the world where the rain falls on the just and the unjust, the
world in which God is often silent. Like a Zen koan, it breaks the back of
logic, insists that expecting order and reason from the universe will not
get us far. Maybe in Heaven all will be made clear. Maybe there Dirk has
his reward. But in the meantime, what is there but faith, work, and
hope?[7]

The central passage of Alves's book echoes, uncannily, the moment
when Dirk's pursuer fall through the ice:

> Truth appears as we stumble, when the frozen surface of the lake
> cracks and we hear its voice: dreaming. . . .
>> We are saved by the power of dreaming. Dreaming is the
> power which resurrects the dead. [. . .]
>> So the eucharist: an empty, silent space for our dreaming, be-
> fore the Absent One—like the dead man of the sea.

It is absence, not presence, which performs the miracle, Alves
claims: "God is the absence which saves":

> It is not theology.
> Theology wants to be science, a discourse without interstices. . . .
> It wants to have its birds in cages. . . .
> *Theopoetics* instead,
> empty cages,
> words which are uttered out of and before the void.[8]

Alves offers several metaphors for theopoetics: the empty cage, the empty cathedral, the voice which lives, paradoxically, in the silences within texts.

A poem is like a Gothic cathedral.

What is its meaning? [. . .] it is filled with unexpected worlds . . . in it lives a Stranger—not the architect and his meanings—and when this Stranger speaks, one hears far away bells tolling inside one's soul: and the body trembles. . . . Is the cathedral outside a metaphor of the cathedral inside? Or is it the other way round? I don't know—and the memory of an unknown home comes back to me. My knowledge fails me in that moment, I don't need it—I am possessed by the Wind which moves in the Void.[9]

Anabaptists build no cathedrals—though some of our churches are imposing enough in their own way. The one where I worship has large and beautiful stained glass windows, recently refurbished at considerable expense—one with Jesus the Shepherd holding a lamb, the other with him standing at the door and knocking. But even the hidden churches of the early days, the caves where little groups met in secret, have the elusive surplus of meaning that Alves describes here, the sense of a presence not easily rendered in words, no matter how long learned men argue over them.[10]

God is not a powerful figure on a celestial throne, John D. Caputo suggests in his provocative *The Weakness of God.* "The name of God," he suggests, is better understood as a word that "harbors an event," that is a call rather than a presence:

The kingdom of God is a domain in which weakness "reigns," where speaking of a "kingdom" is always an irony that mocks sheer strength. The kingdom is not the simple weakness that lacks the power of faith or the courage for action, but the provocative and uplifting weakness of God, a sublime weakness that, however weak, should not be underestimated because it is a divine force, capable even of inflicting a divine trauma. (14)

What moved Dirk Willems, Caputo might suggest, is this call to action with no thought of success, without claim on the sort of power that would offer freedom as a reward. In this splitting of cause and effect, of morality and reward, is the mystery of the call of a God whose weakness is inscrutable and yet somehow mighty in its own right, the weakness of Jesus on the cross, crying out in pain and misery.

The thousand-plus pages of the *Martyrs Mirror* offer other kinds of surplus as well. Though its compiler's main aims were clearly to gather together the martyr stories (many predating the Anabaptists), to place the Anabaptists in a tradition of dissenters going back all the way to Jesus Christ, and to inspire new fervor in the prosperous, increasingly worldly Dutch Mennonites of the Golden Age, it includes much more. Early on is a fifteen-page attack on the Catholic church and its claims to authority and apostolic succession. There are poems, letters written from prison, lengthy accounts of trials and conversations between the martyrs and their accusers. The tone and mood vary considerably, as does (sometimes) the outcome. To complicate matters further in what may be instructive ways, let us consider two more stories in relation to Dirk's.

Having spent several months in Austria recently, I naturally found myself interested in the fate of Anabaptists there.[11] Most of the material in *Martyrs Mirror* focuses on Dutch and Swiss Anabaptists, but one lengthy account describes a group of 150 Anabaptists who were imprisoned in 1539 at the castle at Falkenstein, not far north of Vienna. King Ferdinand sent officials to question and instruct them, "especially with regard to their sacrament, which they highly extolled, and would have them believe that the flesh and blood of Christ were present in it, and that it was our Lord God, as they said but the brethren answered that it was a dumb god, and that the Lord's Supper had quite a different signification than, they perversely represented, thus shamefully deceiving and seducing the world."[12]

After several weeks of questioning, ninety of the men were led off, "to be taken to the sea." The narrative offers this editorial explanation:

> The cause of this great distress of the pious was solely, that in antichristendom they testified against the idolatrous and unrighteous life and ways of the priests, for which, as an abomination, God should once severely punish them, and make an end with them and their sins.[13]

The account then describes a long, difficult overland journey, ending at Trieste on the Adriatic Sea. Here the story takes a crucial twist when the prisoners, like Dirk Willems, manage to escape from bondage. But their ending is less dramatic than Dirk's:

Then, on the twelfth night, at Trieste, they were all delivered from their chains and bonds, and went out of prison. Through the providence of God a place was shown them, where they all in the same hour let themselves down by cords from the walls of the city. Thus the very bonds in which they had been brought thither as prisoners, had to minister to their deliverance. [. . .] the greater part of them returned with joy and glad hearts to the church in Moravia.[14]

So, what are we to make of this (relatively) cheerful story of a successful escape and homecoming, amongst the bloody theatre of the martyrs? It seems inappropriate to find myself more interested in that band of Austrians, taken prisoner and hauled around for weeks, apparently, in search of someone willing to buy them as galley slaves, who took the chance when they got it and simply ran away, seizing the chance and transforming the cords of their bondage into means of deliverance. Is it wrong to notice, even, that we have no names and no letters from this unlikely group, only this sketchy narrative, and to point out that unlike Dirk, this group's story did not fire the imagination of the artist Jan van Luyken, whose engravings for the 1685 Dutch edition of the *Martyrs Mirror* have become perhaps even more evocative and iconic than the stories themselves?

I will return to our brave band of Austrians, but first let me summarize the next entry briefly. "Anna of Rotterdam, Put to Death in That Place, A. D. 1539," tells the well-known story of Anna Janz, and includes a long letter to her son, which looks forward to the day when the Lord will "avenge the blood of Thy servants and ministers, and shalt through Thyself gain the victory." Her admonition is fitted together, somewhat haphazardly, from familiar phrases and verses from both Old and New Testaments. She asks him to remember Proverbs 11:31: "Behold, the righteous shall be recompensed in the earth, much more than the wicked and the sinners." But a few lines later she seems to recognize that it may not always be so, as she urges her son to "receive the chastisement and instruction of the Lord, bow your shoulders under His yoke, and cheerfully bear it from your youth." No details of her life, imprisonment, or death are given, only this: "Thereupon she sealed this with her blood, and thus, as a pious heroine and follower of Jesus Christ, she was received among the number of the witnesses of God who were offered up."

And where is God in all of this? The author-narrator of the story of the Austrians insists that providence was there at every step: "From this it can be seen, that, though the ungodly devise many things against the pious, God always turns it for the best to His people."[15]

One wonders if those lines were written with Anna Janz and all the other martyrs in mind. Could it be that our narrator was resisting the turn toward the weakness of God that I have followed Caputo in making, unwilling to acknowledge that whatever "the best" might have meant amid all these captivities, tortures, and evasions, the call of God remained a holy inscrutability, its rewards often sparse and thin gruel indeed?

I still find my interest fired by those enterprising souls who seized the chance to escape their captors and high-tail it back to Moravia. Was it also an act of faith to seize the moment, to be bold, careful and sneaky in preserving their singular lives? Similar stories turn up throughout the *Martyrs Mirror;* in one, two "rough fellows" whose brother is among a group imprisoned in Amsterdam devise an elaborate plan to free him while drinking in a tavern, and swear a solemn if un-Anabaptist oath to carry out their plan at all costs. Using a rope, pulley, boathook, and crowbar, they gain access to a high window and break in, lowering the brother and a number of others using the rope.[16] In a case in Antwerp in 1559, a margrave and some others arrest a man named Andries Languedul after a meeting at his house; they plan also to arrest his wife, who has just given birth, but her nurse delays them by "entertaining them very liberally, and plying them with wine," until the woman can be carried away on planks.[17]

Clearly such stories were valued by those who told, retold, recorded, and collected the martyr tales, or they would have been edited out, sooner or later. The theme of running away, of living to carry on the work, is found throughout Anabaptist folklore, sometimes overshadowed by the emphasis on spectacular deaths. Ervin Beck retells the folk tale of Menno Simons bending the truth to elude the authorities:

> Menno was riding on a stagecoach one time and instead of being in the coach he was riding up front, up high, with the driver. And the authorities dashed up on horses to arrest Menno if they could find him. And they said, "Is Menno Simons in that coach?" And Menno turned around and yelled into the coach, "Is Menno Simons in there?" And they said, "No, he's not in here." So Menno

told the authorities, "They say Menno's not in the coach." So he lived to die in bed.[18]

The book of survivors would be even longer than the *Martyrs Mirror*, and far less spectacular, though it also would have its moments of drama and poignance.

The mystery of how to do God's will—the great practical day-to-day struggle—is at once heightened and simplified by martyrdom, given a definite though painful resolution. The poignance of early death lends the martyr stories a cachet and potential authority not unlike that attached to military heroes in societies like mine; I write this on Memorial Day, having avoided the parades but hardly escaped the inevitable, formulaic praises for fallen soldiers that fill the media. Yes, I am grateful to live in a country that allows me to work and write more or less freely, in return for taxes that support the empire's military endeavors . . . though conscious, always, of how deeply strange and perverse this culture is, how deeply in bondage to violence and money and things, how far from any dream of beloved community.

In *Foundations of Violence* Grace Jantzen offers a compelling account of the "necrophilia" of Western culture, tracing a fascination with death, violence, and warfare through Greek and Roman culture and philosophy. Jantzen argues that the grisly spectacle of the Coliseum, far from being mere "entertainment," represented "key aspects of the Roman ideology of gender, violence and empire," with their emphasis on masculinist combat and "penetration." She touches only briefly on the early Christian martyrs, but points out that in important ways they subverted these values by their refusal to swear oaths to the emperor, to recognize his omnipotence, or (most crucially) to fear death: "The power of the Empire was exerted in violence crystallized in spectacle. By despising death, the martyrs despised also that power and that violence, and by despising power they rendered it powerless. It could kill them, but it could not overcome them. On its own terms, the violent ideology of omnipotent empire was undone."[19]

As Jantzen acknowledges, however, while the martyrs "radically reconfigured constructions of death and gender," martyr ideologies remain preoccupied with death even as they configure it differently. Still, she also finds in early Christian writing "metaphors of seeds and plants and flourishing" that provide "possibilities for a symbolic of natality."[20]

While the imagery is different, I would argue that the picaresque tale of the traveling Austrians is a hint of a similar natality even among the burnings and beheadings of the *Martyrs Mirror*. Yes, we might conclude, some of us are bound to suffer and die for the faith—but it can also be faithful to run away, to join the brothers and sisters in Moravia or Newton or Winnipeg and follow the great and mysterious call of God as best we can, from this side of the Great Divide. Even Menno himself, we know, died a natural death, and while his stagecoach evasion may be folklore, it suggests that the small secret voice may speak many and various commands—some of them as simple as "Run away!"

Given the "dulce et decorum" symbolic of the Roman Empire—and more or less all the other worldly empires—with its glorification of death in battle, given as well the martyr symbolic with its glorification of "defenseless" death, we might here only imagine a supplement, another strong vision that looks to life rather than to death for meaning and value. John D. Caputo also ponders what use might be made of the disasters of history:

> The radical historian can only offer hope and a future *for* the dead, on their behalf, pleading on their behalf for the future, . . . What remains now is to *hope*, and to hope, Levinas says, requires first to be driven into a state where, calculatively speaking, it is hopeless. . . . Hope requires blindness. Hence, the work of the historian is the impossible one of giving comfort to the dead by way of memory and hope for the coming of the messianic time. (256)

Both the martyrs and those survivors who escaped to Moravia are long dead, and to redeem or to comfort them is equally impossible. Caputo is surely right, following Levinas, to say that hope requires the blindness of not knowing, especially in reference to the future. Yet we must add that this not-knowing is precisely the condition of all true art, which comes into being when the artist opens the creative space for the inbreak of a voice that will speak what the artist did not know.

A recent anthology edited by Kirsten Beachy, *Tongue Screws and Testimonies: Poems, Stories, and Essays Inspired by the Martyrs Mirror*, offers a rich trove of many such voices, varied and passionate, and even in its title suggests that issues of voice, repression, and expression were and are crucial—as is the question of what meaning(s) we attach and construct with these stories in mind. A full accounting of this book would be a book in itself; here I can only single out a few especially relevant pieces. Some authors are earnest believers; James Lowry offers a deeply traditional "Meditation on Dirk Willems" that imagines him thinking his way through both the Old and New Testaments as he ponders the thief-catcher's predicament at great length, then somehow turning back "in a flash" to save him.

In "A Bonfire of Books" Joseph Stoll, an Old Order Amish minister, retells the martyrdom of Joriaen Simons in Haarlem from the point of view of his frightened but faithful son:

> A lad walked home alone toward the weaver's shop. He clutched in one hand the letter his father had written from prison. In the other hand he held a booklet, its edges browned by the flames of his father's funeral pyre.[21]

Others are far more equivocal; Stephanie Krehbiel describes the trauma she felt in considering the martyr stories in post-9-11 America. She is especially troubled by the "breathtaking confidence" displayed by martyrs such as Maeyken Wiens: "The Lord takes away all fear; I did not know what to do for joy, when I was sentenced." "Joy?" Krehbiel writes, "Now looking back, I think this is the cruelest use of the *Martyrs Mirror* to which I fell prey: the idea that not only do our beliefs invite painful death, but that we should give it a rapturous welcome. Jesus Christ himself didn't live up to these standards."[22]

In a shift at once shocking and provocative, Krehbiel describes finding relief from her martyr complex in the television series *Buffy the Vampire Slayer*, whose teenage heroine experiences a "tangle of humility and hubris, alienation and obligation, in the world but not of the world" that resonates with her own. Seizing on the "warrior archetype" as a model of "action and resistance," even while she resists Buffy's pervasive use of violence, Krehbiel calls for stories that "offer me agency, the power to act and create change. The best stories, the honest ones, won't hide the sometimes deadly cost of defying oppression. . . . Death may be a consequence, but death is not the point."[23] This call clearly resonates with Jantzen's analyses of "necrophilia," though Krehbiel does not refer to Jantzen directly.

Debate, discussion, and efforts to reclaim, resist, and reframe the legacy of the martyrs will surely continue. There is no "pure" martyrology, we should remember, no objective place to stand; there are as many particular locations as there are commentators. It is no accident, surely, that Grace Jantzen and Stephanie Krehbiel, both well-educated women, draw on wide-ranging sources from both within and outside Anabaptism. Conscious of centuries of patriarchy, repression, and psychic violence done especially to women, they remind us that the gap between celebrating the courage and conviction of the martyrs and making the martyr's death a frightening marker of faithfulness is narrow.

On another hand, James Lowry and Joseph Stoll have no use for postmodern theory, much less televised vampire serials. Conservatives who retell the stories to reinforce larger communal narratives of separation from worldly culture, they would surely claim to follow more closely in the footsteps of the men and women who suffered for the faith—even in their commitment to patterns of gendered authority that seem deeply flawed to contemporary feminists.

As I argued earlier, I do not think a simple continuum of assimilation does justice to the complexities of identity among contemporary Anabaptists, especially if (as is often the case) the assumption is that the "unassimilated" are somehow better, purer, and closer to God and tradition. My own sympathies are most fully with those who seek to reimagine and reinvent the tradition for each new day, those who recognize that no sect or church holds the entire truth and seek to find what is nurturing and vital wherever it may be found. Yet I would also argue that *everyone* who chooses to claim access to these stories deserves that access, no matter what their agenda, no matter how earnest or ironic, intellectual or pious, conflicted or nostalgic their account may be. If there is truth within their new constructions, it will find its way; if there is not, eventually it will fade and be forgotten. At least, this is my faith.

The final piece in *Thumbscrews and Testimonies*, written by Dallas Wiebe (himself both marginal and brilliant as any Mennonite writer of the last fifty years) is "The Anabaptist Radiance," a poem that also remembers the martyrs but focuses finally on action and resistance, even as it acknowledges inter-Anabaptist "squabbling" and schisms. Wiebe's complex yet finally affirmative meditation on this "radiance," with all its refusals and affirmations, may serve as a fitting end for this chapter.

> They are marching on in us in our squabbling,
>   in our schisms,

in our refusals of each other,
in our refusals of the world,
and in our persistent, religious democracy. . . .
The radiance of the Anabaptists
still shines out in our lives
when we say to those about us,
"Not us, friends. Not us."[24]

Notes

1. Rubem Alves, *The Poet, The Warrior, The Prophet: The Edward Cadbury Lectures 1990* (London: SCM Press, 1990), 99. My discussion of the Dirk Willems story is deeply indebted to Julia Spicher Kasdorf's keynote presentation "Mightier than the Sword: *Martyrs Mirror* in the New World," presented at "*Martyrs Mirror:* Reflections Across Time," Elizabethtown College, June 8-10, 2010. I am also grateful to Gerald Mast for his generous reading of this chapter, and his pointing me to further incidents of escape and evasion in the *Martyrs Mirror.*

2. An icon of Willems was the first in a series offered through the Anabaptist Images Series, an official project of Mennonite Church USA which began in 2003. The irony of Mennonite icons for sale at lofty prices ($295 for an 8" x 11" print) has not escaped notice, but will not be labored here. See http://graberfound.com/Icon/Anabaptist_Images.

3. Thieleman J. Van Braght, *The Bloody Theater or Martyrs Mirror of the Defenseless Christians,* trans. Joseph F. Sohm (1660; Scottdale, Pa.: Mennonite Publishing House, 1984), 741.

4. Among many other classic lines, my sons and I excessively savor the repeated refrain of the knights in the film *Monty Python and the Holy Grail* when faced with overwhelming danger: "Run away! Run away!"

5. For an especially resistant reading of the story of Abraham and Isaac, see Jantzen, *Violence to Eternity,* ed. Jeremy Carrete and Morny Joy (London and New York: Routledge, 2009), 121-6. "God is, throughout, represented as having the absolute right to demand anything without explanation," Jantzen notes, "whether it goes against the grain of moral sensibilities or not. Moreover . . the willingness of Abraham to commit the act of violence is held up not as a paradigm of sacrilege or as a crime, but as a paradigm of religious righteousness." (124)

6. Van Braght, *Martyrs Mirror,* 741-2.

7. In a recent poem, Franz Wright points out that the infamous slogan at Auschwitz is a "satanically / sarcastic take / on Christ's "The truth / will set you free" ('*Wahrheit macht frei*'): '*Arbeit / macht frei.*'" Franz Wright, *God's Silence,* (New York: Knopf, 2004), 125.

8. Van Braght, *Martyrs Mirror,* 99.

9. Van Braght, 101.

10. I meditated on such spaces and related matters in the first chapter of *Scattering Point: The World in a Mennonite Eye* (Albany: SUNY Press, 2004), 5-36.

11. Austria was a bastion of the Counter-Reformation and generally hostile to all of its manifestations, but goodly numbers of Lutherans and others were to be found there. As early as 1527, 38 Anabaptists were killed in Salzburg, according to an account in *Martyrs Mirror*. The most famous incident occurred in 1731, when Archbishop Count Leopold Anton von Firmian expelled 21,000 Protestants from Salzburg.

12. Van Braght, *Martyrs Mirror*, 452.

13. Van Braght, 452.

14. Van Braght, 453.

15. Van Braght, 453-4.

16. Van Braght, 483.

17. Van Braght, 633.

18. Ervin Beck, "Mennonite Trickster Tales: True to be Good," *Mennonite Quarterly Review* 61.1 (January 1987): 67-8.

19. Grace Jantzen, *Foundations of Violence* (London and New York: Routledge, 2004), 336.

20. Jantzen, *Foundations*, 338.

21. Kirsten Beachy, ed., *Tongue Screws and Testimonies: Poems, Stories, and Essays Inspired by the Martyrs Mirror* (Scottdale, Pa.: Herald Press, 2010), 51.

22. Beachy, 136.

23. Beachy, 142.

24. Beachy, 28-7.

FIFTEEN
CHAPTER

WHO KNOWS WHO IS CALLING?

The world quivers quietly under the weak force of an event, made restless by the silent promptings of God's divinely subversive call. But is it really God who calls? Who knows who is calling?...

No matter. We have been delivered from the search for the name of God by the event.... The truth of the event releases us from the order of names and transports us to another level, where truth does not mean learning a name but making truth come true, making it happen.
—John Caputo[1]

Surely "orthodoxy" is a nearly empty concept, though human religious institutions abound, with varying histories and dogmas, some vast, others very small. Yet for all their pomp and circumstance, the dogmas and creeds that are deployed in the service of institutions feel like mere calcified remnants, the living faith they once served lost beneath accreted layers of abstraction and reification. And all too often those struggling to claim space on the mountain of orthodoxy seem just a gaggle of feuding pretenders, each claiming sole possession of the Truth like boys playing Capture the Flag or King of the Hill.

The theopoets—even the most grandiose, like Blake and Whitman and Stevens—admit that they have no certainties but only voice, no Truth but only truths. Their first confidence is that what has been revealed before is not final, that there is space in the universe for more beautiful things made of words, that the God who seems to have fallen silent left us voices to sing and lament and praise until further notice. "Inside human beings," Rilke suggested, "is where God learns."

There are plenty of "Christian poets," some of them fine enough, and yet their work often seems to me constricted by the very willingness to be tagged by such a term.[2] For many such poets, as James Baldwin said, The Answer tends to cover up the questions, to short-circuit their explorations of the mysteries, to cause them to scurry back toward the comforts of official doctrine. So the theopoets who interest me most often count themselves among the "lingering bad ones," those convinced they aren't going to be saved. There is Emily Dickinson of course, the source of this phrase. Walt Whitman, putting all doctrines and creeds in abeyance. Wallace Stevens and Robinson Jeffers, both worshippers of something other than the Christ of American Christianity in any of its forms. Among the many variations on this theme, some are jubilant, some deviant, but others are anxious and harrowed by this uncertainty and doubt. Consider Anne Sexton's wrenching complaint: "need is not quite belief," and Dickinson, in many of her moods.

In these final chapters, then, I will suggest that the voice as deed is at the heart of poetry and of the quest to speak what we can of the unknowable God. This is not "negative theology" of the conventional sort; at least, I will attempt to avoid quickly bouncing away from the proclamation of mystery and back into proclaiming just what it means to be the right sort of Christian. As T. Wilson Dickinson notes, apophatic theology faces "suspicions of mystification and deception, as its excess is often read as only a momentary deferral of the metaphysical grounds that it appears to deny."[3] In epistemological terms, Dickinson points out, as long as apophasis is viewed as a primarily a "delimitation of one's rational capacity," it is caught in a paradox: "the invocation of the unsayable logically necessitates a bait and switch in which the human conceptualization of God and the descriptive power of language is not blocked *from* but even more absolutely conferred *to* the possession of the apophatic theologian."[4]

How, then, to avoid slipping into "a deceptive and mystified return to a discourse of static metaphysical claims?"[5] I am more interested in claiming the poetic voice as ground for discourse that offers metaphysical potentials without sliding into static or absolute claims. The next pages will offer a series of poems and poets who give up dogma and the Truth to dwell in the contingent, the possible, the uncertain sentence, the dubious assertion that nonetheless finds its way to the page as utterance.

Yet I must admit my apophatic theopoetics also has its limits. In some ways, I may be no more rigorous or consistent in my dwelling on mystery than the Old Fathers, though I hope my claims are differently based and less coercive. If the only truth is Mystery, after all, there is little point in writing books or poems. I'm with Jesus and Whitman and John Howard Yoder and John Lennon, all of whom insisted that it all comes down to loving one another, and I am all with the poets and the others who find themselves compelled to make both new wine and new wineskins for the examination and proclamation of exactly what it means to attempt to live within that great commandment. Some products of the human imagination deserve to be disentangled from the everyday welter as especially rich efforts in that direction, I am convinced, lifted up and offered for more general contemplation. So here are a few glimpses of what my School of Theopoets might teach.

Jantzen, Whitman, and Flourishing

To set up a School without merely introducing a new orthodoxy and a new Chosen People is daunting, and even the effort to imagine it so flies in the face of much tradition. As Grace Jantzen points out, in both the Genesis creation accounts and the visions of a new Jerusalem in Isaiah and Revelation, "peace and beauty prevails only because of the expulsion of those who would wreak havoc." The enemies of God's people must be either crushed or forcibly excluded, it seems, and "violence and beauty appear in tension: a tension that becomes unbearable if we put ourselves into the position of those who are outside rather than those whom God has favored."[6] When we construe the Other as dangerous— and when have we not?—we enable ourselves to overlook or at least to blur the violence in the most familiar stories.

How can it be, as Jantzen remarks, that we read of Noah and the covenant of the rainbow without stopping to notice or to mourn the manifold men, women, children, and other creatures that the story tells us were drowned in the flood, brutally, because Yahweh found them insufficiently obedient? Who would make up such a story, and for what purpose? And how have so many argued earnestly, or at least accepted willingly, that their just and loving God has created a vast torture chamber in which some obscure but large proportion of God's creatures will be burned and tormented for eternity, for crimes as small as failing ever to hear the gospel?[7]

True creativity, Jantzen suggests, "celebrates the beauty of particularity" and "invites harmony and flourishing": difference leads to violence, in gender relations and all others, when it is "treated as a danger rather than as a resource, so that hostility rather than mutuality characterizes the interaction."[8] Thus in this School we will look to those who draw wide circles rather than narrow ones, those whose creeds are not meant to set Others outside, violently or not.

Where else to begin such a list but with Walt Whitman, with his grand catalogs and equally grand insistence that none can be excluded, that the creation is *one*?

> Swiftly arose and spread around me the peace and knowledge that
>   pass all the argument of the earth;
> And I know that the hand of God is the promise of my own,
> And I know that the spirit of God is the brother of my own;
> And that all the men ever born are also my brothers, and the women
>   my sisters and lovers;
> And that a kelson of the creation is love;
> And limitless are leaves, stiff or drooping in the fields;
> And brown ants in the little wells beneath them;
> And mossy scabs of the worm fence, and heap'd stones, elder, mullen
>   and poke-weed.[9]

> These are the thoughts of all men in all ages and lands—they are not
>   original with me;
> If they are not yours as much as mine, they are nothing, or next to
>   nothing;
> If they are not the riddle, and the untying of the riddle, they are
>   nothing;
> If they are not just as close as they are distant, they are nothing.

> This is the grass that grows wherever the land is, and the water is;
> This is the common air that bathes the globe.[10]

But here I go again, citing texts that make truth-claims, that assert the common unity of all beings. . . . as noted in an earlier chapter, Whitman works up to these visionary pronouncements, embedding them in a context of considerable uncertainty and self-questioning.[11] Yet Whitman knew, even amid such grand moments, that to proclaim the unity of all being changed nothing, did not free one slave or cure one case of consumption, or any of the other horrors and shames he catalogs. To fix things, in the short term at least, is not the point; the point is to accept the Other, all of the Others, from human enemies to plants and animals and minerals, to exclude nothing on the grounds that it is too painful or too awful or too disgusting.

Jantzen argues, in a critique of René Girard, that his theory of mimetic violence overlooks that desire often does *not* lead to rivalry and violence. Her examples are female: a mother and child, a teacher who delights in the learning of "her" pupil. There is also creative desire, which she suggests "bespeaks fullness that overflows, that wants to give of its resources, express itself."[12] She mentions music, painting, and the writing of books; Whitman surely is a paradigmatic example of this urge.

Jantzen also argues for the centrality of narrative in the construction of social identity, and that the narratives of Christendom and the Hebrew Bible, which combined with the Greek and Roman narratives "form the self-identity of the West," incorporate both gendered violence and the idea of "being the specially chosen people of God": "Whatever cruelties or injustices Christians visited upon the peoples they conquered or colonized, they could represent themselves as bringing a generous mission to people less fortunate than themselves, civilizing them in this world and saving them in the next."[13] Whitman, for all his celebration of America, also subverts this "chosen people" myth: *everyone* is both special and equal, he insists; there is no distinction.

Jantzen's re-examination of the Hebrew Bible is little short of devastating. She foregrounds a narrative in which Yahweh "is represented as having a virtually insatiable desire for blood."[14] This God constantly demands gendered violence and blood sacrifice, destroys enemies by the thousands simply because they are not of his "chosen people," kills the first-born of Egypt, and demands the sacrifice of Isaac for no reason beyond his own stubborn will. In their insistence that only the "chosen" are worthy of God's notice and protection, and their blindness to the suffering of those others whose only failing is happening, for example, to live in Canaan when the Israelites invade, these stories establish a precedent for the worst excesses of religious war:

Taken at face value, the biblical stories of the covenant present a divine mandate for religious intolerance and ethnic cleansing. If the endless ritual slaughter of the sacrificial system is the preoccupation with death turned inwards, the holy warfare against the indigenous people of the land turns the violence outwards. The religious violence of the West has repeatedly been legitimated by appeal to the constellation of ideas linked in this narrative: the idea of covenant and chosen people, a promised land, purity and sacrifice, adherence to one god and warfare against those who worship differently.[15]

Jantzen believes that "the marginalized theme of the beauty of the divine, and the resultant beauty of divine creation" offers a possible alternative to "a symbolic obsessed with destruction and death. . . . it is a theme of resistance which is always in the margins. . . . Through the divine beauty newness enters the world and makes it sing" (138). Strikingly, the examples Jantzen mentions of this beauty and natality breaking through in the Hebrew Bible are all cast as poetry: the Genesis creation account, where the newly created world and its creatures are pronounced "very good," and passages from Isaiah, Job, and the Psalms in which the beauties of God's creation are invoked and praised.

In creation there is beauty and newness and delight; it is "very good." "Creation recreates; life and beauty shine with hope."[16] What might it mean, that in the poems the beauty and fruitfulness of the natural world emerges from the bloody narrative of warfare, sacrifice, and masculine competition? It would be genre-prejudicial, and invite all sorts of counter-examples, to make broad claims about poetry as the language of beauty, life, and peace. But at least since the Romantics, it seems to me, the broad impetus of poetry has been toward the sort of inclusive, generous, life-affirming vision that Jantzen and Whitman share. That such visions, poetic and otherwise, have been marginalized and attacked from all sides by "realists" and proponents of the just war and the necessary evil is, perhaps, only more evidence of the threat that they pose to the domination system that still rules this world.

How *did* the followers of Jesus–that tiny band of rebels, peaceniks, ultimate outsiders—evolve into Christendom and produce the Crusades, the Inquisition, and the notion that America is uniquely favored by God? Jantzen's archeology of the violence, misogyny, and necrophilia that became embedded in Christian thought and practice is compelling, as is her insistence that throughout this long and often dismal history the hints of resistance and counter-practice can be found. The transformation of Jesus' message of resistance and mutuality into empire and orthodoxy was, Jantzen believes, the product of choices that might have been made otherwise, from the selection of the biblical canon to the Constantinian compromise that Anabaptists have long regarded as a crucial turning point. Yet none of this was inevitable, and sometimes different choices *were* made, "so that Christendom itself is the resource for peace, justice, egalitarianism, and beauty."[17]

Among the most troubling aspects of standard Christian practice are its de-emphasis of the life and teachings of Jesus and its ubiquitous embedded metaphors of warfare, violence, and blood sacrifice. Even the familiar communion liturgy, Jantzen notes, refers implicitly to violent death, as of course does the symbol of the cross. While the New Covenant ends the practice of blood sacrifice of animals, it is replaced with "a theology of atonement, in which Jesus the Lamb of God is sacrificed for the sins of the world. And the holy war against others and their gods become generalized to a fight against 'the world, the flesh and the devil': the whole life of a Christian is warfare against enemies without and within."[18]

This "holy war" is, precisely, the struggle that Whitman refuses to fight in "Song of Myself." He declares that the soul and the body are equal co-partners, not enemies, and so are the other beings and creatures of the earth, including men and women. His true radicalism lies in his reaching back for the actual figure of Jesus, and his rejection of the accreted hierarchical, gendered power structures erected in Jesus' name by the men who came after.

48

I have said that the soul is not more than the body,
And I have said that the body is not more than the soul;
And nothing, not God, is greater to one than one's self is,
And whoever walks a furlong without sympathy, walks to his own
    funeral, drest in his shroud, [...]
And I say to any man or woman, Let your soul stand cool and com-
    posed before a million universes.

And I say to mankind, Be not curious about God,
For I, who am curious about each, am not curious about God;

(No array of terms can say how much I am at peace about God, and
about death.)

I hear and behold God in every object, yet understand God not in
the least,
Nor do I understand who there can be more wonderful than myself.

Why should I wish to see God better than this day?
I see something of God each hour of the twenty-four, and each mo-
ment then;
In the faces of men and women I see God, and in my own face in the
glass;
I find letters from God dropt in the street—and every one is sign'd
by God's name,
And I leave them where they are, for I know that wheresoe'er I go,
Others will punctually come forever and ever.

"I hear and behold God in every object, yet understand God not in
the least." Yahweh is not the only face of God, and it is best not to grasp
for intellectual knowledge about God, but to see the evidence of God
everywhere, and to leave God's letters where they are so that others may
find them as well. No wonder the earnest Christians of his day found
Whitman so frightening, so dangerous; he refused the tribalism and
blood sacrifice and patriarchy of their creed, of those who insisted that
they understood exactly what God demanded of them and (especially)
of others—and worshiped instead in a church of his own, a church of
life, beauty, and interrelation, one startlingly like the one Jantzen imagines a century and a half later.

Anne Carson and the Decreated Self

Anne Carson's "The Truth about God" is a long poem in seventeen
named sections whose immodest title is immediately undercut by the
opening lines: "My religion makes no sense / and does not help me /
therefore I pursue it."[19] Like Grace Jantzen, Carson is an encyclopedic
scholar, a committed feminist, and quite obviously brilliant; if Jantzen
had written poetry, we might imagine it having something of Carson's
tone. Both authors share the sense of God's mystery, but Carson finds
nearly unbearable the conviction that when someday we discover "what

God really wanted" it will be "some simple thing":

> The thought of it
> (this simple thing)
>
> is like a creature
> let loose in a room
> and battering
>
> to get out.
> It batters my soul
> with its rifle butt.[20]

Here and now, though, the aspects of God she explores are, to say the least, troubling, and raise similar questions to those found in Jantzen's work. "The Grace That Comes By Violence" deals with the New Testament story of Jesus healing a man possessed by spirits by casting them into a herd of swine: "I saw you // at the bottom of the cliff of pity / diving in pig blood—/ 'cleansed' now."[21]

Along with the anger, however, are many more complicated moments and small-scale, nearly parabolic narratives. In one of my favorites, titled "God's Justice," God gets distracted by the fine details of making a dragonfly on the day He is supposed to create justice, and (it seems) never quite gets around to it. But the dragonfly, with "turquoise dots all down its back like Lauren Bacall" and "tiny wire elbows," is beautiful. The final poem, "God's Work," ends with seeming acceptance even of sadness and "the blind alleys that run alongside human conversation" as signs of God, and of God's work as necessary: "God's own calmness is a sign of God. The surprisingly cold smell of potatoes or money. / Solid pieces of silence."[22]

Perhaps even more relevant is Carson's more recent essay "Decreation." The title essay (subtitled "How Women Like Sappho, Marguerite Porete and Simone Weil Tell God) compares these three women authors, widely separated in time and culture but united, Carson argues, by their sense that the most intense love, whether its object is human or divine, requires leaving the self behind. The key figure of jealousy connects Sappho and Marguerite, the latter of whom speaks of "her self being pulled apart from herself and thrown into a condition of poverty, to which she consents," and imagines that God asks her "how would I fare if I knew that he preferred me to love another more than himself?"[23] Marguerite is pinned by this thought, Carson thinks, because she realizes that "loyalty to God is actually obstructed by her love of him because this affection, like most human erotic feeling, is largely self-love; it puts Marguerite in bondage to Marguerite rather than to God."[24]

Similarly, Simone Weil "feels herself to be an obstacle to herself inwardly," and wishes to dislodge herself, to "withdraw her own soul" to arrive at God. Weil's desire to somehow disappear is extreme: "If only I knew how to disappear there would be a perfect union of love between God and the earth I tread, the sea I hear . . ."[25] Elsewhere in this book I have indicated my respect for much of Weil's work, but this thread within her thinking troubles me considerably. For one thing, the lines resonate uncannily with a well-known poem from the Sixties by Mark Strand, "Keeping Things Whole," which though secular in its language contains a very similar sense that the speaker's presence is somehow an alien intrusion in an otherwise whole universe. "In a field," Strand's speaker proclaims, "I am the absence / of field. . . . Wherever I am / I am what is missing." "We all have reasons / for moving," the poem concludes, "I move / to keep things whole."[26]

I have thought about this poem for many years; both it and Weil's idea that her disappearance would somehow heal the separation between God and the earth seem to me to display a parallel and remarkable sort of alienated arrogance, a kind of perverse self-regard and self-pity reminiscent of the old Puritans bragging each that he was the humblest of all, the very lowliest of all the worms groveling in the dust. The most cursory glance around would suggest that neither Weil's nor Strand's particular bodies are in fact keeping things from being whole. If Weil's eventual disappearance restored some perfect union to the earth, the rest of us are still waiting to discover it.

Carson reads Weil more sympathetically on this point than I do, as part of Carson's putting forward of what she terms "a profoundly tricky spiritual fact, viz. that I cannot go toward God in love without bringing myself along. And so in the deepest possible sense I cannot be alone with God."[27] I understand this idea—that the "self" is a barrier or an unwanted companion on the quest for mystical union with the Other, whether God or lover—though I am not sure that I agree with it, and Carson does not make very clear how she or her three sources would divide up the various interior components of the psyche, who is the "I" that would rightly be alone with God, or which parts of the self must be left behind. Still, she is right in her appreciation of Marguerite Porete's account of a soul who swims so completely in the sea of joy that she "feels no joy for she herself is joy, and swims and floats in joy without feeling any joy because she inhabits Joy and Joy inhabits her."[28]

The condition Carson describes is somewhat akin to the apophatic elusiveness of God that I have been exploring at various points of this book, but with the key difference that here the absence, and the mystery, have as much to do with a sensed need to empty or "decreate" the self as they do with the mystery of an unknowable God. Yet (as Carson also notes, in an important turn) to convey these ideas, even the most mystical and self-decreating of writers must take on the "brilliant self-assertiveness" required for the "writerly project" they share: "To be a writer is to construct a big, loud, shiny center of self from which the writing is given voice and any claim to be intent on annihilating this self while still continuing to write and give voice to writing must involve the writer in some important acts of subterfuge or contradiction."[29]

To pursue the decreation of self in mystical communion is all well and good, then, but to testify to the experience, one must put that decreation aside even while describing it. One can offer hymns, or prayers, or poems—as did Marguerite, Weil, and Sappho—and when the self has indeed dissolved from its being here on earth, into what we know not, those texts remain, etchings of experiences and intimations that become, if we allow them, experiences of our own, perhaps secondary and faint, the world seen in a clouded mirror, but the most that we can save and carry forward from those moments when the gap between self and God seems to close.

Carson notes that her three heroines were all judged harshly, accused of being "fake women," and lived difficult lives: Sappho was accused of "unrestrained and incoherent sexual indulgence," Marguerite Porete was burned in 1310 as a heretic, and Simone Weil died at thirty-four, refusing to eat in solidarity with the hungry people of occupied France. Yet Carson stands with them all: "they know what love is. That is they know love is the touchstone of a true or a false spirituality; that is why they play with the figure of jealousy." Even so, Carson admits that their words are not to be taken as final or absolute truth; Marguerite herself acknowledges that everything we might say about God "is as much lying as it is telling the truth."[30]

Where are we left, then? With the word, I think, and the myriad supplements and improvisations that are apparently required around the primal I Am that is both ground and mystery. With the voices of women and men, fakers and poseurs that we may be, pursuers of the bird that has flown the cage, inventors of stories that we dream may be true. And, again, with love as the touchstone, the elusive element that must be pursued and enacted even though, like God, it is not to be fully grasped or possessed, but only experienced in the moment of its event, its breaking into the world, like a sunset or a cry or a glance exchanged between two people who realize that with one look their lives have suddenly and forever changed. In the next chapter I will look further into these questions of voice, authority, mystery, and love within some recent poems.

Notes

1. John D. Caputo, *The Weakness of God: A Theology of the Event* (Bloomington: Indiana University Press, 2006), 299.

2. See David Craig and Janet McCann, eds., *Odd Angles of Heaven: Contemporary Poetry by People of Faith* (Wheaton: Harold Shaw, 1994); David Impastato, ed. *Upholding Mystery: An Anthology of Contemporary Christian Poetry* (New York: Oxford University Press, 1997); and Gerry LaFemina and Chad Prevost, eds., *Evensong: Contemporary American Poets on Spirituality* (Huron, Ohio: Bottom Dog, 2006), for anthologies of contemporary American religious poetry. There is very little overlap of poets or poems among these three gatherings, and even the varied descriptive terminology of the subtitles suggests considerable uncertainty. Gregory Wolfe, editor of the influential journal *Image: A Journal of the Arts and Religion*, was recently heard to proclaim that he considered himself "religious but not spiritual."

3. Dickinson, T. Wilson. "Emptying Apophasis of Deception: Considering a Duplicitous Kierkegaardian Declaration," in *Apophatic Bodies: Negative Theology, Incarnation, and Relationality*, ed. Chris Boesel and Catherine Keller (New York: Fordham University Press, 2010), 252.

4. Dickinson, 252-3.

5. Dickinson, 254.

6. Grace Jantzen, *Violence to Eternity* (London and New York: Routledge, 2009), 16.

7. I had several memorable conversations a few years ago with a former Pentecostal preacher, a gentle true spirit who had been driven from his church and separated from his family for failing to preach the Gospel as his church understood it. When he thought he could trust me, he said as if in confession that the real breaking

point came when he realized that he could no longer tell his congregation with conviction that most of the people of the world were bound for hell. We have lost touch, but the last I heard he had become a writer.

8. Jantzen, *Violence*, 21.

9. Walt Whitman, "Song of Myself," sect. 5, *Leaves of Grass and Selected Prose*, ed. John A. Kouwenhoven (New York: Modern Library, 1950).

10. Whitman, sect. 17.

11. See Chapter 4.

12. Jantzen, *Violence*, 17.

13. Jantzen, *Violence*, 45.

14. Jantzen, *Violence*, 129.

15. Jantzen, *Violence*, 73-4.

16. Jantzen, *Violence*, 143.

17. Jantzen, *Violence*, 154.

18. Jantzen, *Violence*, 157-8.

19. Anne Carson, *Glass, Irony and God* (New York: New Directions, 1995): 39.

20. Carson, *Glass,* 40.

21. Carson, *Glass,* 45.

22. Carson, *Glass,* 53.

23. Anne Carson, *Decreation: Poetry, Essays, Opera* (New York: Vintage, 2005), 164, 165. The second quotation is from Marguerite.

24. Carson, *Decreation*, 166.

25. Qtd. in Carson, *Decreation*, 168. Ellipses in Carson.

26. Mark Strand, *Selected Poems* (New York: Knopf, 2002).

27. Carson, *Decreation,* 169.

28. Qtd. in Carson, *Decreation*, 170.

29. Carson, *Decreation* 171.

30. Carso, *Decreation* 180-81.

SIXTEEN

VOICE AND IMAGINATION: MEANING BESIDES TRUTH

THE WRITING OF POETRY IS NOT A CRAFT.
WE ARE MAKING BIRDS, NOT BIRDCAGES.
There will be no music made from chains except they be cast off.
—Dean Young, The Art of Recklessness[1]

Perhaps the hand in dreaming
of being a star sower
made forgotten music echo
like a note from an enormous lyre,
and to our lips a tiny wave
came with a few true words.
—Antonio Machado[2]

We commonly acknowledge that fiction is made-up and that nonfiction is "true"—though both of these claims are too simple, and under constant and intense debate among serious practitioners of fiction and nonfiction. Poetry is less often interrogated for its relation to reality, I think, though it needs to be. A large school of earnest authors practice poetry as a more or less direct transcription of events from their daily lives onto the page (a critic once memorably parodied this school in a poem that began something like "I look out the window and I become / important . . ."). But this work is rarely memorable, or perhaps I should say I rarely find it interesting.

The poems that *do* interest me are, almost always, very clearly *made* rather than merely recorded; they do things with words that take us both deeper into the day-to-day world and beyond, beside, and around it. They are performances in which a voice—or, often, voices—speak in contingent ways of things that are familiar and strange at the same time. They make claims and tell stories whose value is not in their being "true," for they are often untestable, but in their *ringing* true, or at least carrying a certain momentary authority, however contingent and provisional. The source of this authority is itself elusive, but I think it has a great deal to do with an interest in the manifold manifestations of beauty, and with attention to the actual things of the world, and with a certain stance that is at once humble and willing to risk absurdity in the pursuit of glimpses of mystery, traces of the deep songs of the universe.

Consider Emily Dickinson, who almost certainly did not have Death kindly stop for her in a carriage, nor find herself transformed into a rifle. And Walt Whitman, whose barbaric yawp was an act of self-fashioning that he fully recognized was something far different than, though incorporating, his everyday, walkaround self. Even that antiromantic T. S. Eliot found in the figure of J. Alfred Prufrock an imagined voice and a set of astonishing images for his deep sexual anxieties and fears—one far more interesting and worthy of study and contemplation than any mere confession.

These examples could be multiplied endlessly, but instead I focus this final section on William Stafford, Li-Young Lee, and Jack Gilbert, poets whose work I have found especially intriguing and nourishing as theopoetic voices. All of them speak contingently and provisionally; in fact, all foreground a poetic voice that is at once vivid in its presence and tentative in its truth-claims.

William Stafford: "God is not big . . ."

Throughout his long career, William Stafford returned again and again to questions of faith and value—typically presented with a shifty reluctance to embrace large-scale institutions or solutions. Stafford's "Graffiti" ponders how to respond to unwelcome, often violent or demanding but inescapable messages, from "Kill the tyrants" to "Jesus saves" to "I waited an hour." The poem comes down firmly against graffiti, it seems:

But the trees not carved and walls undefaced
mean "Not even Kilroy was here,"
and millions of us haven't killed anyone,
or a bear, or even an hour. We haven't
presumed. And—who knows?—maybe we're saved.[3]

His claims are characteristically modest, yet subtly bold: how might refusing to kill "even an hour" save anyone? I think Stafford has something in mind here very like Grace Jantzen's effort to shift attention away from future-oriented salvation and toward natality and community. It is how we live, not what we believe, that will save us, he suggests—maybe.

The early poem "On a Church Lawn" also shows Stafford imagining an "other" voice that offers an alternative view of ultimate things. (While riding through his neighborhood once, Stafford pointed out to me the nondescript Lutheran church that had triggered the poem.) The focus of the poem is on dandelions on the church lawn, and their perspective, which seems not to require a building nor an elaborate creed:

Dandelion cavalry, light little saviors,
baffle the wind, they ride so light.
They surround a church and outside the window
utter their deaf little cry: "If you listen
well, music won't have to happen."

After service they depart singly
to mention in the world their dandelion faith:
"God is not big; He is right."[4]

Here Stafford reminds us of John Caputo's interest in the "weakness" of God. Stafford was himself, all his life, both something of a loner and one who formed multiple alliances; he resisted formal religious allegiances, though he joined the Church of the Brethren during the year he spent teaching at Manchester College. But he cooperated and mingled freely with a wide range of groups, including the Fellowship of Resistance, a Christian-based pacifist organization. A full treatment of the unsystematic but highly nuanced theopoetics that emerges in his hundreds of published poems, most of them composed during his trademark daily early morning writing sessions, would require another book. A summary, though, might begin with Stafford's consistent suspicions of mass movements and structures, especially nationalist but also religious, an attitude deeply shaped by his experience as a conscientious objector in World War II, when he experienced the pressure of being one of a relative handful who resisted a war most saw as necessary.

Always skeptical of orthodoxies, fascinated by the natural world, Stafford saw himself as simultaneously an outsider and a member of a scattered, small band committed to finding "what the world is trying to be," as he put it in "Vocation."[5] In this poem and many others the epiphanic moments occur outdoors, as in "Earth Dweller," which begins with a catalog of homely things become precious, but becomes a kind of prayer to the earth:

> If I have not found the right place,
> teach me; for somewhere inside, the clods are
> vaulted mansions, lines through the barn sing
> for the saints forever, the shed and windmill
> rear so glorious the sun shudders like a gong.[6]

This is romantic, surely, but with a decidedly home-grown, agrarian sort of sublimity: what is glorious is not the spectacular and exceptional, but an exceptional moment within the everyday and ordinary. It is, literally, a barnyard experience rather than a mountaintop one. While the poem ends with one of Stafford's strongest statements of conviction, the belief he offers is decidedly not Christian in any conventional way:

> Now I know why people worship, carry around
> magic emblems, wake up talking dreams
> they teach to their children: the world speaks.
> The world speaks everything to us.
> It is our only friend.[7]

He is often playful, flirting with irreverence; God enters many poems, but more as a problem or a category to be examined than as a reliable marker for deity. In "Ultimate Problems," which contrasts an Aztec design in which "God crowds / into the little pea that is rolling / out of the picture," while in the White man design, "God is everywhere, / but hard to see." Characteristically for Stafford, the "outsider" voice gets the last word, which is a question, not quite rhetorical and making no definite claims, yet pressing against everyday complacencies: "The

Aztecs frown at this. // *How do you know He is everywhere? / And how did he get out of the pea?*"[8]

"Allegiances" begins with a brusque dismissal: "It is time for all the heroes to go home / if they have any." This poem sides with the "common ones" who may travel to encounter the strange and marvelous but are content to come back:

Suppose an insane wind holds all the hills
while strange beliefs whine at the traveler's ears,
we ordinary beings can cling to the earth and love
where we are, sturdy for common things.[9]

Examples could be multiplied, but I must end with a look at "Sky," composed in 1992, shortly before Stafford's death, and the first poem in the posthumous *The Way It Is: New and Selected Poems*.

I like you with nothing. Are you
what I was? What I will be?
I look out there by the hour,
so clear, so sure. I could
smile or frown—still nothing.

Be my father, be my mother,
great sleep of blue; reach
far within me; open doors,
find whatever is hiding; invite it
for many clear days in the sun.

When I turn away I know
you are there. We won't forget
each other: every look is a promise.
Others can't tell what you say
when it's the blue voice, when
you come to the window and look for me.

Your word arches over
the roof all day. I know it
within my bowed head, where
the other sky listens.

You will bring me
everything when the time comes.[10]

This poem, like so many of Stafford's, is a sort of prayer, not to God but to an aspect of the world. The blankness and magnitude of the sky ("great sleep of blue") inevitably reminds of the vast inscrutability of God, but the poet here finds comfort in that blankness—"I like you with nothing." At the same time, he is hardly content with it; the second stanza is filled with requests—demands?—for relations that are far more than nothing. Familiar and less familiar God-language abounds (father, mother, "great sleep of blue"), and the opening of the inside, the invocation of what is hidden within, is nearly Gnostic.

Of course the sky is always present, however silent—what then is its word? The poem does not speak it, only asserts its existence and that the poet knows it, his head bowed as if in prayer, listening with the "other sky" within. True prayer, it is often said, is listening, and the finding of a promise even in silence. Is there a faith here? If so, surely, it is an elusive, austere one—Wallace Stevens suddenly comes to mind, for all their differences—with little dogma and no systematic theology. It is premised instead on action and allegiance: "never to kill and call it fate," ("Objector"), "cling to the earth and love / where we are" ("Allegiances").[11] And do not forget to play, to make, to invent. The retrospective "In Camp," after remembering the wartime Civilian Public Service camp where Stafford and others who refused military service were more or less imprisoned, ends with these beautiful lines: "In camps like that, if I should go again, / I'd still study the gospel and play the accordion."[12]

It is fairly certain that Stafford and his fellow COs did study the gospel—but it also seems clear that he did not, technically, play the accordion. Somehow that little invention seems a fitting place to end our short time with him, remembering, as he wrote in "Believer," that "there are ways for lies to be so." "I leap through doubt," he writes there, "eager to find / many more truths to tell," and "I am the one / to live by the hum that shivers till the world can sing."[13]

Li-Young Lee and Mobile Voices

Although Li-Young Lee's own poetic voice is unmistakable, the signal note of his recent book *Behind My Eyes* is its multiple voices, its constant conversation with others who are (apparently) both real and imagined, both remembered and invented. The dialogic interplay of these voices creates a dazzling field of possibility and conjecture, offering many lovely openings into theopoetic spaces. In the first poem, "In His Own Shadow," this interplay is established, as the poem offers a third-person persona "seated in the first darkness / of his body sitting in the lighter dark / of the room," where his body throws shadows both onto the paper before him and onto his mind:

> One makes it difficult for him to see
> the words he's written and crossed out
> on the paper. The other
> keeps him from recognizing
> another master than Death. He squints.
> He reads: *Does the first light hide*
> *inside the first dark?*
>
> He reads: *While all bodies share*
> *the same fate, all voices do not.*[14]

The layering here is complex and beautiful: the "he" who is surely (no?) the poet, the shadows, the written words, his reading of them and our own, deferred until the poem arrives in our hands. The final claim, that at least some voices may outlast the body's inevitable end, is both softened and reinforced by its placement, which is itself complicated; it is hard to read on the paper, within the poem's narrative, and yet it is offered to us in emphatic italics as the end of the poem, where it comes as a strong, even if tentative, claim.

Such maneuvers (I use the word with admiration, not reserve) are common in *Behind My Eyes,* and well suited to the exploratory nature of Lee's theopoetics, which are at once intricate and delicate. (Lee has other thematic preoccupations, including his refugee immigrant heritage and his complex family history, but I will not foreground them here.)

In a very different mode, "Have You Prayed" examines interior mysteries, and the difficulty of speaking clearly even of one's own feelings and thoughts. It opens with a question that readers of Lee's work will find unsurprising, returning to his long preoccupation with his father, now dead for some time: "When the wind / turns and asks, in my father's voice, / Have you prayed?" Lee begins to answer with characteristic indirection, but immediately finds himself lost in hesitations and self-corrections, at once amusing and poignant: "I know three things. One: / I'm never finished answering to the dead. / Two: A man is four winds and three fires. . . ."

Or maybe he's seven winds and ten fires.
And the fires are seeing, hearing, touching,
dreaming, thinking . . .
Or is he the breath of God?

When the wind turns traveler
and asks, in my father's voice, Have you prayed?
I remember three things.
One: A father's love
is milk and sugar,
two-thirds worry, two-thirds grief, and what's left over

is trimmed and leavened to make the bread
the dead and the living share.[15]

There is a lovely blend of surprise and precision in these lines, an inventive boldness even within the apparent indecision, along with a witty, self-aware disregard for mathematics ("two-thirds worry, two-thirds grief") and, again, multiple voices engaging in a kind of quasi-conversation, even while we know they are all in some way situated within the poet's mind. "When the wind / asks, Have you prayed? / I know it's only me," the poem continues, but Lee is not satisfied with such "realistic" reductionism either, and the poem ends on what is not exactly a correction, but more like a supplement:

It's just me

in the gowns of the wind,
or my father through me, asking,
Have you found your refuge yet?
asking, Are you happy?

Strange. A troubled father. A happy son.
The wind with a voice. And me talking to no one.[16]

How is it that the presence of loved ones remains, long after their death? The poem is about a truly ghostly encounter, not the sensationalist reality-show kind, but one of those moments when we find ourselves speaking, silently or on the page, to presences that are no one, that are not there. And yet . . . who is he speaking to? What is that voice, if it cannot be his father, if it cannot be the wind? Lee traces these mysteries with a lovely tact and craft, with no hint of mystification or sensationalism.

The long poem "Lake Effect" is constructed as a dialogue between "I" and a "she" who is at least tentatively identified as a sister. They begin with the lake (quite likely Michigan, given Lee's home in Chicago), but the conversation quickly becomes a series of floating, lyrical observations and assertions about books, minds, voices, arrayed in a constellation of simile and metaphor around the first image of the lake:

I said, "The mind like a lake,
and your voice a figure of the foam."

She said, "The book a voice, its pages
burning in rooms birds foretell every evening."[17]

In what seems clearly a biblical echo/revision, the "I" offers this sequence: "Therefore, a voice was first, the world comes after, / and the book comes last." But what about the relations between them? Though the book comes last, it is perhaps more permanent than the transient voice . . . the book says, *"Ash and dew sing the founding notes / of world, book, time, and body. // The page remains the place where we can hear them."*[18] Yet even the boldest assertions are presented provisionally, less as Truth than as voice, and the poem ends with questions that pose the worldly, enduring lake against the transience of words and people:

She said, "The lake, the first and last page of the day,
overwhelms every word written there."
I said, "So who was running down the steps
in front of the museum in the rain?
Who woke up sitting in the window of a moving train?"[19]

Once again, I cannot provide anything like a full account of Lee's richly evocative, subtly speculative theopoetics, and must concentrate on his approach through multiple voices and layered narratives. Perhaps the *tour de force* in *Behind My Eyes* is "Virtues of the Boring Husband," in which the speaker speculates over six pages about love and God, all as a way to help his weary wife fall asleep: "Whenever I talk, my wife falls asleep. / So, now, when she can't sleep, I talk. / It's like magic."[20] This self-deprecating, humorous frame allows Lee to carry on in a voice more abstract than he might dare otherwise:

> "Or maybe God says *I love you!* and the whole
> universe, consciousness included, is a shape
> of that pronouncement.
>
> Or maybe there's no *You* in that,
> but only *I love!* ringing,
> engendering all of space, every quadrant
> an expression of God's first nature: *I love!*"[21]

The speculations continue—the speaker uses the word "maybe" fourteen times—culminating in a lovely passage in which the wife drifts fully off just as the poet's thoughts reach a peak of intensity—while becoming even more tentative:

> "Maybe it's true, what sages have said,
> I don't know if I'm remembering it right.
> Something about moving up a ladder of love.
> Maybe we learn
>
> to love a person, say, first as object,
> and then as presence, and then as essence,
> and then as disclosure of the divine,
>
> or maybe all at the same time,
> or discovering over time
> each deeper aspect to be true.
>
> And maybe our seeing it in another
> proves that face inside ourselves.
> Oh, I don't know. You sleep now."[22]

All this grand speculation, Lee suggests through the narrative frame, is indeed just speculation, and may be mainly useful for putting one's beloved to sleep. Is that sad? Perhaps. And yet the poem's tenderness toward the wife, the poet's acceptance of her need for rest and his own role, at this moment, as comforter, make it seem also entirely right. And, of course, what happens within the frame of the poem is quite different than what happens to a reader, who is offered two things at once, both the quiet domestic scene and the poet's ruminations—in a moment, Lee surely hopes, when the reader is not so much in need of rest as the wife, and ready to follow to the end. If the action of soothing is more important than abstraction and theorizing when it comes to love and God, if such talk puts many good people to sleep, still it may serve its purpose. The act is a blessing, even if as words and ideas it passes on quickly and vanishes, as all speech does, as inevitably even our written words must, sooner or later. And isn't it marvelous?

Near the end of *The Weakness of God*, John Caputo takes up Jacques Derrida's use of of the ubiquitous French "*adieu*," which translates literally as "I commend you to God" (a Dieu). Derrida makes the complicated confession that he "rightly passes for an atheist," yet argues earnestly for hospitality in a way he partly learned from Levinas, but which aligns with Caputo, with Grace Jantzen, and to much other recent thinking as a key element of any meaningful effort to follow God. "How can someone who rightly passes for an atheist rightly commend someone to God?" Caputo asks:

> The answer lies in the event. For the event that overtakes us in "*adieu*" slips across the border erected by the name of God. On the one hand, how can one say and pray *adieu*, practice the mad hospitality of the kingdom, and not be *in* the kingdom of God? But, on the other hand, how can one rightly pass for an atheist and not be *outside* the kingdom, since the kingdom is God's, which seems very theistic? But then again, is not the kingdom precisely for outsiders (while the insiders who take it for granted are out) and who could possibly be more outside the kingdom of God than one who rightly passes for an atheist? So by the mad para-logic of the impossible, rightly passing for an atheist is no obstacle, and might even be an advantage, while rightly passing for one of the inside crowd could spell trouble.[23]

This fascinating passage envisions a kind of inverted or transposed Catch-22. In Joseph Heller's now-famous original version, World War II pilots must keep flying dangerous missions as long as they fear them, because their fear is entirely rational; if they aren't afraid to fly, that indicates they are crazy, but in that case, they are willing to keep flying. So they are stuck, either way. But Caputo's version is the opposite of a bureaucratic maneuver to make men keep serving the murderous state; it suggests that membership in the kingdom might belong to those who practice true hospitality, even if they will never be admitted to the "inside crowd" of those who believe "properly." Might all those who respond to the mysterious event we point to with the word "God" be themselves made welcome into the company of the hospitable?

Jack Gilbert and the Sacrament That Is Neither Flesh Nor Spirit

Jack Gilbert's long career provides an excellent example of one whose refusals of the orthodox and conventional have fired, rather than cooling, his interest in ultimate questions. Shortly after his first book, *Views of Jeopardy*, won the Yale Younger Poets Prize in 1962 and threatened to turn him into something of a celebrity, Gilbert left the U. S., initially with the aid of a Guggenheim fellowship. He lived abroad for nearly twenty years, often on very little money, and published little. During his time in the Greek islands and other European places, though, he developed a distinct vision and sensibility. The title poem of his 2005 *Refusing Heaven* makes clear that the "refusal" he has chosen is not made lightly, nor is it a simple one:

The old women in black at early Mass in winter
are a problem for him. He could tell by their eyes
they have seen Christ. They make the kernel
of his being and the clarity around it
seem meager, as though he needs girders
to hold up his unusable soul. But he chooses
against the Lord. He will not abandon his life.[24]

Just what does Gilbert mean by choosing "against the Lord"? Like Dickinson and Whitman, like Stevens and Carson, like Stafford and

Lee, he remains deeply engaged, if not obsessed, with religious questions. And like all these others (however polyglot they are in every other way) his poems approach large questions through the physical, tangible things of the world, through the mysteries of the actual, of time, of sex and love. "Moreover" makes several bold assertions: "We are given the trees so we can know / what God looks like," Gilbert claims, "And rivers / so we might understand Him." And, even more provocatively, he suggests that it is through women that "we" gain our closest experience of divinity: "We are allowed / women so we can get into bed with the Lord, / however partial and momentary that is."[25]

What most sets Gilbert apart from the other theopoets I have been examining is his love of the grand, definitive-sounding generalization, grounded (it seems) in nothing more than his experience and his convictions. For all his doubts about God, he retains an unshakable and unshaken belief that this life *does* mean something, however difficult and painful it might be. Yet in "A Walk Blossoming" he offers a formulation that would fit well into John Caputo's view of God as event and call rather than mighty power:

> The spirit can know the Lord as a flavor
> rather than power. The soul is ambitious
> for what is invisible. Hungers for a sacrament
> that is both spirit and flesh. And neither.[26]

What we hunger for is elusive, a sacrament neither and both spirit and flesh, something that dwells invisibly within the everyday, a flavor rather than a power, a gift that we can request but not demand, prepare to receive but not predict. This is the difficulty of what the liturgical calendar calls "ordinary time," not the magical entry of Christmas nor the pain and triumph of Easter. Its mysteries are less exotic, but no less deep. Its beauties are less spectacular, those of the open prairie rather than mountains and shore lines.

The call to live in the everyday mystery is a strange one, involving all those days when the bushes do not burn, when no voice demands that we take off our shoes, when the preachers are not invoking the spectacular mysteries of birth and death and resurrection, when all we have is the world and its ten thousand things going on into time, moment by moment, hour by hour.

What of all those days when God seems silent, when the stones do not speak? As Annie Dillard writes in *Teaching a Stone to Talk,* "The silence is all there is. It is the alpha and the omega. It is God's brooding over the face of the waters; the whine of wings."[27] But even this silence, perhaps, is not final. For the world still shines forth around us, in all of its ten thousand things. Some of them say very little in English, it is true, and the problems of translation are formidable. We know so little of the mute things of the world, and when we gaze at the stars, or at open field filling with snow, or into the desert places within, we cannot escape the sense of just how narrow and small our knowing remains. Still, what we have is a great deal more than nothing. "I am trying to use what I have / to invent what I need," Adrienne Rich once wrote. This work must go on, in poetry and in prose.

And with this, perhaps, this chapter and this book have reached a stopping place—how to "finish" a text on mystery? Know at least that many meandering and ponderous paragraphs, overextended quotations, and repetitive, marginally defensible assertions that once had tentative place in this compendium of the wild, the willful, and the wistful have been removed, consigned to the dark silence of patterns stored in tiny, obscure spaces where the mysteries are both large and very small, manipulated and governed somehow by tools that I employ without any understanding of their fundamental workings. What remains still seems to me willful, wistful, dubious, and clumsy by turns—but for now it is the best I can do.

What do we know? A great deal, and very little. What can we do? Something, every day, never enough. Praise, and lament, and resist, and come together to lift up what is good and true, what makes for more abundant life. For now, let us sing together despite it all, and allow Gilbert to lead us.

> We must risk delight. We can do without pleasure,
> but not delight. [. . .] To make injustice the only
> measure of our attention is to praise the Devil.
> If the locomotive of the Lord runs us down,
> we should give thanks that the end had magnitude.
> We must admit there will be music despite everything.[28]

Notes

1. Dean Young, *The Art of Recklessness Poetry as Assertive Force and Contradiction* (St. Paul: Graywolf, 2010), 47, 88.

2. Antonio Machado, *Border of a Dream: Selected Poems*, trans. Willis Barnstone (Port Townsend, Wash.: Copper Canyon, 2004), 125.

3. William Stafford, *An Oregon Message* (New York: Harper & Row, 1987), 45.

4. William Stafford, *The Way It Is: New and Selected Poems* (St. Paul: Graywolf, 1998), 55. For a fuller treatment of his work and its relation to peacemaking, see my *Walker in the Fog*, 74-96.

5. Stafford, *The Way It Is*, 102.

6. Stafford, *The Way It Is*, 129

7. Stafford, *The Way It Is*, 129.

8. Stafford, *The Way It Is*, 222.

9. Stafford, *The Way It Is*, 129.

10. Stafford, *The Way It Is*, 3.

11. Stafford, *The Way It Is*, 181, 128.

12. Stafford, *The Way It Is*, 250.

13. Stafford, *The Way It Is*, 112, 113.

14. Li-Young Lee, *Behind My Eyes* (New York: Norton, 2008), 15.

15. Lee, *Behind My Eyes*, 23-4.

16. Lee, *Behind My Eyes*, 24.

17. Lee, *Behind My Eyes*, 36.

18. Lee, *Behind My Eyes*, 39.

19. Lee, *Behind My Eyes*, 40.

20. Lee, *Behind My Eyes*, 92.

21. Lee, *Behind My Eyes*, 95.

22. Lee, *Behind My Eyes*, 97.

23. John D. Caputo, *The Weakness of God: A Theology of the Event* (Bloomington: Indiana University Press, 2006), 266.

24. Jack Gilbert, *Refusing Heaven* (New York: Knopf, 2005), 60.

25. Gilbert, *Refusing Heaven*, 65.

26. Gilbert, *Refusing Heaven*, 67.

27. Annie Dillard, *Teaching a Stone to Talk: Expeditions and Encounters* (New York: Harper & Row, 1982), 76.

28. Gilbert, *Refusing Heaven*.

BIBLIOGRAPHY

"The Gospel of Thomas." Trans. Stephen Patterson and Marvin Meyer. *The Gnostic Society Library.* 1994. Web. 14 June 2010.

Abram, David. *Becoming Animal: An Earthly Cosmology.* New York: Pantheon, 2012.

———. *The Spell of the Sensuous: Perception and Language in a More-Than-Human World.* New York: Vintage, 1977.

Agee, James, and Walker Evans. *Let Us Now Praise Famous Men: Three Tenant Families.* New York: Ballantine, 1939. Reprint ed. 1966.

Alves, Rubem A. *The Poet, The Warrior, The Prophet: The Edward Cadbury Lectures 1990.* London: SCM Press, 1990.

Antinoff, Steven. "Spiritual Atheism: Part One: Reading Kafka for Breakfast, Swallowed Up for Lunch: A Special APR Supplement." *American Poetry Review* (May/June 2006): 27-32.

———. "Spiritual Atheism: Part Two: The Quest for Atheistic Salvation." *American Poetry Review* (July/August 2006): 23-35.

Auden, W. H. "Epitaph on a Tyrant," *Selected Poetry of W. H. Auden.* New York: Random House, 1970.

Baldwin, James. *Creative Process.* New York: Ridge Press, 1962.

Bangs, Jeremy Dupuis. *Letters on Toleration: Dutch Aid to Persecuted Swiss and Palatine Mennonites 1615-1699.* Rockport, Maine: Picton Press, 2004.

Barnstone, Willis. *The Other Bible.* New York: HarperCollins, 1984.

Barthelme, Donald. "Not-Knowing." In *The Art of the Essay*, ed.Lydia Fakundiny. New York: Houghton Mifflin, 1991, 485-498.

———. *Sixty Stories.* New York: Dutton, 1982.

Beachy, Kirsten, ed. *Tongue Screws and Testimonies: Poems, Stories, and Essays Inspired by the Martyrs Mirror.* Scottdale, Pa.: Herald Press, 2010.

Beck, Ervin. "Mennonite Trickster Tales: True to be Good." *Mennonite Quarterly Review* 61.1 (January 1987): 58-74.

Biespiel, David. "This Land Is Our Land." *Poetry* (May 2010). Web.

Blake, William. *Jerusalem, Selected Poems and Prose.* Ed. Hazard Adams. New York: Holt, Rinehart, and Winston, 1970.

Bly, Robert. "Looking for Dragon Smoke." In *Naked Poetry: Recent American Poetry in Open Forms.* Ed. Stephen Berg and Robert Mezey. Indianapolis: Bobbs-Merrill, 1969, 161-4.

———. *The Kabir Book: Forty-four of the Ecstatic Poems of Kabir.* Boston: Beacon, 1977.

———. *News of the Universe: Poems of Twofold Consciousness.* San Francisco: Sierra Club: 1980, 1995.

———. *Selected Poems.* New York: Harper & Row, 1986.

———. *The Soul Is Here for Its Own Joy: Sacred Poems from Many Cultures.* New York: Ecco, 1999.

Bloom, Harold. *Agon: Towards a Theory of Revisionism.* New York: Oxford, 1982.

Blum, Peter C. "Foucault, Genealogy, Anabaptism: Confessions of an Errant Postmodernist" Dula and Huebner, *The New Yoder,* 90-105.

Boesel, Chris, and Catherine Keller, Eds. *Apophatic Bodies: Negative Theology, Incarnation, and Relationality.* New York: Fordham University Press, 2010.

Borges, Jorge Luis. "John Wilkins' Analytical Language." *Jorge Luis Borges: Selected Non-Fictions.* Trans. Eliot Weinberger, Esther Allen, Suzanne Jill Levine. New York: Penguin, 2000.

Brandt, Di. *Now You Care.* Toronto: Coach House, 2003.

———. Review of *The Wing-Beaten Air* by Yorifumi Yaguchi. *Mennonite Quarterly Review* 84.3 (July 2010): 462-4.

Breton, Andre. "Manifesto of Surrealism: Three Excerpts." *Poems for the Millenium: The University of California Book of Modern and Postmodern Poetry.* Ed. Jerome Rothenberg and Pierre Joris. Berkeley: U of California P, 1995. 468-70.

Caputo, John D. "On Being Clear About Faith: A Response to Stephen Williams." *Books & Culture: A Christian Review.* Posted 11/01/2006. http://www.christianitytoday.com/bc/2006/novdec/18.40.html?start =1. 11 August 2009.

———. *The Weakness of God: A Theology of the Event.* Bloomington: Indiana University Press, 2006.

Carson, Anne. *Decreation: Poetry, Essays, Opera.* New York: Vintage, 2005.

———. *Eros the Bittersweet.* Princeton: Princeton University Press/Dalkey Archive, 1998.

Carson, Anne. *Glass, Irony and God.* New York: New Directions, 1995.

Cohen, Leonard. *Songs of Leonard Cohen.* Columbia Records, 1967.

Cohn, Norman. *The Pursuit of the Millennium: Revolutionary Millenarians and Mystical Anarchists of the Middle Ages.* Oxford: Oxford University Press, rev. ed. 1970.

Coles, Romand. "The Wild Patience of John Howard Yoder: 'Outsiders' and the 'Otherness of the Church.'" Dula and Huebner, *The New Yoder*, 216-52.

Coward, Harold, and Toby Foshay, Eds. *Derrida and Negative Theology.* Albany: SUNY Press, 1992.

Craig, David, and Janet McCann, Eds. *Odd Angles of Heaven: Contemporary Poetry by People of Faith.* Wheaton: Harold Shaw, 1994.

Crane, Stephen. *War Is Kind and Other Lines.* 1899. About.com. Web. 27 July 2010.

Davis, Todd. *The Least of These.* East Lansing: Michigan State University Press, 2010.

Denck, Hans. *Selected Writing of Hans Denck.* Ed. and trans. Edward J. Furcha and Ford Lewis Battles. Pittsburgh: Pickwick, 1975.

Dickens, A. G. *Reformation and Society In Sixteenth-Century Europe.* New York: Harcourt, 1966.

Dickinson, T. Wilson. "Emptying Apophasis of Deception: Considering a Duplicitous Kierkegaardian Declaration." In Boesel and Keller, 251-72.

Dillard, Annie. *Teaching a Stone to Talk: Expeditions and Encounters.* New York: Harper & Row, 1982

Dostoyevsky, Fyodor. *The Brothers Karamazov.* Trans. Andrew R. MacAndrew. New York: Bantam, 1970.

———. *The Idiot.* Trans. Eva Martin. (Project Gutenberg, 2001). http://www.gutenberg.org/files/2638/2638-h/2638-h.htm. 17 July 2010.

Dula, Peter, and Chris K. Huebner. *The New Yoder.* Cambridge, UK: Lutterworth, 2011.

Dylan, Bob. "Mr. Tambourine Man." bobdylan.com. 25 May 2004.

Eliot, Thomas Stearns. *The Sacred Wood.* London: Methuen, 1920; Bartleby.com, 1996. http://www.bartleby.com/200/. 26 May 2006.

Emerson, Ralph Waldo. *Selected Writings of Emerson.* Ed. Brooks Atkinson. New York: Modern Library, 1940.

"Ernst Troeltsch." *The Boston Collaborative Encyclopedia of Modern Western Theology.* Web. July 23, 2007.

Espada, Martin. *The Republic of Poetry.* New York: Norton, 2006.

Fisher, John. "Making Something Happen: Toward Transformative Mennonite Peace Poetry." *Mennonite Quarterly Review* 82.1 (Jan. 2008): 27-42.

Fox, Matthew. *Original Blessing.* New York: Tarcher/Putnam, 1983, 2000.

Frazier, Charles. *Cold Mountain.* New York: Vintage, 1997.

Friesen, Patrick. *Interim: Essays & Meditations.* Regina: Hagios Press, 2006.

Frost, Robert. "Education by Poetry." *The American Literature Archive.* Ed. Brian A. Bremen. http://www.en.utexas.edu/amlit/amlitprivate/scans/edbypo.html. October 16, 2006.

Gass, William. "Rilke's Rodin." Introduction to *Auguste Rodin.* Rainer Marie Rilke. Brooklyn: Archipelago Books, 2004.

Gilbert, Jack. *Monolithos, Poems 1962 and 1982* Port Townsend: Graywolf Press, 1984.

————. *Refusing Heaven.* New York: Knopf, 2005.
Gilchrist, Alexander. *Life and Works of William Blake.* 2nd. ed. London, 1880. Reissued Cambridge UP, 2009.
Goddard, Harold C. *Blake's Fourfold Vision.* Wallingford, Pa.: Pendle Hill, 1956.
Goering, Mel. A One-Sided Diet: Martyrdom and Warriors," *Mennonite Life* 61.4 (Dec. 2006), n. p. Web. 26 July 2010.
Goldstone, Lawrence and Nancy. *Out of the Flames: The Remarkable Story of a Fearless Scholar, a Fatal Heresy, and One of the Rarest Books in the World.* New York: Broadway Books, 2002.
Goodin, David K. "Sinners, Satan and the Insubstantial Substance of Evil: Theodicy within Orthodox Redemptive Economy." *Theandros—An Online Journal of Orthodox Christian Theology and Philosophy* 6.1 (Fall 2008). Web. 3 June 2011.
Gundy, Jeff. "A Certain Courtesy of the Heart: A Conversation with William Stafford." *Artful Dodge* 18/19 (1990): 5-10.
————. "Arrogant Humility and Aristocratic Torpor: Where Have We Been, Where Are We Going?" In *World, Self, Poem: Essays on Contemporary Poetry from the "Jubilation of Poets."* Ed. Leonard Trawick. Kent, Oh.: Kent State University Press, 1990, 20-27.
————. *Deerflies.* Cincinnati: WordTech Editions, 2004.
————. *Flatlands.* Cleveland: CSU Poetry Center, 1995.
————. *Inquiries: Poems.* Huron, Ohio: Bottom Dog, 1992.
————. *Rhapsody with Dark Matter.* Huron, Ohio: Bottom Dog, 2000.
————. *Scattering Point: The World in a Mennonite Eye.* Albany: SUNY Press, 2004.
————. *Spoken among the Trees.* Akron: University of Akron P, 2007.
————. *Walker in the Fog: On Mennonite Writing.* Telford, Pa.: Cascadia, 2005.
Hafiz. *The Subject Tonight Is Love: 60 Wild and Sweet Poems of Hafiz.* Versions by Daniel Ladinsky. North Myrtle Beach, S.C.: Pumpkin House, 1996.
Heidegger, Martin. *Existence and Being.* Trans. Werner Brock. Chicago: Henry Regnery, 1949.
————. *Poetry, Language, Thought.* Trans. Albert Hofstadter. New York: Harper, 1971.
Hildegarde of Bingen. *Scivias.* Trans. Mother Columba Hart and Jane Bishop. New York: Paulist, 1990.
Hölderlin, Friedrich. *Hyperion and Selected Poems.* Ed. Eric L. Santner. New York: Continuum, 1990.
Holland, Scott. "The Coming Only Is Sacred: Self-Creation and Social Solidarity in Richard Rorty's Secular Eschatology." *Cross Currents* 53.4 (Winter 2004). Web. 2 August 2010.
————. "Communal Hermeneutics as Body Politics or Disembodied Theology?" *Brethren Life and Thought* 40.2 (Spring 1995): 94-110.
————. "Response to Gordon Kaufman," *Conrad Grebel Review* 14.1 (Winter 1996): 51-6.

————. "Theology Is a Kind of Writing: The Emergence of Theopoetics." *Mennonite Quarterly Review* 71 (1997): 227-41.

Hopper, Stanley Romaine. *The Way of Transfiguration: Religious Imagination as Theopoiesis.* Ed. R Melvin Keiser and Tony Stoneburner. Louisville, Ky.: Westminster/John Knox, 1992.

Hostetler, Ann, Ed. *A Cappella: Mennonite Voices in Poetry.* Iowa City: University of Iowa P, 2003.

Howe, Arthur. "The Arc of the Universe Is Long But It Bends Towards Justice." *Slate* Jan. 9, 2009. http://open.salon.com/blog/arthur_howe/2009/01/18/the_arc_of_the_universe_is_long_but_it_bends_towards_justice27. 31 May 2012.

Huebner, Chris K. *A Precarious Peace: Yoderian Explorations on Theology, Knowledge, and Identity.* (Scottsdale, Pa.: Herald, 2006).

Huelsenbeck, Richard. "We Hardly." *Poems for the Millenium: The University of California Book of Modern and Postmodern Poetry.* Ed. Jerome Rothenberg and Pierre Joris. Berkeley: University of California Press, 1995, 306-07.

Impastato, David, Ed. *Upholding Mystery: An Anthology of Contemporary Christian Poetry.* New York: Oxford University Press, 1997.

Jantzen, Grace. *Becoming Divine: Toward a Feminist Philosophy of Religion.* Bloomington, Ind.: Indiana University Press, 1997.

————. *Foundations of Violence (Death and the Displacement of Beauty).* London and New York· Routledge, 2004.

————. *Violence to Eternity.* Ed. Jeremy Carrete and Morny Joy. London and New York: Routledge, 2009.

Janzen, Jean. *Elements of Faithful Writing.* North Newton, Kan.: Bethel College, 2004.

————. *Paper House.* Intercourse, Pa.: Good Books, 2008.

————. *The Upside-Down Tree.* Winnipeg: Henderson Books, 1992.

Kaplan, Benjamin J. *Divided by Faith: Religious Conflict and the Practice of Toleration in Early Modern Europe.* Cambridge: Harvard UP, 2007.

Kasdorf, Julia Spicher. *Eve's Striptease.* Pittsburgh: Pittsburgh University Press, 1998.

————, Moderator. "Literature, Place, Language, and Faith: A Conversation between Jean Janzen, John Ruth, and Rudy Wiebe." *Conrad Grebel Review* 26.1 (Winter 2008): 72-90.

————. "Mightier than the Sword: *Martyrs Mirror* in the New World." Keynote presentation. "*Martyrs Mirror*: Reflections Across Time," Elizabethtown College, June 8-10, 2010.

————. *Poetry in America.* Pittsburgh: Pittsburgh University Press, 2011.

————. *The Body and the Book: Writing from a Mennonite Life.* Baltimore: Johns Hopkins University Press, 2001.

Kaufman, Gordon. *In Face of Mystery: A Constructive Theology.* Cambridge: Harvard University Press, 2006.

————. *In the Beginning . . . Creativity.* Minneapolis: Fortress, 2004.

————. *Jesus and Creativity.* Minneapolis: Fortress, 2006.

Keats, John. "Ode to a Nightingale." *The Oxford Book of English Verse*, ed. Arthur Quiller-Couch (1919). http://www.bartleby.com/101/624.html. 31 May 2012.

————. *Selected Letters of John Keats.* Ed. Grant F. Scott. Cambridge: Harvard University Press, 2002.

Keefe-Perry, L. B. C. "Theopoetics: Process and Perspective. *Christianity and Literature* 58.4 (Summer 2009): 579-601. 11 May 2012.

Klassen, Peter J. *Mennonites in Early Modern Poland and Prussia.* Baltimore: Johns Hopkins University Press, 2009.

Krehbiel, Stephanie. "Staying Alive: How Martyrdom Made Me a Warrior," *Mennonite Life* 61.4 (Dec. 2006), n. p. Web. 26 July 2010.

Laird, Martin. "The 'Open Country Whose Name Is Prayer: Apophasis, Deconstruction, and Contemplative Practice." *Modern Theology* 21.1 (January 2005): 141-55.

LaFemina, Gerry, and Chad Prevost, Eds. *Evensong: Contemporary American Poets on Spirituality.* Huron, Ohio: Bottom Dog, 2006.

Lammert, The Rev. Sarah. "Unitarianism and the Radical Reformation." The Unitarian Society of Ridgewood, January 12, 2003. Web. 12 August 2004.

Lao Tzu. *Tao Te Ching.* Trans. D. C. Lau. New York: Penguin, 1963.

————. *Tao Te Ching.* Trans. Stephen Mitchell. New York: Harper Perennial, 1992. http://academic.brooklyn.cuny.edu/core9/phalsall/texts/taote-v3.html#29. 31 May 2012.

Lawrence, D. H. *Studies in Classic American Literature.* Thomas Seltzer, 1923. *American Studies at the University of Virginia.* http://xroads.virginia.edu/~hyper/LAWRENCE/lawrence.html. October 16, 2006.

Lee, Li-Young. *Behind My Eyes.* New York: Norton, 2008.

Levine, Julia. *Ask.* Tampa: University of Tampa Press, 2003.

Lopez, Barry, and Christian Martin. "On Resistance: An Interview with Barry Lopez." *Georgia Review* 60.1 (Spring 2006): 13-30.

Lorca, Federico Garcia. "The Duende: Theory and Divertissement." *Margin: Exploring Magical Realism.* Ed.Tamara Kaye Sellman. http://www.angelfire.com/wa2/margin/LorcaDuende.html. 17 July 2010.

Machado, Antonio. *Border of a Dream: Selected Poems.* Trans. Willis Barnstone. Port Townsend, Wash.: Copper Canyon, 2004.

Marcus, Greil. *Lipstick Traces: A Secret History of the 20th Century.* Cambridge: Harvard University Press, 1989.

Merton, Thomas. *New Seeds of Contemplation.* New York: New Directions, 1961.

Metres, Philip. *Behind the Lines: War Resistance Poetry on the American Homefront since 1941.* Iowa City: University of Iowa Press, 2007.

Miller, David L. *Hells & Holy Ghosts: A Theopoetics of Christian Belief.* Nashville: Abingdon, 1989.

Miller, Keith. *The Book of Flying.* New York: Penguin, 2004.

Miller, Keith. *The Book on Fire.* Stafford, UK: Immanion Books, 2009.

Moore, Marianne. "Poetry." *The Norton Anthology of Modern Poetry,* 3rd. ed., Vol. 1. Ed. Jahan Ramazani, Richard Ellman, and Robert O'Clair. New York: Norton, 2003: 439.

Neruda, Pablo. "Childhood and Poetry." *Neruda and Vallejo: Selected Poems.* Ed. Robert Bly. Boston: Beacon, 1973.

Norris, Kathleen. *Dakota: A Spiritual Journey.* New York: Houghton Mifflin, 1993.

Nye, Naomi Shihab. *You & Yours.* Rochester, N.Y.: BOA Editions, 2005.

O'Connor, Flannery. *A Good Man Is Hard to Find and Other Stories.* New York: Mariner Books, 1977.

O'Connor, Flannery. Letter to Louise Abbot. *The Habit of Being: Letters of Flannery O'Connor.* Ed. Sally Fitzgerald. New York: Vintage, 1979.

Oliver, Mary. *Evidence.* Boston: Beacon, 2009.

Pagels, Elaine. *Beyond Belief: The Secret Gospel of Thomas.* New York: Random House, 2003.

———. *The Origins of Satan.* New York: Vintage, 1996.

Paine, Ed J. *The Poetry of Our World: An International Anthology of Contemporary Poetry.* New York: Harper Perennial, 2001.

Pascal, Blaise. *Penseés,* Trans. W. F. Trotter. New York: Dutton, 1958. http://oregonstate.edu/instruct/phl302/texts/pascal/pensees-contents.html. 26 July 2010.

Paul, Garrett E. "Why Troeltsch? Why Today? Theology for the Twenty-First Century." *The Christian Century,* June 30-July 7, 1993, 676-681. Web. July 23, 2007.

Ratzlaff, Keith. *Then, a Thousand Crows.* Tallahassee: Anhinga, 2009.

Redekop, Calvin. *Mennonite Society.* Baltimore: Johns HopkinsUniversity Press, 1989.

Revell, Donald. *Invisible Green: Selected Prose of Donald Revell.* Richmond, Calif.: Omnidawn, 2005.

Rilke, Rainer Maria. *Selected Poems.* Trans. Robert Bly. New York: Harper & Row, 1981.

———. *Selected Poems of Rainer Maria Rilke.* Trans. David Young. Oberlin, Ohio: Field Translation Series 20, 1994.

Robinson, James R. ed., *The Nag Hammadi Library,* revised edition. HarperCollins, San Francisco, 1990. http://www.gnosis.org/naghamm/nhl.html. 4 April 2012.

Roth, John. "In This Issue." *Mennonite Quarterly Review* 82.1 (Winter 2008): 3-6.

Rumi, Jelaluddin. *The Essential Rumi.* Trans. Coleman Barks. New York: HarperSanFrancisco, 1995.

Ruth, John. "Lecture for a Limited Audience," *Mennonite Life,* March 1983, 24-6.

Sider, Alex. "Friendship, Alienation and Love: Hauerwas and Yoder." *Mennonite Quarterly Review* 84.3 (July 2010): 417-40.

Shindell, Richard. *Blue Divide*. Shanachie Records, 1994.

———. *Reunion Hill*. Shanachie Records, 1997.

Shklovsky, Victor. *Art as Device*. Trans. Benjamin Sher. Normal, Ill.: Dalkey Archive Press, 1990.

Smith, Ann, Philip Metres, and Larry Smith, Eds. *Come Together: Imagine Peace*. Huron, Ohio: Bottom Dog, 2008.

Stafford, William. *Another World Instead: The Early Poems of William Stafford, 1937-47*. Ed. Frederick Marchant. Minneapolis: Graywolf, 2008.

Stafford, William. *An Oregon Message*. New York: Harper & Row, 1987.

———. *The Way It Is: New and Selected Poems*. St. Paul: Graywolf, 1998.

Steenberg, M. C. "Gregory Palamas: Knowledge, Prayer, and Vision." *Monachos.net: Orthodoxy through Patristic, Monastic, and Liturgical Study*. 15 May 1999. http://www.monachos.net/content/patristics/studies-fathers/62. 3 June 2011.

Stevens, Wallace. *The Palm at the End of the Mind: Selected Poems and a Play*. Ed. Holly Stevens. New York: Vintage, 1972.

Strand, Mark. *Selected Poems*. New York: Knopf, 2002.

Thoreau, Henry David. *The Illustrated Walden*. Ed. J. Lynton Shanley. Princeton: Princeton University Press, 1973.

Tzara, Tristan. "Dada Manifesto on Feeble and Bitter Love." *Poems for the Millenium: The University of California Book of Modern and Postmodern Poetry*. Ed. Jerome Rothenberg and Pierre Joris. Berkeley: University of California Press, 1995. 299-305.

Van Braght, Thieleman J. *The Bloody Theater or Martyrs Mirror of the Defenseless Christians*. 1660. Trans. Joseph F. Sohm. Scottdale, Pa.: Mennonite Publishing House, 1984.

Vaneigem, Raoul. *The Movement of the Free Spirit: General Considerations and Firsthand Testimony Concerning Some Brief Flowerings of Life in the Middle Ages, the Renaissance and, Incidentally, Our Own Time*. Trans. Randall Cherry and Ian Patterson. New York: Zone Books, 1998.

Wahlberg, Patrick. *Surrealism*. 1965; reprint New York: Thames and Hudson, 1997.

Weaver, J. Denny. *Anabaptist Theology in Face of Postmodernity*. Telford, Pa.: Pandora Press U.S., 2000.

———. *Keeping Salvation Ethical: Mennonite and Amish Atonement Theology in the Late Nineteenth Century*. Scottdale, Pa.: Herald Press, 1997.

———. *The Nonviolent Atonement*. 2nd. ed. Grand Rapids: Eerdmans, 2011.

Weil, Simone. *Waiting for God*. Trans. Emma Craufurd. New York: HarperCollins, 1951, 2001.

Whitman, Walt. *Leaves of Grass and Selected Prose*. Ed. John A. Kouwenhoven. New York: Modern Library, 1950.

Wilde, Oscar. *Collected Works of Oscar Wilde*. Ware, Hertfordshire: Wordsworth Editions, 1997.

———. *De Profundis*. Methuen, 1913. Project Gutenberg, 2007. http://www.gutenberg.org/files/921/921.txt. 23 July 2010.

Wojahn, David. "Maggie's Farm No More: The Fate of Political Poetry." *The Writer's Chronicle* 39.6 (May/Summer 2007): 21-31.

Woodman, Marion. "Men Are from Earth, and So Are Women: Marion Woodman on the Inner Marriage of the True Masculine and the True Feminine." Interview by James Kullander. *The Sun* 368 (August 2006), 4-13.

Wright, James. "Ten Letters." Ed. Jonathan Blunk. *The Georgia Review* 59.1 (2005): 19-39.

Wright, Franz. *God's Silence.* New York: Knopf, 2004.

Yaguchi, Yorifumi. *The Wing-Beaten Air: My Life and My Writing.* Intercourse, Pa.: Good Books, 2008.

Yeats, W. B. *Essays and Introductions.* London and New York: Methuen, 1961.

———. *Per Amica Silentia Lunae,* New York: McMillan, 1918.

Yoder, John Howard. "Armaments and Eschatology." *Studies in Christian Ethics* 1.1 (1988): 43-61.

———. *Body Politics: Five Practices of the Christian Community Before the Watching World.* Scottdale, Pa.: Herald P, 1992.

———. "Creation and Gospel." *Perspectives: A Journal of Reformed Thought* 3.8 (Oct. 1988): 8-10.

———. "On Not Being in Charge." *War and Its Discontents: Pacifism and Quietism in the Abrahamic Traditions.* Ed. J. Patout Burns. Washington: Georgetown University Press, 1996. 74-90.

———. "That Household We Are." Typescript of presentation at Bluffton Believers' Church Conference, 1980.

———. *The Priestly Kingdom: Social Ethics as Gospel.* Notre Dame: University of Notre Dame Press, 1984.

Young, Dean. *The Art of Recklessness: Poetry as Assertive Force and Contradiction.* St. Paul: Graywolf, 2010.

Young, Dean. *Beloved Infidel.* Middletown, Conn.: Wesleyan University Press, 1992.

INDEX

A

Abram, David, 34, 37-8, 192-4
Agee, James
    Let Us Now Praise Famous Men,
        67-8
Alves, Rubem A., 17, 36, 206-210,
    224-7, 230, 233-4
Anabaptist Surrealism, 66
Antinoff, Steven, 23
Antinomianism, 113, 115-7, 121
Apophatic theology, 216-8, 245-6,
    254 *See also* Negative theol-
    ogy
Assimilation, 33, 43, 46-8, 103, 241
Auden, W. H., 75
Austrian Anabaptists, 235-7, 243 n.
    11

B

Baldwin, James, 83, 138, 215, 245
Bangs, Jeremy Dupuis, 121 n. 3
Barks, Coleman, 196-7
Barlaam of Calabria, 216
Barthelme, Donald, 75, 215
Baumgartner, Jill Pelaez, 146
Beachy, Kirsten, 239
    Tongue Screws and Testimonies,
        239-42
Beauty, 86 n. 24, 110, 204-12, 213
    n. 16, 221-2, 249. *See also*
    Dostoyevsky, Fyodor;
    Jantzen, Grace; Weil, Simone
    and death, 205-6, 210
    and desire, 205-6
    and flourishing, 246-7, 250-1
    and God, 206-8, 211-12, 249,
        251
    and institutions, 208-10
    and music, 170, 179
    and peace, 249-50
    and poetry, 205, 249
    and power, 208
    and romanticism 205-7
    and sadness, 205-7
    and truth, 19, 38, 205, 221-2
    and utility, 129
    and the world, 205-7, 210, 258
Beck, Ervin, 237-8
Belief, 21, 38, 55-9, 70, 108-9, 173-
    6, 194, 209-10, 217, 245,
    260-1, 269. *See also* Jantzen,
    Grace
    and martyrdom, 240

and poetry, 23, 150
and theopoetics, 32
and Dirk Willems, 231
Biespiel, David, 146, 150-1
Blake, William, 17, 18, 20, 32, 37,
    110-6, 143-6
    "Garden of Love, The," 112
    "Jerusalem," 110
    "London" 111
    The Marriage of Heaven and Hell
    25, 83-4, 111-3
    Milton 143-4
Bloom, Harold, 23-4
Blum, Peter C., 186
Bly, Robert
    "Six Winter Privacy Poems,"
    106-7
Boehme, Jacob, 97
Borges, Jorge Luis, 74-5, 84
Brandt, Di, 50, 158-9, 163 n. 12,
    169
    "Interspecies Communication"
    158-9
    Jerusalem, beloved, 158
    "nonresistance, or love Mennon-
    ite style," 158
    Now You Care, 158
    questions i asked my mother, 50
Breton, Andre
    Manifesto of Surrealism, 130
Buffy the Vampire Slayer, 240
Bush, George W., 60, 127, 156

C
Calvin, John, 70-1
Caputo, John D., 40, 85 n. 9, 116,
    234-5, 239, 244, 267-9
    Weakness of God, The, 234-5
Carson, Anne, 109, 172-4, 251-5
    "Decreation," 252-5
    Eros the Bittersweet, 172-4

"Truth about God, The" 251-2
Cohen, Leonard, 71, 169-70
    "Anthem," 71
    "Suzanne," 169-70
Cohn, Norman, 61-2
    Pursuit of the Millenium, The, 61
Coles, Romand, 187
Crane, Stephen, 173

D
Dada, 128-34
Davis, Todd, 154-5, 159
    "Can We Remember?" 154-5
    "Migration," 159
Denck, Hans, 66
DePiero, W. S., 149
Derrida, Jacques, 267-8
Desire, 22, 32, 35, 63, 69, 84, 109,
    143, 172-81, 226-7, 248. *See
    also* Blake, William; Carson,
    Anne; Jantzen, Grace; Erotic
    and religious desire
    and beauty, 204-6
    and community, 174-5
    and language, 109
    and reason, 83, 114
    and religion 171-3, 197, 225
    and repression, 111-12
    and theology, 109-10
    and theopoetics, 35-40, 95-7,
    204
    as malady, 81
Dickens, A. G., 58
Dickinson, Emily, 23, 245, 258
Dickinson, T. Wilson, 245
Dillard, Annie, 270
Dostoyevsky, Fyodor, 199-201,
    210-11
    Brothers Karamazov, 199-201
    "Grand Inquisitor, The," 199-
    201

Idiot, The, 210-11
Dula, Peter, 185-6, 187
Dylan, Bob, 133, 205
   "Mr. Tambourine Man," 133

E
Eastern Mennonite University, 50
Edwards, Jonathan, 70
Eliade, Mircea
   The Myth of the Eternal Return,
   62
Eliot, T. S., 110, 113-14, 258
Emerson, Ralph Waldo, 55
   "Compensation," 71-2
Erotic and religious desire, 109,
   171, 172, 176, 253. *See also*
   Desire
Espada, Martin, 144
   "The Soldiers in the Garden,"
   144

F
Falwell, Jerry, 25
Fisher, John, 146, 147-8, 156, 164
   n. 29
Flourishing, 177-80, 194, 209, 238,
   246-8. *See also* Jantzen, Grace
Forché, Carolyn, 148
   Against Forgetting, 148
Fox, Matthew, 38-9, 191
Francis, Saint, 89
Frazier, Charles, 178
   Cold Mountain, 178
Free Spirit movement, 56, 61-6, 69
Friesen, Patrick, 79
   Shunning, The 50
Frost, Robert, 45

G
Gass, William, 127-8
Gilbert, Jack, 258, 268-70

Refusing Heaven, 268-70
   "Walk Blossoming, A," 269
Gilman, Charlotte Perkins
   "The Yellow Wall-Paper," 83
Girard, René, 248
Gnosticism, 23, 55, 63, 68-70, 77,
   190, 262. *See also Gospel of
   Thomas; Gospel of Philip*
Goddard, Harold C., 114-16
Goodin, David K., 217
Goshen College, 50
Gospel of Philip, 68-9, 89, 91, 96
Gospel of Thomas, 46, 68, 77
Gregory of Palamas, 217
Gundy, Jeff
   "Arrogant Humility and Aristo-
   cratic Torpor," 148-9
   "Autobiography with *Blonde on
   Blonde*," 189
   "Contemplation at the Bar R
   Ranch," 91-2
   "Damselfly," 119-20
   "Epiphany with Sirens and
   White-Tail," 156
   "His Name Was Gerdon and He
   Ran a Hatchery in Graymont,
   Illinois," 211
   "How the Boy Jesus Resisted
   Taking Out the Trash," 88
   "How to Write the New Men-
   nonite Poem," 44
   "Letter to Students Gone for
   Summer," 135-6
   "Second Morning Song from
   Oneonta," 141-2
   "Where Water Finds an Edge,"
   99-100

H
Hafiz, 97
Halfway Covenant, 69-70

Hamill, Sam, 149-50 *See also* Poets Against the War
Hass, Robert, 205
  "Meditation at Lagunitas," 205
Heidegger, Martin, 106, 108
Hegel, George, 224-5
Heresy, 17, 21-2, 55-72, 102-21, 172, 254
  heretical pastoral, 104
  heretical sublime, 102 ff.
Hinz-Penner, Raylene, 154
  "Inside, after September 2001," 154
Hölderlin, Friedrich, 86 n. 24
Holland, Scott, 22, 31, 75, 85 n. 4
Hopper, Stanley Romaine,102, 104-7, 116. *See also* Theopoetics
Hostetler, Ann, 146-8, 157
  A Cappella, 146-7
Huebner, Chris K., 185-7
Humility, 81-2
Hulsenbeck, Richard, 132
  "We Hardly," 132

I
Irigaray, Luce, 210

J
Jantzen, Grace, 38, 48, 109, 175-8, 194, 209, 238-9, 246-52, 259
  Becoming Divine, 175-8
  flourishing, 177-80, 194, 209, 238, 246-8
  natality, 176-7, 209-10, 238-9, 259
  necrophilia, 175-8, 238-40
Janz, Anna, 236-7
Janzen, Jean, 35, 49, 118-9, 153, 159-60
  "Five Lessons in Piety," 118-9
  "Liminal," 119

"No Stars for Me," 153
Paper House, 118, 159-60
"Peaches in Minnesota," 82
"Penitential Psalms," 159-60
Janzen, Rhoda
  Mennonite in a Little Black Dress, 49, 50
Jeffers, Robinson, 173, 245
Johnson, Ronald, 120-21
Joris, Anna, 225-6

K
Kabir, 35
Kafka, Franz, 104
Kaplan, Benjamin K., 121 n. 3
Kasdorf, Julia Spicher, 50, 117-8, 147, 157-8, 242 n. 1
  "Baby Screaming in the Back Seat, The," 147
  "Bat Boy, Break a Leg," 117-8, 157-8
  Poetry in America, 157
  Sleeping Preacher, 50
  "When the Stranger Is an Angel," 117
  "Writing Like a Mennonite," 157
Kaufman, Gordon, 76-9, 104-5, 177, 223-4
  In Face of Mystery, 223
  reification, 104-5, 223
  serendipitous creativity, 104-5, 177, 223-4
Keats, John, 38, 106, 192-4, 205
  negative capability, 106, 195
  "Ode on a Grecian Urn," 205
  "Ode to a Nightingale" 192-4
Keefe-Perry, L. B. C., 31
King Jr., Martin Luther, 195
Klassen, Peter K., 121 n. 3
Krehbiel, Stephanie, 240

L

Lacan, Jacques, 175
Laird, Melvin, 217
Lammert, Sarah, 59
Lawrence, D. H., 81
Lederach, John Paul, 146
Lee, Li-Young, 258, 262-8
  Behind My Eyes, 262-8
  "Have You Prayed?" 263-5
  "In His Own Shadow," 263
  "Lake Effect," 265
  "Virtues of the Boring Hus-
    band," 266-7
Levine, Julia
  "On the 12:50 Out of Fairfield,"
    94-6
Lindsay, Nicholas, 110
Lopez, Barry, 75, 85 n. 6
Lorca, Gabriel Garcia, 218-9
  Duende, 218-9
Lowell, Robert, 164 n. 21, 221
  "Skunk Hour," 221
Lowry, James, 240-1

M

Machado, Antonio, 17, 214, 257
Manz, Felix, 57
Marcus, Greil
  Lipstick Traces, 62-6
Marquez, Gabriel Garcia
  "Handsomest Drowned Man in
    the World, The" 227
Martyrs Mirror, 22, 33, 43, 84, 134,
  225, 230-42. *See also* Thiele-
  man J. van Bracht
Mast, Gerald, 242 n. 1
Melville, Herman
  Moby-Dick, 60, 82
Merleau-Ponty, Maurice, 193
Merton, Thomas, 89, 92-3
Metres, Philip, 151-2, 159

Behind the Lines, 151-2
Militarization, 143-4
Miller, David,117
Miller, Keith
  Book of Flying, The, 82
Missional, 33
Münster rebellion, 57-8, 61-63, 113
Mystery, 231-42, 246, 251, 257-70

N

Narrative, 32, 75-8, 231-42, 248-9
Negative capability, 106, 195 *See
  also* Keats, John
Negative theology, 216-18 *See also*
  Apophatic theology
Neruda, Pablo, 134, 144
Nerval, Gérard, 38
Norris, Kathleen, 181 n. 9
Nye, Naomi Shihab
  "I Feel Sorry for Jesus," 138

O

O'Connor, Flannery, 87, 98, 178-9
  "Good Man Is Hard to Find,
    A," 178-9
Oliver, Mary, 219-21
  "At the Pond," 219
  "At the River Clarion," 220-1
  Evidence, 219-21
  "Mysteries, Yes," 221
  "Spring" 220
Opposition ,18-19, 147, 174
Ordnung, 34, 45

P

Pagels, Elaine
  Beyond Belief, 68
  Origin of Satan, The, 68-9
Parker, Theodore, 195
Pascal, Blaise, 214
Pacifism, 113 ff.

and teaching, 127-36
Peace, 179, 184, 194, 246, 249-51,
    See also Beauty; Flourishing
    and beauty 249-51
    and poetry, 143-62
Pinsky, Robert, 192-3
Plato, 109, 185
Poe, Edgar Allen, 205
    "Philosophy of Composition,
    The," 205
Poets Against the War, 149-156. See
    also Hamill, Sam
Porete, Margaret, 69, 252-5
    Mirror of Simple Souls, The, 69
Pound, Ezra, 182

R
Ratzlaff, Keith, 153-4, 160-1
    "July 4," 153-4
    "What Kind of Guy Are You?"
    160-1
Rebellion, 18-19
Redekop, Calvin, 129
Regier, Ami, 164 n. 29
Reiss, Haydn, 164 n. 21
Revell, Donald, 81, 120-1
    Invisible Green 120-1
Rilke, Rainer Maria, 37, 106, 128,
    131, 245
    "Eingang" ("Entrance"), 131
Rook, 188-9
Roth, John, 43-51
Rotten, Johnny, 62-3
Rumi, Jelaluddin, 196-201
Ruth, John, 49

S
Saint Augustine, 173, 191
Saint Gregory of Nyssa, 216
Sappho, 252-5
Schleitheim Brotherly Union, 132

Servetus, Michael, 70-2
Sex Pistols, 65-6
Sexton, Anne, 245
Shindell, Richard, 171-2
    "Ballad of Mary Magdalene,
    The," 171-2
    "Reunion Hill," 171
Shklovsky, Victor, 215-6
    defamiliarization, 215
Sholl, Betsy, 155
    "Back with the Quakers," 155
Simons, Menno, 237-8
Split This Rock, 151
Stafford, William, 34, 151, 164 n.
    21, 218, 258-62
    "Allegiances," 261, 262
    "Believer," 262
    "Earth Dweller," 260
    "Graffiti," 258
    "In Camp," 262
    "Objector," 262
    "On a Church Lawn," 34, 259
    "Sky," 261
    "Vocation," 260
    "Ultimate Problems," 260
Steenburg, M. C., 216
Stein, Kevin, 150
Stevens, Wallace, 75-6, 107, 205,
    221-3, 245, 262
    "Final Soliloquy of the Interior
    Paramour," 222-3
    "Notes Toward a Supreme Fic-
    tion," 76
    "On the Road Home," 221-2
    "Sunday Morning," 205
Stoll, Joseph, 240-1
Strand, Mark, 253
    "Keeping Things Whole," 253
Surrealism, 66, 84, 128-34 See also
    Anabaptist Surrealism

T

Tao Te Ching, 60, 189
Tertullian, 216
Theopoetics, 18-24, 31-41, 103-10,
    117-21, 189, 215-230, 233-
    4, 246-55, 259-70
Thoreau, Henry David, 34, 36, 64,
    120
    Walden, 64
Tiessen, Hildi Froese, 44
"Thunder, Perfect Mind, The," 36
Toews, Miriam
    A Complicated Kindness, 49, 50
Transgression, 17-19, 23, 102-4
Turner, Brian, 159
Tzara, Tristan, 132

V

van Bracht, Thieleman, 33-34, 43
    See also *Martyrs Mirror*
van Leyden, Jan, 61-2, 63
van Luyken, Jan, 236
Vaneigem, Raoul, 62-5. See also Free
    Spirit

W

Wahlberg, Patrick, 128-30
Watts, Alan, 102, 104
Weaver, J. Denny, 24, 87-8,93-4
Weil, Simone, 22, 204-7, 226-7,
    252-5
Wiebe, Dallas, 241-2
    "The Anabaptist Radiance,"
    241-2
Wiebe, Rudy, 49, 157
    Peace Shall Destroy Many, 49,
    157
White Christmas, 143
Whitman, Walt, 64, 74, 79-81, 90,
    173, 182, 205, 245-51, 258
    Leaves of Grass, 78

"Out of the Cradle Endlessly
    Rocking," 205
"Song of Myself," 40, 247-51
Wilde, Oscar, 81-2, 140
Willems, Dirk, 63, 226, 230-4
Wojahn, David, 146, 149-50
Wolfe, Gregory, 255 n. 2
Woodman, Marion, 79
Wordsworth, William, 223
World War II, 143
Wright, Franz, 242 n. 7
Wright, James, 94

Y

Yaguchi, Yorifumi, 146
Yeats, William Butler, 126
Yoder, John Howard, 24, 39, 107-8,
    116, 182-201
    "Armaments and Eschatology,"
    108, 183-4, 194-5
    Body Politics, 199
    "But We Do See Jesus: The Par-
    ticularity of Incarnation and
    the Universality of Truth,"
    187, 189-92
    didaskaloi, 184-5, 195
    Priestly Kingdom, The, 184-5
Young, Dean, 41, 205-6, 257
    "Rothko's Yellow," 205-6

CREDITS AND AND PERMISSIONS

THE AUTHOR

Jeff Gundy, born in 1952 near Flanagan, Illinois, grew up among Mennonites, corn, soybeans, and chickens in the prairie country that remains his psychic home. He earned an English degree from Goshen College in 1975 and graduate degrees in creative writing and American literature at Indiana University. After four years at Hesston College in Kansas, he has taught at Bluffton College since 1984, where he founded the writing program and teaches literature, writing, and American Studies. He has also taught at Goshen College, Ohio Northern University, and the University of Salzburg, where he was a Fulbright Lecturer in 2008.

Gundy's books include the pathbreaking *Walker in the Fog: On Mennonite Writing* (Cascadia, 2005), winner of the Dale E. Brown Award for Anabaptist and Pietist scholarship and one of the first critical texts on American Mennonite literature, and two books of creative nonfiction—*A Community of Memory: My Days with George and Clara* (Illinois, 1996) and *Scattering Point: The World in a Mennonite Eye* (SUNY, 2003).

He has also published four chapbooks and five full collections of poems—*Spoken among the Trees* (Akron, 2007), chosen for the Society of Midland Authors Poetry Award; *Deerflies* (winner of the Nancy Dasher Award); *Rhapsody with Dark Matter; Flatlands;* and *Inquiries.* Anhinga Press will publish *Somewhere Near Defiance,* a new collection of poems, in 2014.

His poems and essays have appeared in dozens of journals, including *The Sun, Kenyon Review, Nimrod, Cincinnati Review, Image, The Mennonite, Witness, Shenandoah, Antioch Review, Poetry Northwest, Pleiades, Mennonite Life, Creative Nonfiction, Mennonite Quarterly Review,* and *Conrad Grebel Review.* His work has been anthologized in *The Rose Metal Press Field Guide to Flash Nonfiction, Fast Break to Line Break: Poets on the Art of Basketball, Making Poems: Forty Poems with Commentary by the Poets, A Cappella: Mennonite Voices in Poetry, Sweet Jesus: Poems about the Ultimate Icon, Food Poems, Modern Poems of Ohio, Illinois Voices,* and several volumes in the yearly series *What Mennonites Are Thinking.*

Gundy has served on the faculty of the Antioch Writers Workshop and the Language of Nature workshop, and led numerous other writing workshops and seminars across the country. Since 2001 he has served on the planning committee for the Mennonite/s Writing conference series, and was chief local organizer for the 2006 conference at Bluffton University. For twenty years he has regularly reviewed poetry and nonfiction for *The Georgia Review,* including an extended review of five books by Mennonite authors in 2004.

Other honors and awards include six Ohio Arts Council fellowships, two C. Henry Smith Peace Lectureships, and numerous Pushcart Prize nominations. He has served as an evaluator for Fulbright awards and as division and department chair at Bluffton University, where he also directs the Bluffton University Research Center.

He and Marlyce (Martens) Gundy are members of First Mennonite Church in Bluffton, and have three grown sons and a grandchild. His hobbies include playing guitar, songwriting, biking, and jogging.

CPSIA information can be obtained at www.ICGtesting.com
Printed in the USA
BVOW03s2028101113

335964BV00001B/25/P